S0-BEX-206

The Church of the Lepers is one of countless Taiwan landmarks bearing witness to the dedicated work of Lil Dickson and her Mustard Seed mission.

Angel at Her Shoulder

Angel at Her Shoulder

Lillian Dickson and Her Taiwan Mission

by Kenneth L. Wilson

Foreword by Daniel A. Poling

HARPER & ROW, PUBLISHERS
New York, Evanston, and London

ANGEL AT HER SHOULDER. *Copyright © 1964 by Kenneth L. Wilson. Printed in the United States of America. All rights reserved. No part of this book may be used or reproduced in any manner whatsoever without written permission except in the case of brief quotations embodied in critical articles and reviews. For information address Harper & Row, Publishers, Incorporated, 49 East 33rd Street, New York 16, N. Y.*

FIRST EDITION

LIBRARY OF CONGRESS CATALOG CARD NUMBER: *64: 10757*

B-O

Big angels visit in our sore dismay,
But little ones go in and out all day.

—Author Unknown

Special credit, or blame, must go to Dr. Daniel A. Poling, who pushed me into this writing project; to my wife, who pulled me through it; to Campiox, which, as my associates will understand, is both a place and a telephone number; and of course to Lillian Dickson, without whom there would have been nothing to write.

K. L. W.

Contents

Foreword

by Daniel A. Poling

Angel at Her Shoulder is more than the title of an amazing story and the biography of a most remarkable, physically undersized but spiritually large woman.

Lillian Dickson, the irresistible "Lil" of this book, who was for many accurately described by the title "Typhoon Lil," has in a crowded lifetime up to now practiced and demonstrated the faith "once delivered" as no other mortal I have ever known. In these chapters we find her building hospitals, orphanages, schools, a leprosarium, churches, and mountain clinics, with a veritable abandonment of courage—courage that at times plunged ahead against what seemed to be, even to her most devoted associates, insuperable odds.

Between these covers, accurately and with restrained eloquence, has been written the amazing record of this small woman, who was pyramid high in love of the helpless and hapless. Manifestly, the author has been captured by his subject. And Mrs. Dickson of Taiwan, South America, Mainland China, and the World could not have been more fortunate in her biographer.

Dr. Wilson lived with his subject and her family in Taipei, and from that capital city traveled through the lavishly productive paddy and sugar-cane lands of the island's western plain to the offshore, storm-swept Pescadores. He went with her into Taiwan's high mountains and visited the aboriginals there, the tribes of Polynesian origin. He saw her work among the babies and children, the little thieves from the streets and prisons, and the lepers who were without hope until she brought it to them. There is something vastly reassuring about this woman with weatherbeaten cheeks, her accordion and her eyes at times so strangely hypnotic. She literally compels faith, your faith in her, and the faith of all to whom she comes for financial assistance as well as those whom her widely diffused program assists.

In one of his crowded, luminous chapters, the author writes concerning Mrs. Dickson's work:

" 'Where are your projects going to stop?' Lil's sober business friends wondered.

" 'Why should they stop anywhere?' Lil demanded. 'Do we think that God can supply two dollars and not three dollars? Or that, when we see a hungry or sick child, He may say, 'You don't need to care about *that* child—you're doing enough already'? Is any need, anywhere, beyond the love of God? And if it is His concern, should it not be ours?'

" 'You can't take on the whole world!' they argued.

" 'I can't,' Lil agreed. 'God can.' "

I well remember the first time I ran into this "God can" answer. Mrs. Dickson appeared at *Christian Herald* shortly after the establishing of our own orphanage program on Taiwan, a program that she encouraged and indeed made possible. Her work among lepers was just beginning and she needed eighteen thousand dollars for a special building. We were already committed beyond our budget. That was it—or was it? Mrs. Dickson said, "Yes, I understand. But if you *should* receive funds designated for leper work—?" We never had. "Certainly, we will remember," was our reply. That was an easy way out, and I escorted the little woman with the mystical smile to the elevator. Well, within the week eighteen thousand dollars from a giver previously unknown to us, as to her, came to my desk with the request, "Please use this to help lepers." Now the name of *Christian Herald* appears on a building of a leprosarium in Taipei.

Again and again, in project after project, *Angel at Her Shoulder* reveals Mrs. Dickson's unusual pipeline to her Father in Heaven, who is mindful of even the sparrow's fall. At this writing, the up to now unfailing budgets of all "The Mustard Seed" projects directed by this irrepressible woman total considerably more than two hundred fifty thousand dollars annually. It is my judgment, based upon firsthand observation and knowledge of fifteen years, that moneys given for the overseas activities of our Christian churches have never been more wisely and sacrificially disbursed than contributions entrusted to Mrs. Dickson.

There is yet another story to be written about the amazing Dicksons, the story of Jim Dickson—Dr. James I. Dickson—founder and president of the Taiwan Theological College which, from its beautiful mountain setting, looks westward over and beyond the buildings and countryside of Taiwan's picturesque capital city. The husband is as colorful and as dynamic, as wise and as heroic, as his wife. Together they have formed and maintained a service partnership for thirty-five years, which in their field is as perfectly integrated as that of President Chiang Kai-shek and Madame Chiang in the field of politics and government. Always, these Dicksons remind me, not only of the Chiangs, but of the Curies, and of that Ferdinand and Isabella partnership that sent Columbus sailing westward upon uncharted seas.

Finally, this volume reveals one fact in contemporary history that surely needs telling. Had Jim Dickson's warning been heeded when, with Lil, he arrived in Honolulu direct from Taiwan, there might have been no Pearl Harbor debacle.

The ancestry of Lillian LeVesconte places her in the pioneer history of Minnesota and brings her out of Indian warfare and from an abduction that took her grandmother from a home in the State of New York. There are thrills aplenty in Dr. Wilson's book but this Foreword is too long already. Let it conclude with a message Lil wrote her fiancé, Macalester College's long-distance runner, Jimmy Dickson: "We have only one life to live. Let's go where there is the greater need."

And so, trusting in Jesus Christ for strength, they went out, far out and on together.

Preface

In the Amoy dialect of Chinese, which is spoken by native Formosans, *"Ma-ma hoo-hoo"* means "All is confusion." It is an apt characterization of Taiwan itself, whose history has been turbulent and whose soul never its own. It is also a characterization in a quite different way of Lillian Ruth Dickson, one of the most compassionate human typhoons ever to strike this or any other island. The despair of all who pin their faith upon orderly business procedures, she simply pins hers Elsewhere. "We work on a shoestring—but it's God's shoestring." She thinks of herself as housemother for all God's neglected little people of Taiwan.

She never learned to say no to need. Since God supplies the money and physical strength and emotional competence, there are always more where they came from.

If trouble is slow in knocking at her door, this five-foot troubleshooter goes out looking for it. When she quotes "Jesus *went about* doing good," you can see italics that her comfortably seated contemporaries have forgotten. Oblivious of personal slights, she becomes a holy terror when her "humble people" are ill-treated. Tragic need, as well as perils, have put her on friendly terms with the urging and protective presence she calls "The angel at my shoulder."

Hers is not a sterile compassion untouched by human hands and heart. Of her mobile clinic work in an aboriginal mountain village she once said, "If we give them service without love, they would know it. When we give them service with love, they know that too, and they answer with warm impetuous friendship and love that we hope will sweep them into the Kingdom of God."

For her, beauty is as basic as bread. Along with orthodox blankets and vitamins she offers the heresies of candlelight and costume jewelry. And always she offers the simple life-changing Gospel, wrapping all other gifts in it.

But this is not so much the story of a woman who is so utterly dedicated and self-effacing that her name does not even appear on the letterhead of her organization, as it is the story of what God can do and is ready to do when He finds that kind of person. Though focused upon Lillian Dickson, this book is intended as a tribute to all the faithful missionaries who have given and are giving their lives to the people of Taiwan, and whose own stories will perhaps never be told.

Angel at Her Shoulder

I. Among the Headhunters

Something had gone wrong. Lil Dickson, wrapped in a quilt and lying in the chill darkness on the floor of the old Japanese-built house, could sense it. Outside, the rain tapped upon the roof tiles, seeped into the thatched roofs of the bamboo huts huddled in the mountain village of Formosa, rattled upon tree leaves in the dense forest beyond.

Lil tried not to move. She did not want to wake the others—the nurse sleeping beside her, or the doctor, the evangelist, and the other American across the room. Straining every nerve, she listened—nothing but raindrops falling from the roof.

Now wide awake—had she ever been asleep?—Lil sat up quietly. The darkness was thick enough to cut with a knife—a headhunter's knife, she thought wryly, then scoffed at her uneasiness. After all, this was 1947. When she and Jim, her missionary husband, had come to Taiwan twenty years before, headhunting was even then a fading custom. But, Lil recalled, the war years had revived many savage practices, including this one. The Japanese overlords had distrusted and persecuted the mountain people, who had only one way to fight back—by taking heads. With the Japanese gone only two years, they must still be in good form.

Lil lay down again, but sleep would not come. The Japanese house had rustles and creaks all its own. Or *were* they its own?

She had been in the mountains many times, though not often since the war. But never had she felt such cold hostility as in this Tyal village of Sakura. You didn't have to know the language to feel it. Lil had mastered Taiwanese and Japanese before the war. But she couldn't master every language of every tribe. Without the language, one learned to sense attitudes, know what people meant when they talked in words one didn't understand. When there were no words, one sometimes understood even more quickly. A smile needed no interpreter, nor did an anxious mother with a feverish child held tightly in her arms or cradled in a sling on her back, the baby's legs straddling her hips and its head bobbing.

A scowl, with or without words, meant suspicion—and no mistake. The people of Sakura had greeted the Mobile Medical Unit that morning with scowls, and the scowls deepened as the day wore on.

On this trip into the mountains, other villages had received them gladly. Not Sakura. Yet the procedure here had been no different. When they arrived at the little village back in the mountains, not far from where the Tropic of Cancer skewered the island, Lil's eyes lighted up in anticipation as Glen Graber, the Mennonite missionary, assisted her into her accordion straps. She enjoyed bringing music to the mountain people.

The children gathered first. "Nearer, My God, to Thee" was one of the favorites, though the Taiwanese liked the more cheerful words "Come to Jesus." After Lil played for a while, she told Bible stories, the evangelist interpreting. She loved the Bible and she loved children. Her hair was frizzy from the dusty mountain roads and her blue dress wrinkled, but her smile was as bright as ever it was in Taipei, where Jim was head of the Presbyterian seminary.

The children—the smallest ones wearing a romperlike garment conveniently gaping in the rear—listened gladly, but the adults of the village stood remote, glowering. The Tyal tribal tattoo of the married women, an arc of dark purple beginning under the nose and sweeping upward on either cheek toward the ears, and the series of dots the men wore under the lower lips, gave them an alien look. The women wore shapeless but colorful dressees and the men nondescript trousers, some lopped off for freedom of movement. Almost all, young and old, were barefoot.

After the singing and the stories, Lil distributed used Christmas cards to the children who crowded close. Each received two or three, stamped with a Bible verse in Chinese characters. These cards would be the sum total of "literature" in many a Sakura home.

In the afternoon, the clinic was made ready, set up out of cases opened on a commandeered table. The Mennonite Mobile Medical Unit truck had been left far behind. With Rev. Glen Graber in charge, they had come over impossible roads, forded mountain streams or used them as highways, crept through passes on ledges cut out of rock. When they ran out of roads, the five members of the Medical Unit picked up their medicines and walked.

All around them as they had come to Sakura were the mountains, rising sharply against the blue sky—tree-clad, cloud-haloed mountains of such dimension and profusion that they looked, Lil thought, as if God, not knowing what to do with them anywhere else, had flung them down here while He made up His mind. When they labored high enough, breathtaking vistas opened—range upon receding range of purple peaks. Everywhere were the waterfalls, some of them a hundred yards of shimmering gauze from which the wrinkles were being shaken over great rock cliffs. Lil's poetic heart responded to the riotous beauty. Yet she knew that these same mountains spawned sickness and unbelievable poverty. Time had been walled out. The years had managed to get through, but the clock was a century slow.

At Sakura that afternoon, the visitors spread out their medicines —and waited. Slowly, cautiously, the people came. The doctor made the initial examinations, prescribing and dispensing medicines. The simple cases he passed along to Lil, who, with Glen

Graber assisting, bandaged wounds, cuts, and boils, washed out sore eyes with soothing medicine, and tended scabies. Today, when Lil smiled, the patients did not return the smile. They appeared silently like wild forest creatures, took the medicine with no words of greeting and no words of gratitude.

The doctor found just about every disease in the book: great open sores, deep infections, untended wounds. He could only shake his head at symptoms of leprosy and tuberculosis. To pregnant women he gave a supply of vitamins. "Four out of five babies born in the mountains die," he reminded Lil.

One of the most common infestations was intestinal parasites. As a matter of routine, the doctor distributed worm medicine to all comers. It was bitter-tasting stuff—even the men made faces and muttered unhappily; but no one received treatment until taking it.

The clinic staff noticed the distrustfulness of their patients. "*Sakura* is Japanese for 'cherry blossoms,'" Lil remarked to shirt-sleeved Glen Graber, who towered a full fourteen inches over her.

"I don't think our cherry blossoms are happy today," he replied. The native evangelist took it more seriously. He stood off to one side, watching the people come and go, concern growing in his eyes.

Even so, there were so many patients that they were not finished until late in the afternoon—worm medicine for everyone, other medicines according to diagnosis. That evening after a hurried meal prepared by the nurse, the clinic staff held their customary evangelistic meeting. Only a few of the aborigines showed up. Those who did looked more glum than ever.

After the meeting, one of the leaders of the village brought the staff to the old Japanese house where they were to stay overnight. By then the rain had begun; a clammy chill invaded the house. Showing them in, the man stared speculatively at them—at Lil especially, it seemed to her—and commented, "There are lots of snakes around this place—poisonous snakes." Turning to leave, he added, "This is just the kind of night they like to be out."

When the evangelist had translated for Lil, he asked, "Now what do you suppose he meant by *that?*"

"I, for one, have no intention of finding out!" volunteered Lil. "I happen to be allergic to snakes."

The evangelist was not satisfied. "I think there's more to it—"

"You mean," Glen Graber asked, "the way the people have been acting all day?"

"Right. Anywhere else I wouldn't think much about it. But this is Sakura." He went to a window and slid back a panel to look out at the darkness. Turning, he said, "There was a massacre here not too many years ago." He thought a moment. "Fifteen years ago—1932. Foreigners—the Japanese—were responsible."

"And you and I are foreigners," Lil said, looking at Glen. It didn't sound quite as carefree as she had intended it should.

"The Japanese tried to hush it up," the evangelist went on. "But we heard about things, down on the plains. We heard in spite of the fence, three hundred and sixty miles long, which the Japanese built to keep the tribespeople from getting out of the mountains and outsiders, especially missionaries, from getting in. They even electrified more than two hundred miles of it. But we heard."

"The mountain people did not like the Japanese," the doctor continued. "The Japanese sent police everywhere, even into the mountains."

"I thought the mountain men were fighters," said Glen. "Didn't they fight back?"

"They killed thousands of Japanese soldiers," the doctor said quietly, "by taking their heads."

"They were fighters," Glen agreed quickly.

"And still are," the evangelist said.

"Where does Sakura come into it?" Lil asked, lying down in her clothes and pulling her quilt around her. It was getting colder, and the rain was coming down harder now.

"Some of the Japanese police tried to force their attention upon the Tyal women," the evangelist said. "The Tyal men sharpened their knives and planned very carefully a way to avenge themselves." He paused to roll up in his own quilt.

"How did they do it?" Lil wanted to know.

Lifting himself on his elbow, the evangelist went on, "A school near Po-li was holding its sports day and the whole town had turned out to watch. During the festivities, the Tyals slipped into town. First they sent their own children home, then cut communication lines. After they overran the police station, they swept through the crowd, their knives flashing. Every Japanese man, woman, and child was beheaded—more than two hundred in all. Then the raiders retreated—to Sakura, this very village."

Lil's voice was small and sad. "The Japanese followed, of course."

The evangelist nodded. "Planes came, but planes are not of much use in the mountains. Troops came next—on the roads as far as there were roads, and then on foot as we came. The Tyal men who had taken part in the massacre sought refuge on the mountaintop above us. The Japanese saw they could not take the position, and so they sat down and waited, day after day. While the families of the men watched helplessly from here in the village, their fathers and husbands were starved to death."

"The Japanese have gone now," Glen Graber observed.

"But memories stayed," the doctor said. "Relatives of those who died in the siege of Sakura were among those we treated today."

"They didn't like that worm medicine, did they?" Lil smiled. "I don't blame them. There ought to be a worm medicine that tastes good—"

The doctor was thinking about something. "Not only doesn't it taste good—" He left the rest unsaid.

"Well, time to turn in," said Glen. The men retreated to one side of the room with the evangelist, and the nurse wrapped herself up near Lil, on the other side.

Was this the feeling she had sensed, Lil wondered—that what evil foreigners had done once, other foreigners could do again? Were these people held so tightly in the grip of an old hatred that they could not recognize Christian love, much less respond to it? Outside, the rain dripped down, sounding like stealthy footsteps.

About that time there were other footsteps that Lil could not hear. The Tyal who had brought them to this house was even then slipping out of his hut, carrying a long knife, stepping carefully and silently to a bamboo shelter larger than the huts. Moving in among the dozen or more men already there, he felt a sudden wrenching, gripping knot in his stomach. He twinged momentarily as he took his seat on a woven mat. Then the pain was gone. A small flickering fire cast shadows on the tattooed faces around him. A wrinkled old man was talking. "Once we were people of the plains. Then our enemies came and took our good lands and pushed us into the hills. Others followed them and forced us into the high mountains. The Japanese came into the mountains, telling us how to live our lives, what to think, what kind of religion we must believe in. Always evil has come from the plains . . ."

Lying uneasily in the Japanese house, the house that was itself a hated reminder of the past to the people of Sakura, Lil smelled woodsmoke. She was thinking of the comment their host had made about snakes. Was it only this that was troubling her? The stocky woman in her late forties pulled the quilt tightly around her shoulders, wishing for the dawn. Darkness or light, surely it was all the same to God. Surely, too, God had a hand in this. Otherwise, she would have been living a quiet chairman-of-the-ladies'-aid life in America, where, as some other Americans were frank to say, she "belonged." Instead, she was the wife of tall, rugged Jim Dickson, Dakota cowboy turned missionary.

Together they had come to Taiwan in 1927—outsiders called it Formosa—under The Presbyterian Church in Canada, the denomination primarily interested in northern Formosa. Jim was the missionary, Lil the missionary's wife. That was the way their board operated. For several years she had been content to be simply the lady of the house, mothering her children, serving as hostess and general backstop in her husband's work. Then she had decided that she wasn't going to sit out her life. She became a missionary in her own right, an "unofficial" one, with Jim's blessing if not the board's. Jim, a pioneer in the mountain work, and eager to enlist help wherever he could find it, requested the Mennonites to send a medical unit and their missionary Glen Graber from China. Lil, carrying her accordion, often went with the truck into the hills. "Mother on the Medical Unit," the mountain people called her. What would she be doing tonight if she had stayed comfortably at home in Minnesota? Lil wondered. But she had once told Jim, "We are safe only where God wants us to be." This drafty, creaking house in Sakura was that place, she was sure.

A gust of wind brought a damp breath of woodsmoke.

In the council house, smoke from the fire drifted close to the ground, held by the moisture-laden air. Another Tyal was on his feet. "Why did the two foreigners and the others from the plains come to Sakura? Why did they make us drink their foul-tasting medicine? Was it really medicine? Was it—" Suddenly he doubled over as if he had been run through with a spear. A murmur ran through the group and fear showed on the faces in the firelight. The old man who had spoken first stood to his feet, and was himself hit by a wave of pain.

"Poison!" gasped the old man. "They poisoned us! Take their heads! I myself will deal with the foreign woman devil!" He reached for his long knife, but before he could wrest it from its sheath, he fell to the floor. The wail mounted as another was seized, and another. "Kill them! None must escape alive!" the hoarse cries went up.

"We can do nothing now—" the old man moaned, his body racked by waves of fire in his belly.

Lil heard far-off excited voices. But it was the noise at her elbow that brought her full awake.

The snake is in! her nerves screamed. Sitting up, she switched on her flashlight—catching a startled kitten squarely in the beam. Frightened by the sudden light and motion, the kitten leaped, scattering the remains of a bag of peanuts over the floor.

That had been the rustling noise—a curious kitten investigating an intriguing bag! Chuckling softly, Lil picked up the peanuts. Switching off the flashlight, she tucked it away by her side and pulled up the quilt against the night's chill. With a sigh of relief, she closed her eyes. God was awake. There was no use for both of them to lose sleep.

By morning, the fire in the council house had burned out. The Tyal men, weakened by their ordeal of the night, crept back to consult together. The wrinkled old one looked at the others, then at his long knife still lying on the floor. Picking it up, he balanced the sheath in his hand while the barest hint of laughter lit his eyes. "We will not need our knives," he said. "Are there any among you who are not convinced it *was* worm medicine?"

Lil and the others were up, warming themselves in the morning sun, when their host of the night before arrived. In apologetic words he spoke at length to the evangelist.

"What does he say?" Lil wondered.

"He says we'll live," the evangelist assured her, and told what had happened during the night.

"It must have been an angel that held them off," said Lil.

"Or cramps," said Glen, wiping his forehead suddenly—and gratefully.

2. Only One Life

Lil came naturally by her spirit of adventure and "unorthodoxy." Many people, early and late, had a part in making her what she became. There was Jim Dickson, who went from Dalzell, South Dakota, to St. Paul to attend Macalester College, where he met Lillian LeVesconte, the girl he would marry. There was Glenn Clark, her professor of English, who taught her writing and the conviction that "God's power is always available whenever you put yourself utterly and completely in His hands." There were Lil's artist mother and her progressive father, who blessed their daughter with a happy girlhood in Prior Lake, Minnesota. And there was Lil's grandmother.

In 1833, her grandmother, then three years old, was living in New York State. One evening the child's mother fell and cut a gash in her head. The father had to take the mother to the nearest hospital, which was in Albany. Because she would be in the hospital for some time, he had to arrange for the care of the children. When any emergency arose, it was the custom to parcel out the children to neighbors.

The lively three-year-old was given to a German woman.

Several times the child tried to run away home, across the fields. The neighbor grew exasperated.

At this time Rev. and Mrs. Jedidiah Stevens, a missionary couple on their way to the wilds of Minnesota to take up work among the Indians, stopped in the community and stayed at the German woman's house. They were attracted to the little girl, especially because they had lost a child of their own.

"I think the mother will die," the German woman said when the Stevenses were ready to push on. "Why don't you take her?"

It seemed the humane thing to do.

When the father returned home a few days later and heard the story, he sounded a dismayed alarm. Other neighbors rallied and agreed to form a pursuit party. The posse jolted westward along the road the missionary couple was believed to have taken.

Mr. and Mrs. Stevens, with the child, stopped at a tavern in Ohio to spend the night. Mrs. Stevens and the girl went to bed, Mr. Stevens went downstairs to the public room. Seated in front of a trencher of tasty stew, meanwhile engrossed in a book, he tried to pay no attention to the unministerial talk at the bar and was grateful when conversation subsided at the sound of hoof-beats. He looked up from his book when the door was flung open and a rider shouldered his way though the room. At the bar the newcomer announced, "Fast team coming! They're looking for somebody who stole a little girl."

The Rev. Mr. Stevens suddenly choked and his book hit the table with a thud. He walked slowly from the room, but once out of sight, he raced up the stairs and woke his wife. Bundling the child into her clothes, they hurried down to the stable. Even if Mr. Stevens by then had wished to return the child, to do so might have endangered his life; an angry father was likely to shoot first and ask questions afterward.

Soon their pursuers arrived at the tavern. "We're on their heels!" the father reported excitedly. "By this time tomorrow night we'll easily have them."

His neighbors looked at him sympathetically, but shook their heads. "This is as far as we go," one of them said. "Already we've come clear across New York and we've got to get back for spring planting."

The mother recovered, but neither she nor the father ever saw their child again. Mr. and Mrs. Stevens pushed westward and settled in the St. Paul-Minneapolis area. Very few white people were there at that time, but they did find many Indians, and the Stevenses made work among them their vocation.

Lil's grandmother soon learned their language. When the Indians found that Mrs. Stevens was not her mother—she remembered her own mother—they gave her the name "Little Crow Which Has Been Caught." She played with the Indian children; when the braves came back from battle, the little girl saw them dance with bloody scalps at their waists.

Says Lil, "Though some of the Indians proposed to her years afterward, she married a white man, my Grandfather Gibbs. They built a log cabin in a district that was later a part of St. Paul."

At the time of the Sioux outbreak in 1862, young warriors who had been her childhood playmates slipped in to warn her. "You must take your husband and go away. This time they are out to kill all the white people."

Her husband was a stubborn man and would not leave. On the night of the Sioux massacre, he was away. With her wide-eyed little ones she watched houses burning in the distance. Fires blazed up, one after another, coming in her direction. But soldiers from Fort Snelling arrived in time and she was not touched.

When Lil's mother grew up, she took Grandmother Gibbs back to New York State. Of course, Grandmother Gibbs's mother had died, but they did find relatives who had heard of the child who was "kidnaped."

Today in St. Paul, the house of Lil's grandmother still stands. The log cabin later had a house built around it, and the whole structure is a historical museum that school children by the hundreds go to visit.

Lil's mother, Lillie Belle Gibbs, was the youngest of the family. From the start, she was an artist. When she went to school, her schoolmates would offer, "We'll do your arithmetic, if you will draw our pictures." Later on, she could sell any picture she painted. When she married John LeVesconte, whose family had come to America from the English Channel Isle of Jersey when he was nine, she gave up her painting but managed nevertheless to instill an appreciation of beauty in her children.

Lillian, third of John and Lillie's four children, was born at Prior Lake, January 29, 1901. "I had a big brother Harold," she says, "a big sister Amy, and a younger brother Lester. These three had the brains—I was supposed to be the one that was not worthwhile. I think they all hoped I'd get married quickly."

During all her childhood, there were lakes in view. This meant skating in winter, swimming in summer, picnics along the lake shore, boating. "I used to swim down the lake, a mile down and a mile back—two miles without stopping, just for the fun of it. I'm surprised now that my parents let me do it."

Lil's father kept abreast of the times. "We had the first Edison phonograph in the community. We had the first car, too—people used to line the roads to see it go by."

Prior Lake was basically a Catholic community. The Presbyterians had a constituency of about a dozen, of which the LeVesconte family made up a large part. "I never knew until later that sometimes Protestants and Catholics do not get along well with each other." When the Presbyterian Church mortgage was about to be foreclosed, the Catholic young people put on a benefit, raised the needed money, and brought it to Lil's mother. "We'd do as much for our own," they said. Lillie LeVesconte visited the sick as religiously as the local priest; sometimes they would meet across a sickbed.

Professors from Macalester, the nearest Presbyterian college, often preached in the small Prior Lake church. When John LeVesconte insisted that his children attend college, he had Macalester in mind. He himself was in the first class to be graduated from the University of Minnesota Agricultural College. A mail carrier and dairyman, he didn't have enough money to finance their schooling singlehanded. Lillie Belle had inherited a piece of land between the Twin Cities; proceeds from its sale met part of the expenses and the children worked out the rest.

All the children went to college. Today, Harold is a patent attorney in California. Amy has her Ph.D. in biochemistry and teaches at Mary Hardin Baylor College, Belton, Texas. Lester, the "little one" (now six feet tall), lives in Chicago, where he is an electrical engineer.

During her summers at Macalester, Lil worked fulltime as a stenographer, thanks to the business course she had taken after high school. During the college term, she served the board of trustees as secretary, going to classes in the mornings, working afternoons, studying evenings.

Her classmates kept asking her, "Why don't the trustees do something for us? Why don't they give us a better school? Why do we always have a football team that never wins, and no gymnasium?" So one day she went to Professor Glenn Clark and said, "I want your opinion on an idea."

He listened.

"What do you think of the student body giving a thank-you banquet to the trustees?" she said. "We wouldn't say anything about wanting a new gymnasium or anything. We'd just thank them for all the help they've given to the college in the past. The students would be all dressed up and looking their best, and the trustees would be encouraged. It would be good for both groups."

Professor Clark gave her a queer look. "Where did you get that idea?"

"It just came," she replied.

He said, "No, it didn't. It came from God," and he went out and shut the door.

Lil felt baffled. She didn't know how to go on or whether she should try.

A few days later Professor Clark sent for her and said, "Present it to the students at chapel hour. Tell them that the trustees are like a team that has been playing a game with nobody in the bleachers. Let's fill the bleachers for once, and give them a cheer."

Lil secured the reluctant consent of the chapel committee. Speakers were chosen, talks planned and given. She took the college paper containing a report of the chapel meeting to the trustees and said, "See what the students want to do—give a thank-you banquet for you!" The trustees seemed interested.

They had the banquet at the House of Hope church. Trustee George Dayton stood up and said, "For more than thirty-five years I've been a member of this board, and this is the first time anyone has ever said thank you." Lil wasn't prepared for what came a few days later. The St. Paul newspapers blazed in great headlines: "MACALESTER BOARD OF TRUSTEES START A MILLION-DOLLAR BUILDING PROGRAM—NEW GYMNASIUM PROMISED."

Professor Clark doubled as track coach. One of his long-distance runners, Jim Dickson, a lanky boy from a South Dakota ranch, didn't greatly impress Lillian LeVesconte when she first met him. "Jim was just one of the men at college. There were a lot of nice boys there. I became acquainted with him principally in Christian Endeavor work."

It was in his capacity as Christian Endeavor treasurer that she thought he might be useful to her. Out of her monthly earnings of forty dollars she was in the habit of taking "according to Scripture" one-tenth, four dollars, to buy fruit and cakes for the charity basement of the city hospital, where she distributed her gifts from bed to bed.

"But Christmas was coming, and I knew that four dollars would not be enough," she recalls. "Jim had the Christian Endeavor Christmas money to use. So I went to him and asked if some could be used in the basement of the city hospital. He thought it was a good idea, and got it voted. We bought presents and took them down—his first trip there."

Jim ran a furniture moving business on the side. Acquiring a ramshackle truck, he advertised, "We move anything"—an optimistic approach that has never deserted him. Built of sinew and muscle, he had the perfect physique for a mover.

"Jim was an earnest Christian," says Lil. "He was going to be a missionary and go to China. He asked me one time: 'Why don't you be a missionary?' It made me furious. The idea of *my* being a missionary!"

After their graduation from Macalester in 1924, Jim went to Princeton Seminary and Lil taught high school in northern Minnesota for a year. They knew by now that they would be married when Jim completed his three years of seminary training, and that Lil would be a missionary after all. The next year she enrolled in Biblical Seminary in New York and the following year at National Bible Institute. The Institute had four mission halls going every night, and an outdoor meeting every day. Participation in these was a part of her training, as was a medical course for missionaries. In addition, at night at the YWCA, Lil taught English classes for newcomers to America.

Jim did student work in Canada one summer. As a result, The Presbyterian Church in Canada asked him to come and settle in that country. "I'm going to the mission field," he informed them.

"In that case," an official replied, "be our missionary—go out under our church."

"What do you think?" Jim wrote to his bride-to-be. "They want us to go to Formosa, which is a Canadian and English Presbyterian field. They say they have a greater need than the American Presbyterians."

"Fine, if true," Lil wrote back. "So many people say that just to get you. But if it's true, let's go where there is the greater need. We have only one life to live." So it was Formosa.

On May 16, 1927, they were married at Princeton, New Jersey. In a decrepit car—his classmates said they would never make it—they went up through New England, across into Canada, came back down to the States and headed west. At Vancouver, they sold the car and all their possessions to an obliging customs officer and were on their way.

3. "Beautiful Isle"

No steamer went directly from America to Formosa, so Jim and Lillian Dickson honeymooned their way across the Pacific to Shanghai. In 1927 when the Dicksons arrived, Shanghai, a city of foreign concessions, was Chinese only in its Chinatown.

While they waited for a ship to take them the rest of the way, they stayed in the China Inland Mission home where a Princeton classmate of Jim's was living. Lil paid no attention to their lively table talk of barbed wire and bullets.

"Anyway," said the classmate, "I think it's all over now. Let's get a taxi, and I'll take you down and show you Chinatown."

As they drove, the street was suddenly crowded with people.

"I don't know where they came from," Lil recalls. "It was a mob—tightly packed. They surged toward the car and around it, even climbed on the top. A spokesman for the mob yelled something to the driver, and of course I didn't know what he said or what the driver answered. But the crowd fell back, and some of the people even smiled at us."

Some blocks distant, the driver turned to Jim's friend, put what was obviously a question, got in reply a vehement nod.

Jim, in his staccato manner of speaking, snapped, "What did he say? What happened? What's it all about?"

His friend explained, "Back there, they asked if we were English or American. The driver didn't have the slightest notion, but he assured them we were all Americans. Just now he was checking up, and I made an honest man of him. That crowd wanted the blood of an Englishman."

Lil was relieved when a few days later they went down to the wharf to board the boat that would take them on to Formosa. "My, it's little," Lil sighed, as they got their first look at the grubby coastal steamer.

"But," Jim pointed out, "it *does* go where we want to go."

On the boat, to be accommodated, they had to be separated. Lil was put with another woman, who, by way of introduction, said brightly, "I was on a boat that was captured by pirates not long ago—a boat like this." The threat of pirates did not seem as dismaying at the moment as the gagging stench that saturated the ship. It was an inescapable, dominating presence.

"What's that awful smell?" Lil asked Jim, when they had a chance to be together on deck.

"That smell, Lil dear, is *everything*—compounded of all the cargoes that this boat has carried in forty years."

At Foochow, a missionary fellow passenger, a Mr. Christian, who was leaving the boat, invited the couple to come to his house to stay overnight while the ship was in dock. "Little less gamey, you know. Build up your resistance." They gratefully accepted.

"When we reached his house," says Lil, "his wife was surprised to see us but welcomed us in and sent out the soup to be watered again, I guess. Then we sat down to eat."

During the meal, with a spoonful of soup midway between bowl and mouth, Mrs. Christian remembered something. Turning to her husband, she remarked, "Something odd happened while I was having lunch yesterday. I heard a noise outside—like firecrackers, but not quite. I went out and someone shouted, 'Mrs. Christian, go inside! There's a battle going on over at the compound.' " She lifted the spoon. "Sure enough, there was."

"I'm not used to having war every day!" Lil exclaimed to Jim that night when they had turned in.

From Foochow, the ship headed across the Formosa Strait.

"Not far," Jim assured Lil. "Only about a hundred miles." But a few hours later, when the boat began pitching, the distance seemed to approach infinity. The small craft was wrenched high on waves that grew more mountainous by the minute. At each crest, it hesitated a moment, then creaked despairingly and plunged down into the trough.

Climbing into her bunk, Lil watched queasily as trunks skidded from one side of the cabin to the other. Slowly, she became aware of a knock at the door. "Come in," she said feebly.

It was Jim. "Tail of a typhoon," he reported. "Don't go on deck—waves washing over everything."

"I have no intention of going on deck," said Lil, turning her face to the wall.

"You stay right here and I'll bring you something to eat."

"Jim, *please!*"

The next morning there was again a knock at the door.

"We're here, Lil!" Jim called. "Formosa! All out!"

Lil opened her eyes cautiously. The blankets were soaked with sea water that had come in around the porthole. The motion seemed to have stopped—blessed relief. She was alive, she discovered with no little amazement.

Joining Jim on deck, Lil looked out at the land that was to be their home.

"Keelung," he said. "A port city is not the greatest introduction to a country, but it's the best I can do at the moment."

"It's beautiful," Lil whispered. They could see the mountains rising on either side of the Keelung River, terraced part way with yellow-green ricefields and then rising until they were lost in blue haze. On shore, coolies wearing conical straw hats were pulling carts loaded with everything from logs to squealing pigs. Rickshaw men, their arm and leg muscles rippling, jogged along in the shafts of their two-wheeled vehicles, while their passengers sat relaxed and impassive.

The busy port provided an accompaniment of rattling winches and shrill commands shouted in a strange language.

"Did you ever notice," Lil observed, "that when you don't understand the language, everyone sounds angry? As if they're going to tear each other apart—when maybe they're just saying 'Good morning!' " She listened to another sound. "The international distress signal," she said. "A baby crying! Anybody can understand that."

The Japanese authorities, always thorough and wary right now of anyone coming from China, kept them on board until evening. "I want to learn everything about Formosa and see everything," Lil said, refusing to go below. "I want to hear the noises and smell the smells. Although," she added, "right now, the smells of the ship overpower everything else."

"I can tell you a little about the island," said Jim, "but not everything. It's shaped something like a tobacco leaf and is larger than Vermont and Connecticut taken together. As the crow flies, the longest line north to south is some two hundred and thirty miles, but no crow would be foolish enough to try it, for the route goes over one rugged peak after another. Some of them are more than ten thousand feet high. The island's greatest width is about eighty miles. We're east of South China, separated from the mainland by the Formosa Strait—you're already acquainted with *it*."

Lil shuddered.

"Someday," said Jim, "we'll get to the Pescadore Islands, twenty-five miles west. To our east—open ocean, till you reach Hawaii, and that's a long way—almost five thousand miles."

The passengers were eventually cleared, and Jim and Lil went by rickshaw to the railroad station. Few people on the island spoke English, and the two of them could speak no other language. Very slowly, Jim asked the ticket agent, "How . . . long . . . before . . . a train . . . for Taihoku?"

The Japanese agent, proud of his English, answered confidently, "Ten hours." They were still wondering how to put in the time when ten minutes later a train chuffed in and the agent pointed it out to them. He had simply got his words mixed.

At Taihoku—Japanese for Taipei—they telephoned the mission compound and a missionary came to the station to pick them up. The main thoroughfare was then a dirt road and the mission compound stood in a cow pasture. To this day, old Formosan hands greet compound residents with a knowing nod, adding, "Oh, you live in the cow pasture."

While they boarded with a missionary, their first job was to get the language—in five hours of study a day. That would go on for two years. On weekends, they went out to visit country churches, traveling sometimes by train, sometimes by bicycle.

Lil learned something about the history of the island, and on her trips with Jim, saw the amazing mountain barrier that divides it north and south. The western third of the island, she discovered, was a great undulating plain. The eastern two-thirds was filled with mountains, standing side by side and behind each other as if stacked on bleachers. The backs of the last tier were cliffs that plunged sharply into the sea.

"You never understand people anywhere until you understand the geographic forces and also the human forces that influenced them," Jim said to her.

All kinds of forces had influenced Formosa, she learned—Chinese, Japanese, Portuguese, Spanish, Dutch, Chinese again, and then once more, Japanese.

The Chinese came in the sixth century to compel the payment of tribute to the Emperor. Unable to enforce submission, the "Son of Heaven" then simply ignored Formosa. After that nothing much happened until the thirteenth century. Mongol rulers of the Yuan Dynasty, after acquiring complete control of mainland China, looked around for other worlds to conquer. The Pescadores attracted them and they gained control of those islands, using them as a base from which to conquer Formosa. When Formosa had been subdued, a large number of Chinese immigrants came in.

About this time the island became a center for both Chinese

and Japanese pirates. When trade was slack, they sacked and burned mainland coast villages. The Japanese kept to the Keelung area, the Chinese to South Formosa. Despite their mutual unfriendliness, Formosa became a kind of unofficial clearing house for trade between them. This attracted in time a more reputable class of merchants who decided they could do better in legitimate business than in piracy.

The European phase of the island's history began late in the 1500's. The Portuguese had won special concessions at Macao on the mainland coast, not far from the present Hong Kong. One of the Portuguese ships blown off course "discovered" an island that so impressed its captain with its beauty that he exclaimed, "Ihla Formosa!" ("Beautiful isle!") The name of Formosa stuck, at least as far as Europeans were concerned.

"It's almost funny," Lil remarked to Jim. "You hear that the Portuguese 'discovered' Formosa—when the people who lived here knew all the time that it was here!"

In 1612, during the Ming Dynasty, the Chinese gave to the island the name Taiwan ("Terraced Bay"). At about the same time, two Dutch warships arrived at the Pescadores (a Dutch name meaning "fishermen"). In 1624 they landed on Formosa, or Taiwan. There the Dutch built Fort Zeelandia near Tainan, on the southwest coast. In 1626, the Spaniards came to the northern tip of the island, built San Salvador and another city, San Domingo, at the site of Tamsui, where they also built a fort. The Dutch, unnerved by the competition, attacked the Spaniards and drove them out in 1641, ending their fifteen-year stay. In the wake of the traders came the missionaries who were startled by certain prevalent practices.

"Did you know that in those days a married man could not reside permanently with his wife until he was fifty years old?" Lil asked Jim.

"I like our system better," he said with a smile.

"And that"—her expression sobered—"it was a disgrace if a woman gave birth to a child before her thirty-seventh year?" Lil had wondered about children. When would she have her own—and what would it be like, bringing them up in a strange land?

"The Dutch lasted thirty-eight years," Lil declared to Jim, as if he were hearing her lessons.

"And you can thank them for the waterbuffalo you see all over the island," Jim said. "They brought them in from the East Indies."

"You know what caused their downfall?" Lil asked. "A disgruntled employee. See that it never happens to you!"

Ho-ping, the employee with the grievance, was particularly resentful of ill-treatment of the Chinese at the hands of the Dutch. When a Chinese warrior known to Westerners as Koxinga, champion of the Ming Dynasty and unsuccessful fighter against the Manchus, paused in Amoy to lick his wounds, Ho-ping saw in him a way of driving out the Dutch, and refitting Koxinga for a victorious campaign against the Manchus. He told Koxinga: "Take the island. Assemble and multiply people there for ten years. Train and feed them for another ten years. Then—the mainland."

The Dutch with only two thousand troops stood up to Koxinga's twenty-five thousand men and his nine hundred war junks for seven months. Victorious, Koxinga set himself up as ruler of the island. He gave each soldier a plot of land. Foreign trade was encouraged. More than five hundred scholars came over from the mainland to give him assistance.

But after an administration of only five months, Koxinga died in 1662 at the age of thirty-six. His son succeeded him and was in turn succeeded by his son. By that time the Manchus were ready to fight back. In 1683, a Manchu admiral conquered the Pescadores and then Taiwan, which was made a part of the Chinese province of Fukien. Attempts at independence within the decade following American independence were put down. Chinese rule continued for two-hundred thirty-three years, ending only when Taiwan was ceded to Japan at the end of the first Sino-Japanese War in 1895.

The Japanese brought technical skills to the island, Lil soon learned. They knew how to run things. They built roads, dug sewers, developed irrigation, tunneled mountains, flung spider-web cable suspension bridges across valleys, built railroads and rebuilt them when typhoons swept away the roadbed. They introduced and required a common language—Japanese—and then forbade the distribution of Bibles in that language. Trying to squeeze the life out of Christian education, they built Shinto shrines. Increasingly, they restricted the Christian faith that had first come to the island with the Dutch and the Spaniards.

Soon they would conceive their Greater Asia plan and begin to slap and pound and mold Formosa and Formosans into the southwestern anchor point of an Empire that would dominate all of the Pacific. That part of it Lil didn't know yet. All she knew was that she was homesick.

"Formosa was beautiful," she remembers, "but so different! I was homesick every day for the first seven years I was there, thinking of America. I would go to Taipei on the pretext of shopping. Actually I was hoping that perhaps a ship had come in, perhaps some Westerners had come ashore, and I would see one. But I never did. The mail arrived only once every six weeks or so. Sometimes I had the notion that the American continent must have sunk into the sea like lost Atlantis."

As her first Christmas on Formosa neared, one of the missionaries said to her, "Now, Mrs. Dickson, on Christmas Day, we always give a church dinner for the lepers." Across the street from the compound were a leprosy clinic and small church.

In a holiday mood, Lil helped to decorate the church. She had never seen a leper but she faced the prospect with mingled timidity and elation. Lepers seemed so Biblical.

When Christmas Day came, the church was crowded to suffocation. The missionaries, carrying trays of food, moved among the patients. The disease had made a mockery of human features: here a nose had been wasted away, there fingers and hands were gone. Some were blind, their wide-open snow-white unseeing eyes turning toward every nearby sound. Lil suddenly felt sick. She tightened her grip on her tray and forced herself to walk on to the next table and then to smile through her tears at a guest who smiled grotesquely at her.

"That was an experience I'll never forget!" she said to Jim afterward.

"I don't think the Lord Jesus ever did, either," he said gently.

In 1929, the Dicksons moved to Tamsui, the original mission base built on the Tamsui River where it flows into the sea, about fifteen miles northwest of Taipei. Their house was a huge red-brick structure with enormous rooms and windows. "When I first saw it," says Lil, "I wondered what we would use for furniture. The curtains for the first floor alone required thirty-nine yards of material. It took me six months just to save enough money for them."

The great mission house was one of two that sat on a bluff overlooking the river. The sea was on the right and Koan-im Soa—"Queen of Heaven Mountain"—across the river. Before the river silted up, big ships used to go by to their anchorage near Taipei. Sometimes an unidentified ship would slip in furtively and move out in the darkness. The whisper went round, "Pirates!"

Here, Lil began the first phase of her career on Formosa as the wife of a missionary, and it left her feeling empty. Helping Jim as best she could, filling her days with housekeeping and with language study, were not enough. There was room in the big house. Children were needed to bring the house alive.

4. Snakes for Lunch

When Lil realized she was going to have a baby, the ricefields never looked greener nor the mountain haze more lovely. Joyfully she made preparations—clothes for the newcomer, baby things that waiting mothers unfold and look at and pat gently, then fold again and put away for a while. The mission's new doctor in Taipei was young but well trained, they said. There were stars in her eyes the night Jim took her to the hospital in an ancient taxi. "Don't you worry," Lil said to him, in the way of all mothers. In the way of all fathers, he *did* worry—and when an hour later the young doctor put to him the brutal choice, "Do you want your wife or your baby?" Jim replied, "My wife!"

Back from the hospital, Lil placed the baby things on the top shelf of the closet.

When her second baby was on the way, she took them down again with a small knot of anxiety in her heart. Could she dare to hope this time? She stroked the baby-soft garments, and waited. Their little daughter arrived prematurely. Two weeks after she was born, Lil was watching the infant in her crib at the hospital, when the nurse came to her and said gently, "She is dead."

The doctor tried to comfort her. "Missionaries in China lose two out of five."

"I have lost my two," Lil said sadly. "Now I should be allowed to keep the next."

The garments did not come down from the shelf again until Ronald was safely born in 1931. He was a big, husky boy. In 1932, Ronny's sister Marilyn arrived. Even after Ronny and Marilyn were many months old, Lil would wake in the night and steal softly to their beds and listen to be sure they were still breathing.

Jim was not only principal of the big middle school at Tamsui, but later of the theological college, and for a while he held both jobs. At every opportunity, and as the Japanese permitted, he was off in the mountains doing evangelistic work, sometimes for three weeks at a stretch. After the children came, one of the other missionaries said to Lil, "You will never be alone again."

In addition, Jim served on innumerable committees—many of which met at the Dickson home. According to custom, tea was always served. "Tea" included sandwiches, cakes, cookies, all of which had to be made. There were many guests, both expected and unexpected. "Poise," Lil wrote to friends, "is the sense of not being disturbed when sixty people come to your house for meals three times a day!" Besides regular guests, students from the school often seemed to be around at mealtime.

Once, when it was announced that a leaders' conference would be held at the Dickson home, someone asked Lil, "And what do *you* do for the conference?" That gave her pause. It was true that she startled no audience with thrilling words, waved no baton to teach them new tunes. "I am the innkeeper's wife," she replied.

In the local church in which Jim was involved, there were two tongs, or family groupings, that carried on a brisk feud. Even in the work of the church they sparred for power and for position on committees. Sometimes members of both tongs were on the same committee when it met in Jim's study. Lil knew that hot arguments sometimes developed. "They can fight in there," she said to Jim, "but they're *not* going to fight at my table when they come out for lunch!" She developed a plan to forestall any unpleasantness.

"I worked out not only the menu, but the topics of conversation. As we sat down, right after grace I would begin introducing subjects of universal interest—things people could not possibly fight about. If you have twelve men, each one or many of them can contribute something about the last typhoon, for example. Typhoons hit our island almost every year. That's a good topic for talk."

Sometimes to get the stories started, she would tell of the typhoon that hit when Marilyn was just two weeks old. The four of them—Marilyn, Ronny, Jim, and Lil—were in Taipei, planning to take the train home to Tamsui. The classic signs of typhoons had been showing.

First, there was the day or so of uncertain weather. The wind came in horizontal gusts, stopped blowing, started again. There was a mist that became a drizzle. Then rain began in earnest and the wind grew stronger. Wind-whipped, the rain searched out cracks that would let it into buildings, tested roof tiles and swept away any that were loose.

As the wind drove the rain, so it also drove the sea in and over low-lying land areas. When the typhoon coincided with a full moon and tides were highest, rain and wave became brutal allies. Because the valley lying between Taipei and Tamsui, was almost at sea level all the way, it was especially vulnerable to the typhoon-tidal combination.

The water was rising and already boats were being used in the streets, and so Jim took the train ahead of the one they planned to take. "You and Marilyn and Ronny wait in Taipei until I come for you," Jim said in his clipped tones. "I don't think it will amount to much, but you're nervous about it, Lil, so just wait."

By afternoon the water had gone down enough so that Jim could get through by car to pick them up.

"You look paler than usual," Lil said to her blond husband.

He was strangely quiet.

"What happened?"

"When we go by, I'll show you."

As they drove along the valley to Tamsui, Jim pointed. The crumpled coaches of a train were lying in a ravine, where they had been blown from the tracks. Workmen were carrying bodies out of the wrecked cars.

"I made inquiries," said Jim. "That was the train we were all planning to take."

Typhoons took care of the first course at lunch. The choicest topic Lil reserved for "the most dangerous course" which was dessert. By then, the feuding tong members would likely feel so much at ease they would begin unleashing insults.

"I always saved snakes for dessert. I might comment on the fact that at the Taipei compound—floods seemed to hit it especially hard—high water brought out the snakes and rats. In a typhoon they are friendly to each other and even to humans—all they want to do is climb up on you to get out of the water! They see a human being as an island of safety. All things grow tame in the face of natural disaster."

With just a bit of such encouragement, each one of the committee members would tell his own snake story. Everybody had one and enjoyed recounting it. By the time they'd finished their snake stories, dessert was over and they could go back to the study and fight as they pleased. But there had been no fighting at the table.

One of the most startling of Lil's occasional guests was Chi-oang, a tiny woman past middle age. The purple tattoo markings of the Tyal tribe swept upward across her face. Jim had found this Christian aborigine on the east coast, and was able to converse with her because she spoke Taiwanese. He urged her to come to Tamsui to attend the Women's Bible School. At first she hesitated. Was she not too old? Would she not be out of place among the other students? Even her tattoo marks would make her an object of curiosity. But finally she agreed to come.

Lil found a gentle spirit in this unlettered woman from the most savage of the mountain tribes. Chi-oang, she learned, was a woman to be reckoned with: She had negotiated peace between the Japanese army and the Tyals. Lil could not know that this frail, sickly woman would be God's evangelist through whom literally thousands of mountain people would find God during World War II years when no missionaries could be in the country. Lil knew only that this strange little creature needed kindness and love.

Do-wai, a Tyal young man, was another of the students who enjoyed her hospitality. His potential, too, as a channel of God's blessing was unsuspected.

"The mountain people seem different from the people of the plains," Lil said to Jim. "They have different features, not Chinese or Japanese at all. They are taller. And they're darker than the plainspeople."

"But, you see, mountain people *are* different," said Jim, and Lil knew that a lecture was coming on. Not only were his words not tumbling out all over themselves, the way he usually talked, but he was lapsing into his professorial "you see," as if he were speaking to students. "The mountain people, the aborigines, were here before anyone else. No one is positive where they came from. Maybe from the islands of the South Pacific. Maybe they're related to the Dyaks of Borneo—who, by the way, were also headhunters."

"I'm glad you said *were,*" said Lil.

"It's not altogether *were* here, from what I gather. And when you think of it, headhunters are doing—did—with their three-foot curved knives only what 'civilized' nations do with bullets or bombs, except that the knife is a little more personal. In the hands of a mountain man, one swipe and he could sever head from body at a blow." He paused. "Let me get something—be right back."

He returned with a book from his study. "Here's how Dr. George L. Mackay, pioneer missionary in Formosa, expressed it: 'Headhunting may be traced back to the village and tribal wars. As life has no sacredness in the eyes of the savage and an enemy has no rights, it became simply a question of mode as to how their enemies should be put to death and some wrongs atoned for. The bringing back of the head was regarded as satisfactory evidence that the sentence of the tribe had been carried out—a kind of medical certificate.' " Jim explained, "It's the only way the tribespeople knew to settle a grievance."

"A sort of complete solution," Lil observed, hoping meanwhile that none of the aborigines in the school had brought their knives or habits with them.

Jim went on, "Formosa belonged to the tribespeople, when migrants from mainland China began coming in. The aborigines were gradually pushed back into the mountains."

"Like the American Indians," said Lil, thinking of her grandmother and the conquest of the West.

"Exactly. And now the mountain people are shut in and the world is shut out. To the Japanese, they're a nuisance. To each wave of conquerors, the aborigines have been an enemy."

Lil thought of Chi-oang and Do-wai and the other students from the mountains who had come to the schools at Tamsui. "And to us," she said quietly, "they are God's unhappy children."

As she sat on the red-brick colonnaded porch of the house at Tamsui, it was easy to visualize the "waves of conquerors." Next door stood the British Consulate in what once had been the Dutch fort with walls eight feet thick. In front, a rusted cannon pointing seaward had been a weapon of conquest and defense.

But not often was there the chance to sit. When Jim's guests were not keeping her busy, her children needed mothering. The island seemed to be full of children, and most of them looked as if they needed mothering, too.

In the meantime, Jim had asked her to help organize Bible conferences in nearby churches. Shortly after her two children came, she looked in on the conference she had set up in the Bangkah church in Taipei, taking little Marilyn with her. The composure of the whole meeting was threatened by a crying baby in the adjoining manse.

Lil slipped out of the meeting. "What's the matter? What's all the crying about?" she asked.

One of the women explained to her, "It's a very little baby. The mother is out shopping and the baby is hungry."

Lil had just finished nursing Marilyn and she thought she could feed this baby, too. Gathering it up in her arms, she fed the baby and cuddled it to sleep. The Bible conference was not interrupted again.

5. In Perils Often

In 1935, the Dicksons returned from a year's furlough in Canada and the United States. Immediately, they sensed a difference in the Japanese attitude toward foreigners.

Japan had withdrawn from the League of Nations in 1934, following her aggression in the northeast of China. An anti-Christian sentiment had begun to build up in Japan and was being felt in Formosa. Outdoor meetings eventually were banned and indoor meetings could be held only with a police permit. The Japanese demanded that school pupils be taken to Shinto shrines.

Lil wrote to her friends at home:

"We are living through troublous times to be sure, and we could not live among these people without feeling the weight of their burden of anxieties upon our shoulders, too. It is the greatest call upon our morale that we have ever had, but we are still here and carrying on our work as if all were well with the world."

Knowing there was a hard winter ahead because the people were burdened with all kinds of extra taxes which added to their poverty, and with visions of more little urchins than ever on the streets, shivering in their insufficient clothing, Lil called her Formosan neighbors together. They were busy mothers, too, but they offered to come one afternoon a week to make old clothes look almost as good as new. "This may sound like homely, uninteresting work," Lil wrote home, "but, in fact, it takes all one's resources of creative imagination, ingenuity, and diligence to evolve a small boy's pants out of an old winter dress and a little girl's coat out of a flannel middy blouse of bygone days. I deposit the results of our labors in a trunk for later prudent distribution as we find out quietly who really needs them the most."

When the mission council reluctantly announced they had decided to go along with the decree of the Japanese government that all missionaries must speak Japanese, it meant for the Dicksons a return to Japan in 1936 for a year of language study. Ronny was a very grown-up five, Marilyn a toddler of four.

"Mother, why must we go, go, go?" Marilyn asked. "I want to stop."

In Tokyo, Jim went every day to the language school, while Lil had a teacher at home. Once again she was housekeeping in a strange land. She had her address written on a piece of paper to show to the taxi driver after she would be downtown, shopping. She couldn't even pronounce the address, let alone remember it.

Meanwhile, tensions were building up—tensions that would finally explode in a world war.

One day Lil went with her language teacher downtown. Outside the palace moat, a great throng of people had gathered. But this was not a holiday crowd, boisterous, noisy. Though the people were moving about, they were absolutely silent.

"Something has happened," Lil told her teacher. "I don't know what it is, but I'm going home!"

That night, she still had not learned what it was all about. The next day, when the English-language newspaper came, the only headline that sounded exciting was "POLICE HUNT STRAY DOGS." Then a missionary next door, who knew the Japanese language well, came over and told Lil and Jim the news. Rebel soldiers had murdered the whole cabinet and taken over the city. He warned her, "Stay in your house. The radio says the rebels are in charge and that street fighting may break out at any time. If shooting starts, get down behind a large piece of furniture." With that he rushed for the door, tossing over his shoulder the tidbit, "They say the planes are in the hands of the rebels. *Don't get excited!*" The door slammed after him.

Lil looked at Jim. "I wonder if rebels bomb police stations?" she asked. Both of them had a single thought. Their missionary friend lived on one side of them, and the police station was next door on the other side. "If they do," Jim said, "I hope they have good aim."

For the rest of that day, she didn't try to study Japanese. Instead, recalling a line of a poem that counseled, "As the hands toil, so is the spirit raised above the troubled motions of the mind," she tore into housework. Washing clothes, straightening dresser drawers, she vigorously housecleaned her way into peace of mind.

A few days later, loyal soldiers again took over the city, and for a month all lived under martial law. "Martial law," Lil puts it, "means that the bayonet sticks right out toward you! We lived on a little lane that had been laid out a thousand years before and was still very narrow. When you had soldiers holding out bayonets on both sides of the street, you couldn't pass the point of a bayonet and a car at the same time, neither would they move that bayonet one inch. So you would have to look down the street to be sure a car wasn't coming, then go hastily around the point of the bayonet and back in. Weaving in and out among those bayonets gave me bad dreams for years."

During the year, between "revolutions" and the children's bouts with measles and influenza, Lil learned Japanese—not enough to enable her to preach or pray fluently, but enough to carry on conversations. The Dicksons returned to Japan to spend the next two summers at Lake Nojiri. These stays were more utilitarian than vacations often turn out to be. In Formosa, there were few American playmates for the children. At Nojiri, numbers of American missionary families gathered in the summer. Here Ronny and Marilyn learned what other American children were like. Rumors were flying all over, and it was not unusual to be greeted with a firm handshake and the words, "We heard you people had been killed!"

From Formosa, the route to Nojiri was by boat to Kobe, then by train. On their last trip through Kobe, it had rained heavily for three days. When the time came to leave for Nojiri, rain was still falling. The English consul's wife, who had been their friend and neighbor when her husband was stationed in Tamsui, begged them not to go. "It's too dangerous," she said. "You don't know what rains can do here."

Jim, never one to be worried by the elements, and Lil, thinking of the cottage awaiting them in the mountains, decided to go on. At the station, they bought their tickets and boarded the train. Before the train departed, a uniformed Japanese official came into their coach and hurried directly to them. "I am from the Tourist Bureau," he said. "I beg of you, do not go! It is dangerous."

"They're afraid of landslides," Jim explained.

The man seemed so excited that Jim and Lil gathered up their luggage and herded the two children before them off the train. The Tourist representative bowed gratefully and departed as the Dicksons watched the train pull out.

"Well," said Lil philosophically, "there's no point in spending a vacation here on the platform."

"Should we go or should we stay?" Jim asked.

"Whatever you say," Lil replied.

"Let's go on as far as we can," Jim decided. Another train was leaving in an hour. They took it.

All that night they could hear the rain spattering at the car windows. The next morning, they saw the swollen rivers. On either side below the railroad embankment, the water had come up to the tops of houses. But the track was clear, and the train went on.

The following day they heard the shocking news of what happened in Kobe soon after they had left. A flood rumbled down from the mountains, sweeping thousands out to sea, washing away whole blocks of houses. Shoppers in the basement of a Kobe department store panicked at the sight of water flooding down a stairway. Those who rushed for the adjoining subway, rushed to their deaths. Those who fought their way up the stairway were saved, though they were marooned in the store for days. Because Japan was at war with China, the disaster was hushed up.

The Dicksons' narrow escapes began to be a kind of wry joke in the family. In order to keep the children from being frightened, Lil would say with all the heartiness she could muster, "Well, we just missed death *that* time!"

When they returned to Formosa, they tried to continue life as normally as possible, despite the mounting threats. In November, 1938, Lil wrote home, "We still think we are safe here, although I know that our American government looks upon us as one might look with exasperation and embarrassment upon poor relatives who may be a trifle queer in the head, but who cannot be disowned entirely."

The children were now old enough to be left with others for short periods. Lil liked to accompany Jim on some of his trips when she could; they did not know how much longer there would be even limited freedom of movement.

Early one Sunday morning Lil bent over the children and roused them. Ronny and Marilyn ate their rice porridge with sleep still heavy in their eyes, and then all of them took the bus to Taipei. There Jim and Lil left the children at the compound with another missionary and went on into the sunrise on a second jolting bus. The roads became more narrow and stony, but the mountains were beautiful before them. On every hand they saw the harvest fields, golden and fragrant, and people already at work. Their destination was a little village in the foothills, where three rivers and three mountains met.

They walked along the narrow village street, and then turned aside and climbed up stone steps away from the din of the market-place, to a small, low, whitewashed church. The walls of mud and stone were so well made they had stood for forty-three years. The benches were hard and backless; the floor which had been rough red tile was now worn and broken by time. But through the door-way was such a breathtaking view that Lil felt that if her life had been one long search for beauty, here was culmination. The doorway framed the village, the river, and the harvest fields. Beyond, in the delicate blue-rose tinted atmosphere of autumn, were the mountains.

Lil felt close to heaven that morning. "Jim was preaching earnestly and they were listening earnestly," she recalls. "I could see tears in their eyes and I wished passionately that we of the West would bring to these humble people only good teaching and good things and that all the things of harm that our civilization has also bred would somehow never reach them here."

Lil helped with the women's meeting in the afternoon and then she and Jim started home. They were to go part of the way by push car—something like a handcar that runs on a narrow-gauge railroad track. The passengers—four to a car—sit on little benches facing outward. The car often jumps the track, speeding down the steep mountain slopes, and when it does the passengers try to jump first. A man behind pushes, or leaps on to ride.

As they set out, someone assured Lil cheerfully, "The push car will be less bumpy than the bus, but more dangerous."

The car gained speed. The tempo of the click of the rail joints under the wheels was the measure of progress. Jim and Lil held on tightly—but not so tightly they couldn't let go in a hurry—while the push car skittered down hills, hurried through sunny valleys, breathtakingly crossed rivers on rickety trestles where they could not have jumped even to escape a derailment. Where the push car tracks ended they boarded a train that took them to Taipei.

At the compound, Lil reached hungrily for her children. "Did you miss me?" she asked.

They responded blithely, "No."

When Jim informed her that they were facing the possibility of moving again—this time from Tamsui to Taipei—Lil pondered the effect upon the children. Marilyn and Ronny had been shuttled back and forth from Japan to Formosa and over to Canada and the United States, and even in Formosa they wouldn't be able to look back to one home. What would be their heritage of memories? She hoped they would at least remember blue waves tumbling along white sandy shores; palms outlined darkly against a sunset sky; the soft green of waving ricefields with white rice birds rising slowly with supple grace; long brakes of feathery bamboo trees—and always purple mountains piled up against the sky.

During the day, Lil was busy, teaching the children, entertaining guests. But when night fell and the children were bathed and tucked away in bed, then thoughts of the thousands being killed and maimed in the Sino-Japanese War so few miles away overwhelmed her. If she could bind up one person's wounds, she would feel better, she thought. But to do nothing, to stand and wait—that was hard.

Systematically, she reread all her college literature books. In the chinks of time she also made good use of her phonograph. By all rights it should long since have been ushered into decent retirement. "It was old when I first heard it, thirteen years ago when Jim's roommate at Princeton brought it to their room for diversion," she remembered. "My records do not get broken nor are they ever thrown away. They *wear* out. We could manage a new Victrola, I suppose, but we are not buying anything new during the present uncertain conditions. We have had one foot poised for departure so long that I have learned to make the best of what I have."

The foot-in-the-air feeling was not helped by Lil's accidental discovery that she and Jim were being watched.

6. Secret Police

Lil shut the door behind her with a sigh of relief, and stepped out on the big veranda of their house at Tamsui. Across the river rose the almost perfect cone of Koan-im mountain, offering reassurance that some things were the same in spite of the growing tension of the times. Past the old Dutch fort, the river met the sea. To step outdoors in Formosa was to step into an overarching cathedral and be at worship. Yet so few seemed to sense it. Lil had written to her friends back home of the contrasts:

"Sometimes when I am in the ricefields, I am burdened with the beauty of it all, the mountains round about, purple-shadowed, slumbering in the midday sun, the green lushness of the fields, the blueness of the sky—it grips you as if it were too much to bear. And then I wonder about the people who have gazed on all this beauty during the generations that this land has stood, and how strange it is that they have not learned beauty from nature and have not tried to translate some little part of it into their homes. Only where man abides has beauty been defaced. Here are little mud-brick houses with dirt floors, with the pigpen attached and unimaginable filth—even animals and birds live in much cleaner surroundings. I look at their tiny ricefields, furrowed with patience and painstaking neatness, and I wonder—why is it not in their homes?"

Lil was challenged by the fine group of well-educated spiritual-minded young people in the church. They called for her best. But sometimes, in a village that time had forgotten, she wondered what strange paths had led her here—far from all the things she had known and loved. Here beauty abounded in nature, but she seldom found it elsewhere, except in a mother's face. The young mothers had a look curiously like the Madonna, of purity and sweetness, infinite gentleness and love.

Lil could not get accustomed to the clothes. "Their garments are often worn in a sloppy, loose fashion that looks decidedly uneasy," she wrote. "Many a time I have longed for a whole boatload of good strong safety pins and about three years in which to go around and pin up people so that they would know how it feels to be securely dressed!"

Moving from the veranda, Lil went slowly down the wide front steps, wandered toward the divided gate that hung in a graceful curve from two supporting brick pillars. She flung the gates wide and the pillars made a frame for the mountain beyond.

A sudden motion caught her eye. Off to the right, behind a bush, a man was standing, watching her silently. Anyone who had rightful business there would be simply passing by. This man, hat pulled low over his eyes, coat tightly buttoned, was *staying* there. Should she call for help? Her eyes darted the other way down the lane just outside the compound wall. Another man was crouched behind a hedge, unaware that the setting sun sharply silhouetted his figure.

Casually, she swung the gates shut—and hastily slid the bolt. Without seeming to hurry, she strolled back up the walk, up the steps, across the veranda, conscious of eyes boring into her back. Jim needed to know about this.

"Where's Sun Bok-su?" she asked the cook, who pointed to Jim's study. Rushing in, she told him, "There are two men out beyond the compound wall watching every move we make. You had better call the police."

Jim spread his big hands flat on the desk in front of him and pushed back in his chair. "There are not two," he said. "There are eleven. We can't call the police, because they *are* the police. They are Japanese detectives."

"But whom are they watching?"

"They're watching us," said Jim quietly. "We'll have to get used to it, Lil."

The eleven detectives who tried so hard to look like movie versions of secret operatives had their comical aspects; and though the missionaries kept sane by their ability to see humor where it was not intended, the danger was genuine. If the Japanese at any moment of day or night were to decide that the Dicksons had information of military importance, they would simply "disappear" or be wiped out by "smallpox." Jim was directly or indirectly in contact with sixty thousand Christians on the island, in itself cause for Japanese suspicion.

Sometimes Lil felt sorry for "their" detectives who kept watch, come rain, cold, or high water. One wretched night, she turned from the window impulsively. "Jim, couldn't I take some hot tea out to them?"

He shook his head. "They'd think you had put a drug in it."

A visiting missionary from Japan said to them: "You're tense. War nerves, you know. You just imagine that detectives are watching you."

Lil took her visitor by the arm and led her to the gate. "Look, Isabel, over that hedge." Isabel, a tall girl, looked, and gasped. There were three in that one clump, looking out sternly and not the least bit embarrassed at being discovered.

Detectives soon had their fingers in everything. Some came in to look over the magazines on the coffee table and to ask questions. A postmaster advised Lil's cook, "Tell your mistress not to seal her letters. We'll do that after we have read them."

On the train from Tamsui or Taipei, a detective often sat down beside Lil. Sometimes one would introduce himself, unabashed, in his inexpert English: "I am a spy!" Then the questions would begin. Where was she going? Why? Did she like Japan? Why was she in Formosa?

At the compound, one of the missionaries took a load of clothes into her ironing room. A detective who heard her coming had slipped in there to hide. When she opened the door, there he was and she almost dropped the clothes.

"What did you say to him?" Lil asked.

"Well, I just said, *'Konichiwa!'* 'Good afternoon.' If they're under your bed or anywhere, you're still polite!"

After weeks of this, there came a beautiful, clear day. Lil announced to Ronny and Marilyn, "Today, I'm going to take you to Taipei and you may each buy a toy." It was the kind of day that made one wish to celebrate. Besides, they hoped for a few hours of freedom.

Near the gate, they waited for the bus. When it arrived, a man rose out of the grass opposite, his hat pushed down over his eyes. At downtown Tamsui, another detective checked them through. As they began the drive down the valley to the big city, they heard a droning in the sky and saw a formation of planes China-bound. Ronny, squinting upward, used his finger as a counter. "One, two, three, four—"

"Hush!" his mother warned him just in time. Losses had become an embarrassment to the Japanese. In the earlier days of the war, old men would count the planes as they went out, and count them in as they returned. "Ha!" they would jeer. "They lost four." The Japanese had a solution: they made it illegal to count planes.

Near Taipei, soldiers with bayonets boarded the bus and went through all the luggage and packages while Ronny and Marilyn watched with interest. In the city, the three of them located a toy store and the children each selected a toy. Lil gave the man the money and was just reaching to take the change when a heavy explosion shook the building.

"What is it, Mother?" Ronny asked.

"They're just practicing," Lil assured the children.

That night after they returned home, Lil heard that a bomb had been dropped at the airport. She observed to Jim, "If the Flying Tigers had bombed the downtown section—as the Japanese usually do in China—that would have been the end of us. And such a fine day, too!"

The next morning, a hurried note came from the English consul next door. It read: "Mrs. Dickson, the planes are on their way to bomb us again. Prepare to be bombed."

"How do you prepare to be bombed?" Lil wanted to know. "Do you say your prayers, or do you go down to the cellar, or what?" She had three other missionary children with her. It was too nice a day to keep them in the house. She decided that she would take care of just the little ones and let Ronny and Jamie—they were about eight then—play together. "If you hear a siren or planes, come right back," she told them. "And don't go far away."

The three little ones she led to the sandpile outside. A while later, Lil went outdoors to check on them, the magazine she had been reading still in her hand. Behind her she suddenly heard the tread of soldiers' boots. "I didn't want to give the soldiers the satisfaction of knowing that I was frightened," she says, "so I kept on looking at the magazine—though it may have been upside down. I could sense that they were standing right behind me. Finally, I took a sidewise look. They weren't paying any attention to me, but were looking at the three children, whose heads were down as they giggled over the important things they were building in the sand. The children never looked up to see the gleaming bayonets. I think the soldiers were suddenly conscious of their bayonets, too. They went tiptoeing away."

After a while, the two older boys came back to the house. "We had fun," they reported. "Some soldiers let us play with their *guns!*"

The planes never did appear.

Lil's "family" that day, or any day, was made up of whoever happened to need her. When the mother of the "Bible conference baby" that Lil had nursed to quietness years before contracted typhoid fever and entered the hospital, Lil helped again. By now there were several children in that family. Relatives took some of the youngsters, but none of them wanted the baby boy.

"A baby makes lots of trouble," the father told Lil sadly when she went to see what she could do.

"Would you like me to take the baby?"

Tears ran down his face. "That's the one thing that's been worrying me—who would take care of the baby?" He taught school and there was no one else he could trust to do it. So the baby came to the big mission house at Tamsui and Lil cared for him as if he were her own.

The Japanese were strict. Not even a candle or a flashlight was allowed at the time of air raids and air-raid drills, even if the shutters were closed and curtains drawn.

As each alarm began and the big house would be totally darkened, the visiting baby would invariably begin to cry. Lil recalls, "In the darkness I'd have to feel my way upstairs and try to change the baby's diaper in the dark. Have you ever changed a baby's diaper in the dark? It's not easy!"

Newspapers and radio broadcasts were heavily censored. It was forbidden under severe penalty to listen to any but Japanese stations. According to news reports, Generalissimo Chiang Kai-shek's forces in China were demoralized. The Japanese, people of a tiny but industrialized nation, reportedly had a stranglehold on China, twenty-five times larger.

"I can't stand this not knowing," Lil said to Jim on one of the uncertain days. That night when the children had been put to bed and Jim had gone upstairs, Lil made the rounds, trying the door, turning out the lights. Her eyes rested for a moment on the radio before the living room plunged into darkness.

Upstairs, she slid into bed beside Jim. When his even breathing told her he was asleep, very gently she edged out from under the covers. Throwing a big bathrobe around her, she felt her way from the bedroom into the hall then down the stairs. As she approached the living room, she peered around the doorframe. Faint rectangles of light marked the windows. Even as she searched them for shadowed outlines that would mean a detective had come up on the veranda to peer in, she couldn't help thinking, housekeeper-fashion, about the curtains. If they had to move to the compound at Taipei, it wouldn't be too bad. The houses had been built from approximately the same plan. Perhaps the curtains would fit.

The house was silent. From outside, far away, came the sounds of automobiles and the indistinguishable noises of human activity. Together they built up to the heartbeat of a city, rhythm slowed, but inescapably there. A board creaked somewhere. Was one of those shadowy figures patrolling the veranda? Lil stood silent against the door, holding her breath as if it might reveal her presence. It would be more difficult for someone to see in than for her to see out, she decided. Quietly, she crept into and across the living room to the radio. Why had they ever placed the radio so close to the window? She wished it were in a dark corner, although even to rearrange the furniture these days might arouse suspicion.

With a last look toward the window, she slipped off her bathrobe. Draping it behind her shoulders and over her head, she moved close to the radio and brought the robe down over it. Huddling against the speaker, and making sure the glow of the tubes and the light of the dial would be shielded, she cautiously turned on the set. At any moment she expected to hear sudden steps on the floor and feel an arm around her throat, but there was only the slight hum of the radio, indicating it had warmed up.

Turning up the volume just a hair, she twisted the tuning knob, skipping local stations and into forbidden territory on the dial. Suddenly, she heard words that froze her fingers to the knob. A woman was speaking in English. Pulling the robe closer, she strained her ears to listen. "The Japanese have boasted that they will fight until they have brought us to our knees. That may be true, but we will fight on . . . !"

The firm faith in the voice of the woman from Nanking quickened the pulse of the little woman kneeling under the bathrobe in Formosa. Snapping off the radio, and waiting until the glow of the tubes had faded, she flung the bathrobe over her arm and slipped out of the room. Her heart was strangely light as she went up the stairs and then eased gently into bed. She was not startled when Jim whispered gruffly, "Did you find out what you wanted to know?"

"Yes," she whispered back contentedly. "I think the Japanese have their hands full. They're not just fighting soldiers now. They're up against a woman—Madame Chiang Kai-shek."

Jim replied sleepily, "In that case, they can't win."

But it would look as if the Japanese were winning. For a long time, it would look that way.

7. Escape

Surely, the Japanese were reasoning in 1940, the Dicksons must be spies. What else would keep them on Formosa? Many of the other missionaries had left. All the secret police had to do was find the evidence. They tried once more, this time through one of the most trusted members of the Dickson household.

She was an old Formosan woman they had hired to do odd jobs around the house. "Old A-chhia can't get regular work," one of her friends had said to Jim. "She will do anything—scrub floors, wash, do housework." So they took her on, and old A-chhia's wrinkled face became a familiar sight in the big house at Tamsui. Not a Christian, she was an inveterate gambler and besides that, sickly. She had tried the remedies of every herb doctor her friends recommended, to no avail.

"Now that she's scrubbing floors for you, can't you get her into the hospital?" the friend asked Jim. He promptly made the arrangements.

The doctor decided her condition warranted an operation. At the operating table his diagnosis was quick: incurable cancer. There was nothing to do but sew her up again.

Lil, feeling sorry for the woman when she returned to them, put her on very light work so that she could happily fill in the time until she died. Unexpectedly, she did not die, but recovered. Even more unexpectedly, she attributed her healing to Jim, and declared that she would work for him for the rest of her life without pay.

"We can't do it that way," Jim said to her, proffering payment.

A-chhia thrust her hands behind her back. "Because of you, I am well. I will work for you always."

As a solution, Jim opened a savings account for her and deposited her salary regularly.

One day when Jim returned home, A-chhia was unnerved. "The secret police were here," she said, "but I wouldn't let them in."

"It would have been all right to let them in," he answered. "We have nothing to hide."

"Well," admitted A-chhia hesitantly, "I did let them in."

"What did they do?" Jim asked, growing more interested.

"Nothing."

"They could have seen anything they wanted to see," Jim assured her.

"Well," she said, "they did see something."

Jim waited.

"They opened your safe and lifted everything out and laid it on the floor and took pictures with a camera." Her face grew tense. "Don't let them know!" she begged. "They said they would kill me if I told you."

A-chhia decided she wanted to become a Christian. One of the requirements for membership in the local church was an ability to read, so that converts could study the Bible. Try as she would, A-chhia could not learn. "When I look at the book, I keep thinking about floors I should scrub," she explained. The rules were relaxed just enough to let A-chhia squeeze through.

Communications between the mission compounds at Tamsui and Taipei, though they were only fifteen miles apart, grew more difficult. Rumors sprang up. Tamsui missionaries heard that all the Taipei missionaries had been killed, and at Taipei they heard the same of those at Tamsui. The mission council finally asked the

Dicksons to move to Taipei. This did not mean fewer detectives, but it did mean a certain comfort in companionship.

"Lil," Jim said one day, "we must destroy the mission records."

"We're not a foreign embassy," Lil rejoined. "In stories, it's always the embassies that burn their documents."

"The Japanese are interested in anything having to do with the spending of money," Jim replied. "We could get the Formosan church people into trouble if our records fell into Japanese hands. The government officials might ask, 'Where was this money spent? Why was this done?' The less they know, the less trouble the local people will have when we leave."

"Leave—?" Lil spoke the word slowly, almost unbelievingly. *"Leave?"* It was not a real word.

"Not now," Jim assured her. "Someday. But maybe sooner than we think."

Though the house had a fireplace in almost every room, burning papers was not that simple. In summer one would not normally have a fire, except at mealtimes. Lil sorted out papers that had to do with expenditures, crumpled up a few in the fireplace and lighted them, hoping the smoke from the chimney would not look suspicious. Then she swept away the ashes; a detective might come in and see them. She waited a bit and burned another handful, keeping it up all day.

Finding enough food to eat soon became a problem. When Lil went downtown on her bicycle to shop, merchants would pretend they had nothing, because she was a foreigner and thus a potential enemy. She would ride all around town and come home with perhaps a cabbage, and be lucky at that. She recalls, "The last slab of bacon I was able to buy was covered with worms, crawling in and out all over. I cut out the worms, sliced the meat off until I had the heart of the bacon. I boiled that, fried it and gave it to the family. I put out my best linen, best silver, best dishes, trying to hide the fact that there was practically nothing to eat on the table. Never were we served so little in such style!"

Friends were afraid to recognize them, for anyone who spoke to a foreigner was likely to be interrogated afterward by the secret police. Sometimes men and women who had known Jim and Lil for years would give them blank stares when they met. There were some who could not shut off their friendship so easily. One pastor came repeatedly, early in the morning while it was still dark, bringing food. He varied his timing and his route just enough so that the Japanese would not know what he was doing.

In October, a radio report advised that the State Department had requested all Americans to leave Formosa.

"That settles it," Lil said to Jim. "We're going. You and I have a right to risk our lives if we want to. But we don't have a right to risk the children's lives or take the chance of their being put into a prison camp."

"I'm too busy to evacuate," said Jim absent-mindedly.

"*I'm* not too busy!" Lil replied. She began making preparations.

One of the first things she did was to send a cable to Cook's, asking for passage on any ship from the Orient to any west coast port of the United States. When no reply came, she concluded the cable had never left the island. Lil sat down in a rocking chair and did some deep thinking. Then she went to the Japanese steamship company and bought passage on their finest liner across the Pacific —first class. That involved such a big commission they couldn't turn it down.

There was one other matter to be settled, even as the day of departure drew near and the tickets were in hand. "Do we turn the key in the lock and just leave?" Lil asked Jim.

Jim, fortunately practical, said, "We can't do that. We'll sell it all."

"Who'd buy our mess of junk?" Lil wanted to know.

But Jim knew that "foreign things" would be of interest to people who would expect, and probably get, a lot of bargains. He organized the project and announced a sale.

Even now, Lil shakes her head in wonder at the memory of it. "Everybody came. Jim had put prices on things and said it would be a kind of help-yourself operation, and the customers would pay as they went out. They helped themselves, but they didn't always stop to pay! The McMillans, our missionary associates, had left some of their things with us, saying that we could sell them if we had to evacuate. One man walked off with Mr. McMillan's trousers. While I was chasing him to get them back, somebody else took the coat. I lost that whole suit!"

Even so, in a very short time, they were sold out. Some would-be customers felt of the material in the stockings and dress Lil was wearing, hoping to strike a deal. Marilyn sold even her playthings.

"The wildest day in our history!" Lil laughs. "But we had more money than we'd ever dreamed of, and that was all right, because of our having to go home first class."

There was still packing to do, though the sale had drastically thinned out their possessions. Among Lil's keepsakes were books of poetry and clippings of poems she had read through the years and enjoyed, and also copies of the report letters she had begun writing as early as 1936 to people back home.

The American consul's wife gave an "evacuation party" for her departing countrymen, a gesture the Japanese detectives could not understand. "Why do they have a party when they *leave?*" one of them asked the Dickson cook suspiciously. "Why are they so happy?" The cook kept his opinions to himself. "These missionaries must be taking secret information out with them, and are celebrating their success," the detectives mutttered.

Their concern deepened the next morning when Jim and Lil and their two children jammed themselves and their luggage into a taxi and went to the railroad station to take the train to Keelung. Dozens of Christians had come down to see them off, feeling secure against reprisals as long as they were acting as a group. As the train pulled out and the four Dicksons waved from the open window, the church people who had become such an important part of their lives sang hymns. The last haunting strains followed them. "God will take care of you . . ."

"And *you* . . ." Jim and Lil prayed.

At Keelung, their tiny boat reminded Lil of the one that had originally brought them to Formosa.

The local detectives came to pay their parting respects—and to go through all the luggage. There *had* to be something! They could not imagine that Jim Dickson, with a vast network of churches all over the island, could be anything but a spy. But even while two men were still examining the contents of every bundle, their superior called Jim into the corridor.

"We're sorry to have to do this," he said. "We hope you'll be back."

Jim stuck out his hand. *"Sayonara!"*

Just one friend came to the pier to see them off. It was A-chhia, the scrubwoman from Tamsui. She waved as long as the boat was in sight. The Dicksons, who would not return for six years, were never to see her again. Her "cancer" or her old age or the privations of war must have claimed her life—they never could find out.

The bobbing little craft took three days to reach Kobe. There, waiting, was the magnificent new *Yawata Maru,* on which they would make the trip eastward. While their luggage was being transferred, Lil said, "I have a little Japanese money left. It won't be any good to us from now on, so I might as well spend it." She took the two children while Jim stayed by their possessions. When she returned, she was smiling.

"You're feeling better?" Jim asked.

Lil nodded. "We stopped in a store to buy a souvenir. After I had paid the man, he looked all around, behind him, in front. Then he leaned across the counter and said, 'We're sorry you're leaving.' That took the sting away."

On board the big ship, the purser checked their accommodations. First class . . . they must be important. And the ship wasn't crowded. . . . Looking up happily from his papers, he said, "We can let you have the bridal suite."

Jim looked at eight-year-old Marilyn on one side and nine-year-old Ronny on the other, then at Lil, and shook his head. "Somehow," he said, "it wouldn't seem appropriate."

"Then two adjoining cabins?"

"Fine."

They had just located their cabins when a squad of police shouldered their way in. "The Dickson luggage," said the one in charge. "We have orders to take it off."

Picking up everything, they started out. "You, too," said the officer to Jim. "Come with us."

Lil and the children rushed to the deck and watched Jim being escorted down the gangplank with the police carrying the luggage from their stateroom and stevedores bringing up their trunks from the hold. On the dock, they stacked the pieces together and began a methodical search through everything. By comparison, the Keelung inspection was child's play. Even a cake of soap was broken open to see if anything had been hidden inside.

Meanwhile, the ship's whistle blasted its deep warning that visitors must go ashore. As Lil watched from the deck, her anxiety deepened.

She knew this was one of the techniques of the Japanese. Many foreigners "disappeared" just as their ship was leaving. Friends ashore would think they had sailed—they had seen them board. Those who would be waiting for them at their destination would not know until days or weeks later that they were not on the ship.

Scheduled departure time arrived. A whistle blast vibrated the deck. The minutes ticked by. On the dock, Jim stood by helplessly while the police continued their inspection as if they had all the time in the world. He tried to wave encouragingly to Lil, high above. She could only watch—and pray. "God, don't let them haul in the gangplank—"

But even as she watched, there was a sudden order and the rattling of chains as the lines of the gangplank assembly tightened, lifted upward, swung it inboard. The *Yawata Maru* had waited a half hour. She could not wait any longer.

It was then that the police came upon the file of poetry, carefully clipped by Lil, precious to her but of little value to anyone else.

"Translate this into Japanese, and explain," the officer said, thrusting it into Jim's hands.

He began translating, stumbling over the words while also trying to see what the ship was doing.

The officer, like most Japanese, knew something about poetry. Some of it didn't make sense to him, but poetry didn't have to make sense unless you were in the mood for it.

Suddenly he gave a quick order. Everything was tumbled into the suitcases and boxes. Jim, still holding the file of poems, managed to toss it into one of the suitcases. Then all the pieces were bundled over to the ship, flung across open water into a yawning opening in the ship's side. Jim, escorted to a rope ladder thrown over the side, gratefully climbed upward.

There were tears in Lil's eyes when his tall figure came toward her on the upper deck. Rushing to meet him, she fell into his arms. Jim patted her shoulder. "You didn't think I'd make it, did you?" he said. "Well, now I can tell you—neither did I."

"Siong-te an-pai ho-se," said Lil quietly. " 'God has worked it out.' I was praying."

"Good girl. I had no chance. I was busy trying to translate Emily Dickinson."

"It's all right now," said Lil.

But at Yokohama, she wasn't so sure. They were standing by the rail watching the docking routine, when Lil saw three men start up the gangplank. Her hand reached out and clutched Jim's arm. "They are secret police—I'm sure of it."

"Maybe they want to know more about poetry," said Jim, trying to keep the tension out of his voice.

A few minutes later they saw the same three men go back down the gangplank, escorting a middle-aged woman.

"Jim, she's an American missionary from Korea! I talked with her yesterday! I saw Ambassador Grew get on the ship— Let's find him."

But by the time they had located the American Ambassador to Japan, who was seeing off a passenger at Yokohama, it was too late. He could get no information about her; she had been spirited away. Months later, Lil learned that she had been taken all the way back to Korea and put on trial as a spy. Finally released, she eventually made her way to Shanghai and then home to America.

Not even when the big ship turned its bow away from Japan did

Lil and Jim feel secure. "Did you see who was sitting at the table next to us in the dining room?" Lil asked Jim when they returned to their cabin. "Four secret police."

Jim put his finger to his lips. Motioning her into the corridor, he said, "That little gadget on the ceiling of our room—I'm sure it's a microphone. Better not even pray out loud in the cabin! We don't want the Japanese to know some of the things we want God to know."

"Jim was the one who was really in danger," Lil recalls. "The rest of us weren't strategic. If they decided that Jim knew too much, they could push him overboard and say he committed suicide. An incident like that happened later. A Swiss official came down to Formosa from Tokyo to settle the affairs of the English consulate at Tamsui. On the way back, he was found dead, his cabin covered with blood. The Japanese said he had committed suicide. If so, he must have really worked at it." The family never left Jim alone. Either Lil or the children were with him constantly.

Before they had left Kobe, the American consul advised them, "It may be that war will break out while you are at sea. If it does, you will not be told. The ship will simply turn around and bring you back."

So they began each day on shipboard with a quick stroll on deck to check the position of the sun. Seeing the morning sun off the bow, they would breathe in relief, "No war yet."

Between Yokohama and Honolulu, a radio message came from Jim's brother, Sam: "Stop in Honolulu a month." Sam was an officer in the U.S. Army, serving at Pearl Harbor. It was a reassuring message to a family not certain they would ever see Honolulu.

One morning in late November, when Jim found the ship still sailing down a shimmering path into the sunrise, he told Lil, "We're due at Pearl Harbor tomorrow."

They slipped into Pearl Harbor quietly. Lil looked out a porthole and saw American warships everywhere. Jim, behind her, had a sudden thought. "This is Thanksgiving Day!"

"This *is* Thanksgiving Day," Lil said, sudden tears in her eyes. She felt limp. They had lived in tension for four-and-a-half years. Now danger was a thing of the past. They were safe.

When the ship tied up, reporters and photographers swarmed aboard. "They must want to interview somebody," Lil said to Jim. "I wonder who it is." She soon found out. Tipped off by Sam, they wanted to interview the Dicksons, most recent Americans, and almost the last, to leave the mysterious island of Formosa, key Japanese base in the South Pacific. When flashbulbs went off, the mouths of the four secret service men fell open. They had been sure there was more to these missionaries than met the eye!

As Jim and Lil went home with Sam, Jim asked casually, "What are those big tanks?"

"Gasoline, oil."

"But you've got them right down on the beach—and painted white! They could be seen twenty miles out to sea!"

"What of it?"

"You have other tanks hidden back in the hills?"

Sam shook his head. "As far as I know, it's all right there on the beach. What are you so worked up about?"

"You don't understand what's happening in this part of the world," Jim said, his voice coming fast and clipped. "The Japanese don't have *their* storage tanks out in the open. They have them camouflaged—vines growing over them, guards on duty day and night." He shook his head unbelievingly.

"Maybe you had better talk with some of us at the officers' club," Sam suggested.

At lunch Jim told the officers, "The Japanese have always said that war with America is inevitable. They're on their toes, ready to go. I've lived with the Japanese. I know how they think, what they think. They think they're going to fight America and win . . ."

One of the officers said, "Would you like to tell the top brass what you have been telling us?"

"Of course I would!" said Jim, deeply concerned.

At their meeting the next day, Jim began, "One of your officers told me the Japanese couldn't destroy those fuel tanks and get back to their base. They don't *intend* to get back!"

"But, Dr. Dickson," a colonel put in, "after a declaration of war we could intercept the Japanese fleet. They wouldn't be able to get near the Hawaiian Islands."

Jim sat up straight. "In the long fighting history of Japan, never once has she declared war. She has always struck first . . ."

They heard him out, and when he had finished they said, "Nice of you to come."

8. *British Guiana Jungles*

Home at last, Jim and Lil left the children with relatives while they went on to Canada to report to their mission board at Toronto. Lil's was a courtesy call; for in the board's eyes, Jim was the missionary. This understanding had worked fairly well for Lil so far—raising the children and playing "innkeeper's wife" had been just about a fulltime job. But how much longer she would be able to stand uninvolved at the edges of ripe harvest fields, she wasn't sure. She was wondering about something else, too. What do missionaries do when they are chased home by war clouds?

Before a week was out, Jim had the answer. "Lil, they want us to go to South America—until we can return to Formosa." His staccato sentences tumbled over each other. "Place called British Guiana—discouraging mission field—but we have to keep busy—don't know much about it—we have the children to think of—the language there is English, a disadvantage to an American missionary, for he goes in with better command of the language, a better education, than the people, and he tends to 'run' things—" He paused when he noticed that Lil was watching him patiently. "Did you want something?"

"I was waiting for a comma—to say, just give me a little while to get the other side of the world out of my mind."

But in a few days she was asking, "Now, just where *is* British Guiana?"

Together they looked it up in an atlas. It was a small country on the northern rim of the vast South American continent, nestling between Venezuela to the west and Surinam to the east. Lil borrowed books from the library and reported to Jim, "It seems to be a wild and woolly place, not very civilized."

"Not very woolly, either," Jim observed. "Only four hundred miles from the equator."

"Mostly jungle," Lil said, "except for the towns on the coast."

"That's not all," Jim said. "There are no self-supporting churches. No trained pastors. No sanitation or health departments. Missionaries have died there."

Lil looked at Jim keenly. "You want to go, don't you?"

"It's got under my skin," Jim admitted. "Besides, the board says that if we don't go, they'll have to close the mission."

"Then we have no choice, have we?"

Five of the children's most impressionable years were to be spent in British Guiana. Even getting there in the Spring of 1941 was part of their education.

The board booked missionaries by Canadian ships when possible. The Dicksons went to Boston to wait until one bound for South America should come in. Because Canada, along with Britain, was at war with Germany, the ship arrived late at night to avoid submarines, gliding silently through the mist like a ghost. Silently, though there was no need for it in Boston, Jim and Lil and Ronny and Marilyn—now ten and nine—went aboard.

The trip to Bermuda, first stop, was routine. Shortly after they had left Bermuda the family was on deck, taking a last look at the receding jewel-like island.

"I hear an airplane," Ronny said. "There it comes!"

The plane screamed in low, across the bow of the ship.

"American," Jim observed.

An officer rushed by on his way to the bridge. "Is anything—?"

Jim began, but in his preoccupation the officer didn't hear. Lil put her arms on the children's shoulders. "It is time for you two to get ready for dinner," she said firmly. As they started to their rooms, the ship heeled sharply.

"We're turning!" Ronny announced.

Jim looked at the sun. "We've turned west. Back toward the U.S. coast." Then the ship heeled the other way, beginning a pattern of wild zigzagging.

That night when the children were in bed, Jim took a turn around the deck. "The officers are not sleeping tonight," he reported when he came back. "The plane warned us of a German raider."

The next day, one of the ship's officers said to Lil jokingly, "You know, Mrs. Dickson, there is a superstition on the sea that it's bad luck to carry missionaries."

Repeating the remark to Jim, Lil chuckled, "I told him they'd have worse luck if we weren't aboard."

"I wonder if that officer knows his bad-luck story comes right out of the Book of Jonah?" Jim mused.

After delivering the Dicksons safely to British Guiana, the ship turned about and headed into Caribbean waters—to her death. Lil had been more right than the officer.

Their home in New Amsterdam—Georgetown, the capital, was the other principal city—was a stilt-foundation house. The settled area of the country was a narrow strip along the coast, from which four great waterways led into the tangled wilderness. The populace of the country included aboriginal Indians, Africans, and East Indians who had been brought in as plantation laborers. Jim was soon busy training church leaders and encouraging congregations to become self-supporting, an achievement no one had thought possible.

In British Guiana—by a mother's standard, at least—it was lonely for the children. When Pat Magalee, a Lutheran missionary, invited Lil to teach at Christmas, at a deacons' conference he was holding seventy-five miles upriver, she promised Ronny and Marilyn she would take them along.

"And you may invite two of your friends to go with us for the week," Lil said to the children.

"Will we go by train?" Ronny asked.

"No, by boat," Lil said. "And they say the boat is *new*." Ronny had lost his enthusiasm for the British Guiana railroad when he saw a train outdistanced by a dog chasing a butterfly.

The five of them boarded the paddle-wheel steamer. "This is *new?*" Ronny asked, running his finger along peeling paint. Lil had never seen a boat that looked *tireder*.

Making a discreet inquiry, she reported to Ronny, "This boat was used for twenty-five years in South Africa and then discarded. But it is new *here*."

The pilot pulled a bell cord, and the steamer slowly edged out into midstream. Soon the jungle closed in on either side. At midnight, the boat docked at a settlement consisting solely of a rickety store in a clearing at the river's edge and overoptimistically named "Paradise." Hammocks were strung up on the deck crisscross, one above the other, and the lights on the boat suddenly turned out. In the morning, transportation for the rest of the trip arrived—hollowed-out tree-trunk canoes.

When they arrived at the Lutheran compound, Pat Magalee, who had come on ahead, was there to greet them and see that they were settled in a thatched cottage built six feet off the ground.

The four children immediately put their heads together and Ronny came to his mother. "It's *so* hot. We want to go in swimming."

Lil was shocked at the thought of it, but the other three rallied to Ronny's side and assured her that *nothing* could possibly happen to them.

"Well, they can't go in the river," Pat Magalee said firmly. "It's full of piranha and electric eels. But there is a stream back of the compound. There are not so *many* piranha there. I think if they keep splashing and shouting, they will be all right." He went off to make arrangements for the conference.

Lil was in an agony of doubt. "All right," she said finally. "But splash and shout *very* hard."

As they dashed off, Lil shook her head. Flesh-eating piranha, electric eels—what else? Snakes, she thought with a sudden start. She had forgotten about snakes.

When Lillete—Pat's wife—came by the cottage, Lil asked casually, "Are there any snakes around here?"

"We had one longer than the church. Now, about those Bible studies you're going to give the deacons—"

But Lil wasn't listening. The thought of a snake longer than a church was shattering. A little later, walking around the compound, she ran into Pat again. "Pat, *are* there snakes around here? Lillete said something about one as long as the church—" She couldn't bring herself to say "*longer* than the church."

"Since she's told you that much, I might as well tell you the rest. Would you like to sit down?"

"Yes," said Lil weakly, settling herself on the steps of the nearest house.

"Well," Pat began, "on one of our trips up here, some of my aboriginal Indian parishioners came to me and said, 'Pastor, one of our boys has been struck dumb. He went out hunting one day, and since he came back, he won't talk.' I agreed to go see the boy.

"He wouldn't talk to me either, but acted as if he were literally scared stiff of something—and a nineteen-year-old boy down here doesn't scare easily. I said to him, 'Tell me what has frightened you.'

" 'You wouldn't believe me if I told you,' he replied. I assured him I would believe him.

"Taking a deep breath, the boy said almost in a whisper, 'I think I've seen the devil. You don't believe me, do you?'

" 'Well, I'm trying,' I told him. He went on. 'I was out hunting. All of a sudden I saw a head coming toward me through the jungle—a head as high as my head, but bigger than my head. I shot.' The boy was trembling at the memory. 'I shot, then I turned and ran. As I ran, I could hear the devil thrashing down the trees of the jungle.'

"The Indians here use a gun as skillfully as we use our hands," Pat explained to Lil. "I asked the boy where this had happened, and he said it was just a mile up the stream—the stream where the children are now swimming," he added. "I got twelve men to go with me. We found the place—and the body of a giant anaconda. The thing was thirty-six inches around and its head was bigger than a man's. The boy's one shot had hit the brain as the snake, gliding along, head high off the ground, had come for him. It had flattened the undergrowth in its death struggles."

Because Pat knew something about preserving skins, he had the men bring the dead snake to the compound, where he skinned it. Then he tacked the skin to the side of the church, the longest building available. Even so, they had to nail on another board support, for the skin, thirty-three feet long, hung three feet over one end.

"For a preservative," Pat said, "I took all Lillete's salt and rubbed it into the skin. The trouble is, cattle down here—they bring them in from Brazil—are hungry for salt. They came in the night and licked my snakeskin and ruined it. So that's the story—Mrs. Dickson, where are you going?"

"To call the children," she told him. "I think they've been swimming in that stream long enough."

That evening, Pat asked, "How do you like your cottage? Is it comfortable?"

"Oh, it's fine," Lil assured him.

"Just one thing, Mrs. Dickson," Pat added. "Be sure that you and the children sleep under the nets."

"Mosquitoes don't bother us much—"

"It's not the mosquitoes. It's the vampire bats."

"We will use the nets," Lil assured him.

Each day for the six days of the conference, Lil taught Bible at the Lutheran compound, while the children had the time of their lives.

When they returned to New Amsterdam, Lil evaluated her talents. She did not regard herself primarily as a Bible teacher, and certainly not as a preacher. Basically her interests lay in "mother tasks," cleaning up and putting in order, seeing that illness was attended to, leading her larger family to love the Lord and acknowledge His goodness—all mother's work. But when she tried to get across this philosophy to the church women, she ran into problems.

In British Guiana, there was no women's work at all. "And there won't be for another twenty years," the East Indian men said to her. Lil could see the problem. Most of the women spent their days in the fields doing the hardest kind of heavy work. Any organization would have to be very simple, one that would serve the women and not simply add another burden to their already drooping shoulders.

One day she invited a group of the East Indian women to her home. "Everything that a woman does in her home, she should do in the house of God," she said, as one mother to another. "She keeps her home clean—she should keep God's house clean. A woman in her home has to take care of the little ones—in God's house she should do the same. A woman in her home takes care of her young people so that they don't drift away to bad company. In the church she should be equally alert. She should see that the young people's meetings are bright and attractive so that the young people will like to go there, serving cookies and things like that. And in a home, the woman is responsible for the social life of the members of her family, for making them feel free to invite in friends. The women should do the same for the church. God wants our happy service. We could call ourselves Happy Workers."

These were new ideas to the women of British Guiana, but the organization appealed to them. At their first meeting, they adopted the constitution that Lil had prepared.

"The constitution calls for an offering at each meeting," she explained, and picked up a dinner plate she had in readiness. To start things off, she placed a new, bright shilling in the center of the plate and handed it to the woman nearest her. She could hear the clink of coins as the plate passed from hand to hand. When it came back to Lil and she placed it on the table by her side, something didn't look quite right. Then it dawned on her: the bright new shilling was missing. At the next meeting, the offering "plate" was a pickle bottle with a slit in a wired-down cover.

Lil's women were like church women—or church men—anywhere: they were readier to talk about what should be done than they were to do it. "The church is still dirty," Lil said to them a few weeks later. "It is," she chose her word carefully, "a *disgrace*. Who will volunteer to scrub the floor?"

The women were silent.

"Very well," said Lil. "I will scrub it."

The women gasped. Then they relaxed and smiled. Mrs. Dickson was joking.

"You're a revolutionary," Jim admonished her the morning she set out for the church with pail and scrub brush.

"I'd rather be that than have a dirty floor!" she said, flouncing on her way. When she returned, with considerably less flounce and hair askew, she said to Jim, "Scrubbing is awfully devotional. You have to get down on your knees to use a scrub brush."

Lil did not have to scrub that floor again.

Before long the Happy Workers numbered thirty groups. They made garments and sold them and the first year netted five hundred dollars for the church. To teach tithing, Lil said, "If you have ten chickens or ten pigs, tie a string around the leg of one that is for God. Feed that one better, and when they are big, sell that one as an offering."

When the Dicksons had been in British Guiana for almost three years, a letter came from one of Lil's brothers. "Dad is getting along in years," he wrote, "and he has heart trouble. Better come home a little early than just too late." And so six months ahead of Jim's scheduled furlough, she returned to Prior Lake, Minnesota, taking the children with her. During the six months, both her father and mother died. She spoke of it to Jim when he arrived. "We've been on the other side of the world so much, as far as possible from home, yet God worked it out and allowed me to be at their bedsides when they left us."

Lil's major mothering went of course to her own children. All the teaching that Ronny and Marilyn received had to come from their mother. She was not exactly a novice at it, having taught in Aiken, Minnesota, before her marriage. But it was one thing to teach in a well-equipped schoolroom and another to extemporize in the jungle with such textbooks as she could get from the States. In addition to the other subjects they would need later on, Lil wanted to make sure they shared her love of literature and music. Because there was so little poetry in their stilt-house community, Lil pasted verses inside the lids of the jars in which she kept sugar, flour, and other food ingredients. When she made a loaf of bread, baked a cake, prepared a meal, she fed her soul with hyacinths at the same time. Every jar she opened let a stimulating breath of the outside world blow through her mind. When she needed new inspiration, she changed the verses.

If Lil had one extravagance, it was books for the children—storybooks, inspirational books, biographies, classics, all kinds of books, bought usually in fifty-dollar lots. When the shipments arrived, Ronny especially would lose himself in stories of faraway people and places, keeping three books going at once.

To Jim, spending fifty dollars at a clip for books was a prodigality not to be countenanced. So Lil would simply charge them, at the supply houses in America, to her sister Amy. Then all she had to do was say, "Jim, we owe Amy fifty dollars." If there was one thing that appalled Jim more than spending fifty dollars for books, it was owing money to a relative. Always he paid up promptly.

To teach them about poetry, Lil had Ronny and Marilyn write a poem a week. "But first," she said, "you must read the great poets so you will know how to do it." Ronny memorized much of Keats and Shelley.

Lil wanted them both to have piano lessons. As a child, she herself had taken organ and piano. "I got as far as 'Maiden's Prayer,' " she recalls. "Then, away at school and college, I had no chance to play." In South America, she bought a portable organ for her outdoor meetings. She learned to play three or four pieces acceptably and would tell the catechist, "You may ask me for this piece and this piece and this piece—nothing else!"

At one place, they were both double-crossed by the elder who announced a number not on the approved list. Ignoring the catechist's desperate gestures, the elder repeated the number. The catechist sidled over to Lil, "Can you do it?" he whispered.

"Four sharps! But I'll try."

"Fight it out!" he said encouragingly.

But the little pump organ was an unsuitable substitute for a piano for Ronny and Marilyn. Lil wanted them to become thoroughly proficient, which meant finding a piano and a piano teacher. Even if they could have afforded it, the lack of shipping prevented their getting a piano from the States, and none was for sale locally.

But Lil remembered that once she had heard a piano playing. Promptly, she called at the address. Unfortunately, the woman owner had moved upriver, and no one seemed to know just where she had gone.

Determinedly, Lil set out on a bicycle. "Have you heard a piano anywhere around here?" She put the question dozens of times. Finally, the search narrowed down to a particular house.

Going to the door, she asked a pleasant but bewildered woman, "Excuse me, but do you have a piano?"

"Yes, but—"

"I'm not asking you to sell it—I know how scarce pianos are—but would you *rent* it to me—I'll pay the moving costs to my house and back?" The deal was made. A teacher who had studied piano in England was found.

Ronny took to it more readily than did Marilyn, but even his interest soon flagged. "What are we going to do?" Lil asked Jim. "He won't practice the half-hour a day the teacher says he must. Shall we cut it down?"

"He doesn't practice because he hasn't reached the place where he enjoys playing," Jim diagnosed. "The way for him to reach that point is not to slow him down but to speed him up. Don't cut practice. Extend it to an hour a day!"

Jim was right. Ronny soon was playing not because he had to, but because he enjoyed it.

Immediately after the war, Jim returned to Taiwan from British

Guiana for a survey trip. The children went with him as far as the United States—Ronny to Elmhurst, Illinois, to live with his Uncle Lester and attend high school, Marilyn to her Aunt Amy at Belton, Texas, where she took her high school training in three years. When both were made members of the National Honor Society, Lil felt vindicated as a teacher. The crowning touch came when one of Ronny's instructors wrote Lil: "He has a college level background in literature."

Lil was left alone for a while but kept busy and learned a few lessons herself that would soon be useful.

British Guiana was a plantation country, with as many as three to ten thousand workers on a plantation. The laborers from East India were mostly Hindus and Moslems. Lil held ten or twelve outdoor Sunday schools on the plantations each Sunday, followed by a meeting in the hospital in the afternoon and then an outdoor meeting for adults at night. One Sunday school met under a house where a Hindu man lived. When hundreds of little brown-skinned children with great eyes came running, the alarmed Hindu priests advised their man to evict the school. Lil told her Moslem driver, "You Mohammedans will have to rally round—the Hindus are throwing me out!" She didn't realize at the time how concerned they were.

Her evening meetings were arranged by Indian elders of the Presbyterian Church who asked Lil to give the message. Every week she would carefully prepare for the Sunday night service, spending hours on the task because she was speaking to a large crowd of Hindu men and women, mostly men. If they were not active enemies of the Gospel, they were at least not friendly to it.

After some weeks of this, she felt a sudden stab of conviction. Here, I've been always talking about the love of God, she told herself. I should preach about the awfulness of sin and judgment. So that week, she concentrated on the utter blackness of sin.

On Sunday morning and afternoon she was as busy as ever. It was hot. Even the shady areas under the stilt houses were stifling. Lil was looking forward to the evening service. It would be cooler when the sun went down.

There was bright moonlight as her "congregation" gathered. "So many of the old Hindu men have their walking sticks with them tonight," she commented to one of the elders. "I didn't realize they were getting so feeble."

Then it was time for Lil to speak. The sight of the walking sticks had mellowed her. These old men needed more than sticks to help them through the night. They needed the hand of God. Instead of the message she had prepared on the penalty of sin, she found herself telling them once again of the love of God.

Even as she talked, she found herself thinking, This is not what I prepared at all! Why am I saying this? But she went on with it. Never before had the love of God seemed so real to her nor the presence of God so unmistakable. The audience seemed to sense it, too. Lil noticed one of the old men in particular. He was fingering his heavy stick, looking far off into the darkness, deep in thought and totally oblivious of his surroundings.

The Christian elders gathered around Lil and walked with her to an Indian home where the taxi was waiting to take her back to New Amsterdam. As they walked, one said, "The Hindu priests have become alarmed because children all over the plantations are saying, 'We're going to be Christians.' "

Said another elder, "Did you see the sticks? The priests came to the meeting with the intention of making a disturbance. They were waiting for you to say something they could use as an excuse. You didn't say it. You talked about the love of God, and they couldn't disagree with that."

9. *Pentecost of the Hills*

Formosa was a bubbling brew when Jim Dickson returned late in 1945. He went immediately to the mission compound at Taipei. The houses were intact on the outside except for broken windows. Inside, the ceilings were down, and all was a fearful mess. Troops were living on the compound and were also occupying the Mackay Memorial Hospital, even though, before the missionaries left, the property had been turned over to the Formosan church.

Jim went to the hospital to look around. At the door, two soldiers crossed bayonets in front of him and said, "You can't go in."

"I want to see your commander," Jim insisted, and finally they let him go by. He approached the Chinese officer in charge. "The missionaries are coming back," he said. "We will be wanting the hospital in a very short time."

"You can't have it," the officer reported. "It's ours."

"But this hospital belongs to the church," Jim said. "The Japanese recognized our property rights. They used the hospital but they paid rent to the church. I am here by permission of

General MacArthur to make a survey. I would hate to have to report that our allies treated us worse than our enemies!"

Jim wrote to Lil, "I think the house will be ready by the time you get here. They will surely turn over the hospital, too. In a few months I will come back home to make my report to the mission board, then we will return to Taiwan together. . . . The mountain churches have grown amazingly since we left. They call it the Pentecost of the Hills. Remember little old Chi-oang, our unlikely student? She did most of it. Wait till you see . . . !"

Things had changed, and most of the changes were caused in some way by the greatest military cataclysm ever to sweep the globe. A pledge made by America's President Roosevelt and Britain's Prime Minister Churchill to China's Generalissimo Chiang Kai-shek at the Cairo Conference in 1943 became a part of the Tokyo Bay surrender treaty: Formosa and the Pescadores were returned to China. Japanese troops, police, and residents were evacuated from Formosa to Japan with the help of United States ships. Taiwan became a province of the Republic of China.

For fifty years the islanders had been adjusting to Japanese rule. Now they had to accustom themselves once more to a new way of life and to another landlord.

The Taiwanese—these Chinese who had lived on the island for generations—spoke Amoy. The Japanese had introduced their own language into the schools as the official tongue. Now the Chinese coming from the mainland in increasing numbers brought their official language, Mandarin, so unlike the spoken Amoy that the two had almost nothing in common. The islanders did not relish the thought of again adjusting their customs to suit "outsiders," and some of them were frankly appalled at the backwardness of occupying Chinese troops. The Japanese soldiers had been well clothed; many of these newcomers, who came wearing straw hats and sandals, had never seen an electric light or other conveniences that the Taiwanese, under sophisticated Japanese leadership, took for granted.

Chen Yi, the first governor appointed by the Chinese, worsened the problems of the transition period by his harsh misrule. His administration was soon brought to an end by riots, whereupon he was succeeded by the able Dr. Wei Tao-ming, former Chinese Ambassador to the United States.

Jim completed his survey. Then he returned home once more to report. He wrote Lil, still in British Guiana: "Pack up your things; book your passage home as soon as possible. You can see the children and be ready to go back with me to Taiwan." Lil smiled to herself. Husbands safely distant made moving sound so simple! Even if there was little baggage, there were roots to be pulled up, and in five years they go down deep.

After visiting the children in Illinois and Texas, Jim and Lil left for Taiwan by the converted troopship, *Marine Lynx,* but "it wasn't very soundly converted!" All passengers slept in hammocks, men on one side of the ship, women on the other, and lined up for meals and ate from trays. Many missionaries were on board. Those returning to China were fearfully talking about conditions they expected to find there. Lil said, "Why don't you come to Formosa? *We* are never bothered with Communists."

As the ship approached Shanghai, news came over the radio: "Communist-inspired revolution in Taiwan."

"But, Jim," Lil said, "that can't be true! Under the Japanese, not even a breath of communism could get in!" For weeks they were kept in Shanghai, but finally clearance came.

In Taiwan, as soon as they left the ship they noticed changes. Traffic was moving to the right instead of to the left, as had been the Japanese pattern. In Taipei, bomb damage was evident everywhere. Fortunately, no bombs had fallen on the mission compound. The Dicksons' house had been repaired by a Christian Formosan businessman and made ready for their return.

Every day seemed to pump more life—and anxiety—into the city. The handwriting was on the wall. The Communists were taking over the mainland and no one knew what this would mean for the island.

Lil wrote to her friends: "Every day brings new rumors, fresh alarms. It is only because we are under God's care and have our eyes and hearts set on one goal—bringing the good news of the

Gospel to as many as possible while there is time—that we are able to proceed with comparative tranquillity. Refugees are storming our shores by plane and ship by more than tens of thousands. My guests used to come by ones and twos, now and then a group. Last night we had a letter asking if we could give shelter to an orphanage and a whole theological college student body!"

Though the influx of mainlanders and their possessive attitude created problems with the islanders, there were benefits, too. The most immediately obvious gain was simply that the Japanese had not won.

Despite Japanese harassment during the war, a clandestine Christian revival had swept the mountains. "I never saw anything like it," Jim said to Lil. "When I came back, I found at least four thousand believers, and twelve churches already up. At the church in Hwalien, over five hundred aborigines were baptized in less than a year. And," he added, "most of this can be attributed to Chi-oang. You remember her?"

Lil indeed remembered the little tattooed woman who had come to the Bible school at Tamsui.

Jim traced her remarkable adventures. Chi-oang had returned home and began teaching small groups of friends. As interest grew, she went from one village to another. The police, hearing of her activities, ordered the meetings stopped. Though Chi-oang could no longer visit freely, those she had led to faith carried on secret meetings themselves, often at night, setting a guard to warn of approaching police. When she could, she went out among the people.

"One of her journeys sounds like something out of the Acts of the Apostles," said Jim, "as indeed, in a modern sense, it is!"

Her arrival at Mikasa, on the east coast, was reported to the police who suspected that she was planning to hold a meeting without permission. They were right. As the Christians met with her in a home up in the mountains, they heard a bugle call summoning the Home Guard to the police station. They knew that the village would be searched and Chi-oang discovered. Quickly, the meeting broke up and the little group fled back into the hills.

Because Chi-oang was so feeble that she could not keep up with the others, the young men took turns carrying her on their backs. Two scouts going ahead, two bringing up the rear, they followed the mountain trail to the small village of Shimmura. Here, though it was night, the Christians, thirty-four families of them, were waiting to welcome Chi-oang, alerted by those who had gone in advance. After a brief pause, the young men went on with Chi-oang to the little village of Bat-keng, a station on the railroad. They hoped to put her on a train in the early morning hours and send her on to safety.

They arrived at Bat-keng before train time, not knowing that three members of the Home Guard, sent there by the Japanese to arrest her if she came that way, were waiting at a warehouse. The young men carrying Chi-oang approached cautiously, stopping behind that same warehouse to pray. One of them, reconnoitering, found two of the guards. Striking up a conversation, he asked, "Are you Christians?"

"Yes," the two told him, "but the one asleep in there"—they pointed to the open door of the warehouse—"is not."

"If you are Christians," whispered the new arrival, "you will help Chi-oang."

One of the guards padded softly to the door of the warehouse and looked in. "Still asleep," he reported. "What do you want us to do?" Together they worked out a strategy. Presently the train arrived, and they whisked Chi-oang aboard. As they had instructed her, she went into the lavatory and stayed there until the train had gone on some distance.

But she was not yet out of danger. At Mikasa, six men were waiting to search the train. A young Christian, also waiting to board the train, watched the six curiously; it was not difficult to identify those who were in the pay of the police—they had a certain bravado that set them apart.

When the train arrived, the Christian youth swung aboard before it had stopped. Moving through the car, his eyes darted left and right. Then he saw Chi-oang—it must be she the police were after. Sitting down beside her, he said, "Bend over. Quick, I can't explain!" He whipped a large carrying cloth from one of his parcels and flung it over Chi-oang. He piled his other packages helter-skelter over her legs and feet. Scarcely had he leaned back in his seat when the six men entered the car. Though one of them looked sharply at the cloth-draped bundle, the lights in the car were dim and Chi-oang crouched very still and small. They walked by, and soon the train lurched on. Chi-oang smiled her thanks when the youth gently lifted off the covering.

"Just one more stop," she told him. "Mizuhe."

"That will be more difficult," the youth said. "See, it is growing light." In the east, the sky was trembling with the first misty signs of dawn.

But the light, as the darkness, was working for Chi-oang. Police at Mizuhe reasoned that no one would try to escape in broad daylight, and so did not search the train.

Many of the mountain youth paid stealthy visits to Chi-oang's home near Hwalien for Christian instruction. One young man walked twenty miles in the night, once a week for three months, to hear her explain the Bible. "But you are not to begin preaching until you are fully trained," she said to him sternly.

The boy could not wait. Before the three months were up, he had won twenty-five others. The whole village of Gukutsu became a Christian community, thanks to his zeal and courage.

Jim finished his account with a note of sadness: "Chi-oang died just two months before I returned to the island."

Do-wai was another Christian student who had been active in the mountains. Not surprisingly, he was in trouble with the Japanese police even before the missionaries had to leave Formosa. A policeman found a Japanese Bible in a Tyal home; a general search was made, and all Bibles and hymnbooks confiscated and burned. More were brought in; again they were hunted down and destroyed. Three times it happened. At this, the police rounded up Do-wai and the other principal offenders, and made them kneel while they were beaten. "You can cut off our hands—we are still Christians," they said to the police. "You can kill us—we are still Christians."

The police sent them back to their homes with a warning—everyone but Do-wai. Because he was the ringleader, they put him in prison. All he had to do, in order to be free to leave, they said, was to renounce his faith. He would not do it. Later he contracted beriberi. The Japanese doctor who treated other patients refused to treat him, saying, "Pray to your God for help."

"When I made my first trip to the east coast after the war," Jim recounted, "I was awakened at six in the morning by a visitor. It was Do-wai! He had spent years in prison but had won an incredible thousand souls to Christ."

Shintoism never really had a chance in the mountains but the price paid for stopping it was high.

At Mikasa, despite brutal enforcement of the law by the police officer in charge, more and more persons were becoming Christians. He ordered that within three days all believers were to come to the police station and state publicly that they were forsaking the Christian religion. Those who refused, he announced, he would have bound, weighted with a stone, and thrown from the high suspension bridge.

The villagers, well aware that this swaggering little official was equal to any threat he chose to make, met at midnight. "Each must decide for himself," the leader said solemnly.

Someone presented the age-old argument of cornered people: perhaps they had better give up and so live to fight again for freedom and faith. At that, a stripling of a lad stood up and quoted from his Japanese Bible—a Bible that had been smuggled in after three different book burnings. "Fear not them which kill the body, but are not able to kill the soul."

There was a moment of abashed silence, then the terrible choice: "Those who refuse to forsake Christ, raise your hands." In the dim glow of the Japanese electric lamp hanging from the ceiling, every hand was lifted.

The next day they took courage together while their leaders carried the decision to the policeman. "Tonight, I celebrate," he told them. And that night, in a drunken stupor, he decided to go fishing. Out into the rushing river he waded. Before the night air and the icy water could clear his head, a log bounced toward him on the crest of the swift current and struck him a numbing blow. Under the shadowy arch of the execution bridge, he died.

At Tak-kiri, twenty-two believers were forced to kneel while police laid pieces of wood over the calves of their legs, and jumped on the ends of the boards. Four policemen worked in shifts beating other men, stopping only to smoke and rest; one old man died from the beatings. In 1944 an official made the rounds of the villages posing as an evangelist from coastal Hwalien. He called Christians together, preached to them, even took up a collection. When congregations had paid him his round-trip traveling expenses, he wrote down their names and left—stopping at the police station on the way. That night, all who had been at the meeting were rounded up and their leaders stripped, kicked, and beaten.

Near Mikasa, just after the surrender of Japan, the Christians immediately began to build a church. A policeman who did not yet realize that he was out of a job watched the men swarm over the bamboo frame.

"What are you doing?" he demanded. When they told him, he blustered, "I'll burn it down!"

"You will have to burn us with it!" they answered.

Before he went back to Japan the villagers arranged a dinner for him. "This is the way Christians treat those who have treated them badly," they said.

The mountain people moved very rapidly to provide their own church buildings. When the news of V-J Day came through, a delegation of Tyals went down to Hwalien and asked the pastor, "How do you build a church?" He drew a rough sketch and informed them that he would be coming up that way in a few weeks and they could all go into the matter then. When he came, the church was already completed.

One story of his survey trip Jim did not tell but Lil heard from others, the story of the day he was walking with a group of aborigines on a precarious path skirting a cliff. The mountain people, exceptionally sure-footed and accustomed to the sheer rise and fall of their mountains, were bothered by the hazards of cliffs no more than is an American city dweller by heavy motor traffic. But a misstep occurred. A young girl slipped and fell over the edge, her scream following her body down to be ominously silenced seconds later.

The others crept close and peered down; they could not see where the girl had struck.

The leader of the group went to the girl's mother. "She is surely dead," he said sympathetically. "Besides, the way down the cliff is perilous." Shaken by the experience, the group prepared to move on.

"But you can't just walk away!" Jim protested.

"She is surely dead," said the leader. "Besides, the way down the cliff—" But Jim did not stay to listen. Moving carefully to the cliff edge, he found a foothold, then another and another. Slowly, he worked his way down. A rattling pebble drew his attention. A young man was following after him.

The girl, although a mass of bruises and lacerations, was still alive when Jim reached her. The young man picked her up, slung her over his shoulder, and started the climb up. A sigh of relief and wonder went up as the trio pushed over the cliff edge to the trail. Jim examined the girl and found no bones broken. Bandaging her cuts, he made her comfortable.

Journeying on with Jim to the surrounding villages, the chief began every introduction with the story of the white man who went down the mountainside to lead the rescue of an aboriginal girl when everyone else had given up hope.

10. Lil's Black "Lambs"

The house assigned to the Dicksons at the Taipei mission compound had been made habitable; the curtains were up and the household was in running order. Lil, inspired by the stories of Christian sacrifice in the mountains, went to Jim. "I've got my Martha work organized," she said. "I want to do some Mary work, too."

Jim's blue eyes twinkled. "Then I expect you'll do it, Lil."

"I don't want to be just a missionary's wife—I want to be a missionary wife." No one knew better than she how important was her husband's work; Chi-oang was the instrument God had used to bring Pentecost to the hills, but back of Chi-oang was Jim Dickson, another of God's instruments.

"You could do things, unofficially, that the rest of us can't do," Jim mused. "Things that ought to be done—"

"I have a plan—" Lil began. "I had such a happy time in British Guiana with my child-evangelism work and outdoor meetings, that I'd like to continue them here."

"We *are* under martial law, you know," Jim reminded her.

Tireless Lil Dickson rises early to begin a day at headquarters of The Mustard Seed, Inc., nerve center of a far-flung mission of compassion that reaches from the heart of teeming Taipei city to every corner of the island of Taiwan. Soon "Typhoon Lil" will leave her desk to set out on another round of her unending visits to the forgotten lepers, orphans, mountain people, prisoners, newborn babies, and destitute mothers who depend on her for help and hope.

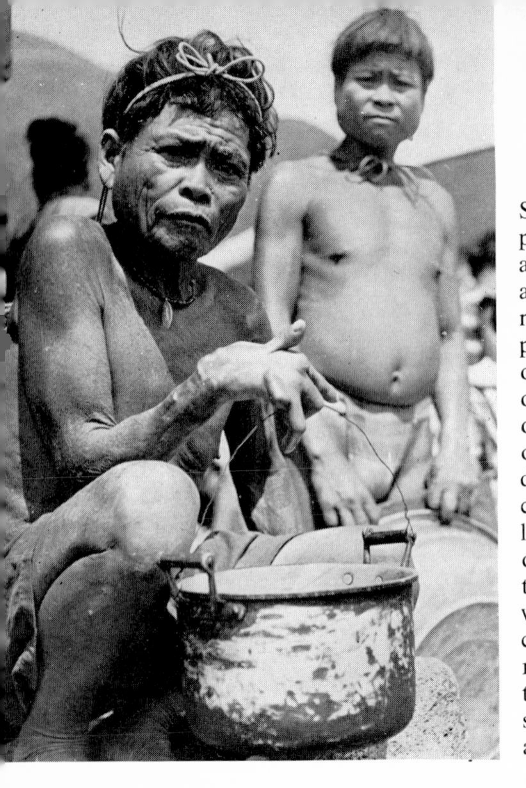

Savage headhunters no longer, the primitive aborigines of remote Taiwan areas now hurry to welcome missionaries arriving with food, clothing, medicine. Jim and Lil Dickson's pioneering treks in the 1930's helped open up the wild mountain territory of the Tyals (opposite, bottom) and other tribes. The Mustard Seed and other mission efforts now provide destitute people with 100 stone churches, like the one on Orchid Island (below) where supplies are being distributed; special medical units, like the mobile clinic on the Pescadores where an aged grandmother brings a child for treatment (opposite, top right); dozens of milk stations, like those on the Great Salt Coast (opposite, top left) where disease and hunger are rampant.

The plight of children has always been at the center of Lil Dickson's heart and work. Just after World War II, her accordion drew hundreds of youngsters to outdoor evangelism services and Sunday schools in the streets of Taipei and in outlying villages (left). In their crowded jail cell (below), prison boys—many of them street urchins who have stolen food to stay alive—crowd around as Lil leads a Bible lesson. Lil founded Boys' Home for unclaimed homeless boys who might be held in prison permanently if she does not "sponsor them out."

When a Mustard Seed milk station opens in Taipei or in a rural village, children scramble to line up for milk, vitamins, and one of the thousands of used Christmas cards on which Lil prints a Bible verse.

Shoes arriving at The Mustard Seed depot are separated into piles for men, women, and children, but each youngster is on his own in the search for a pair that fits. Food and clothing are used not only to supply everyday needs but to meet such emergencies as typhoon disasters (below) and epidemics.

Hun-khai, a crippled orphan imprisoned for begging (see Chapter 21), is one of hundreds of children who have shelter because of Lil Dickson.

Orphan tots at Iro-Iro ("Miscellaneous") Children's Home learn early to join in Sunday morning worship.

To the underfed and untreated patients in a run-down public leprosarium, Lil Dickson has brought food, clothing, medicine, new housing—and hope. The patients (above) receive Christmas presents at a party in the Christian Herald Therapy room. Others who are able to play choose instruments for a band rehearsal (below).

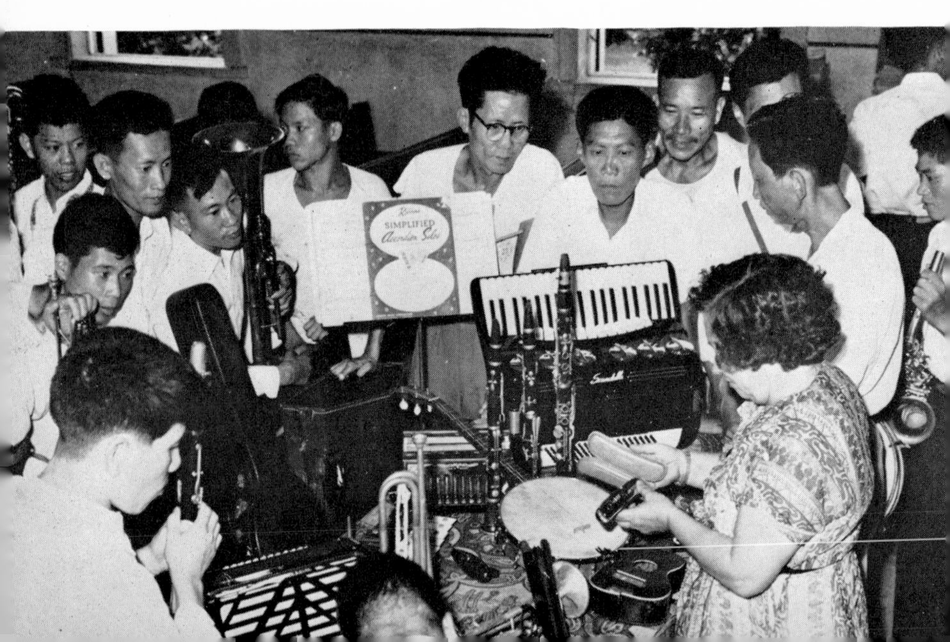

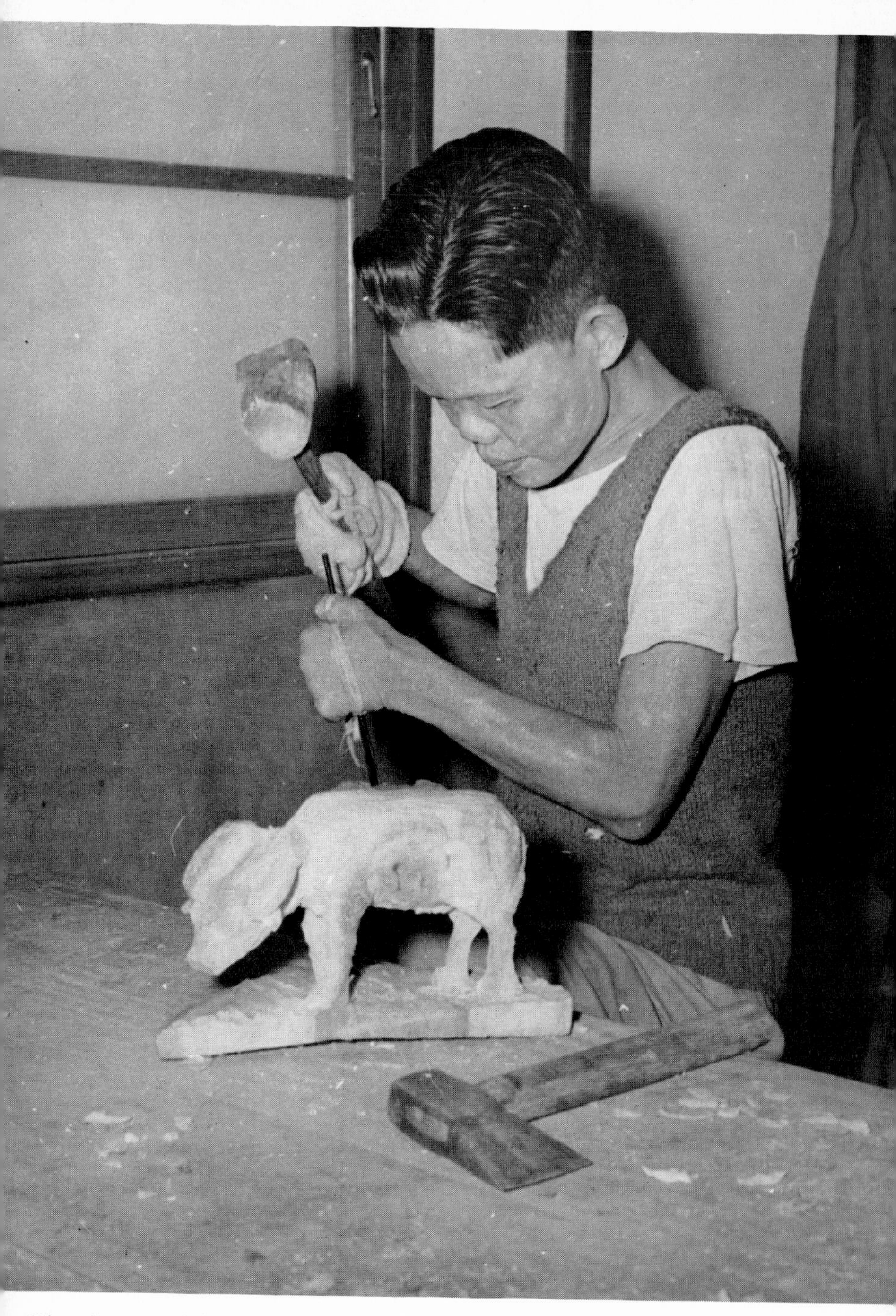

The absence of fingers does not prevent a skilled craftsman from using his chisel in the leper workshop.

Children of lepers, once fated to remain with their parents and contract the disease, are now taken away and cared for in An-Lok Babies Home. Every few weeks Lil Dickson returns the healthy children to see, and to be seen by, their eager mothers and fathers in the lepers' church—from a short distance that seems long.

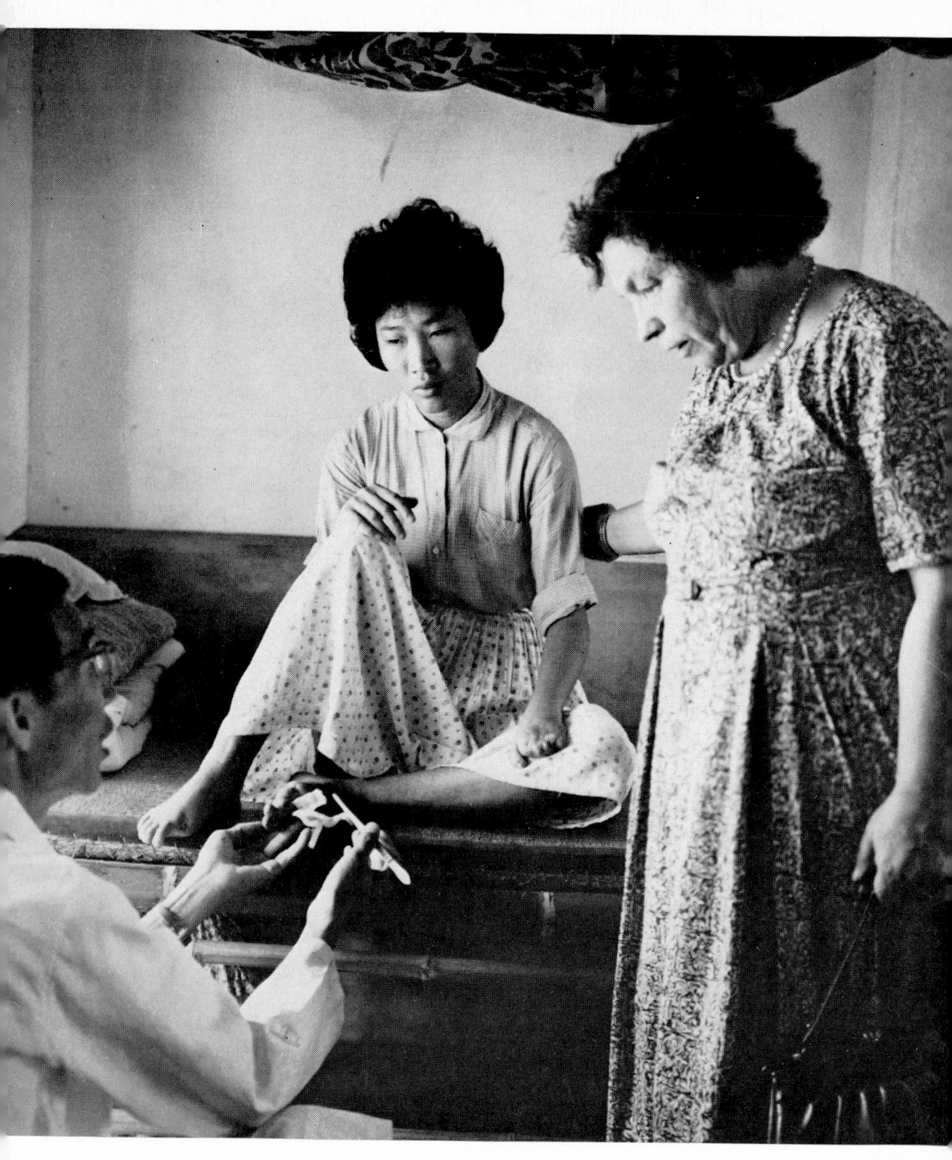

Blackfoot Disease, a strange and cruel affliction of the extremities, is found only on the Great Salt Coast of Western Taiwan. Lil and the doctor visit a young victim at the Mercy's Door Clinic in Pak-mng (above).

Among the Tyals of the northern mountains, 80% of the tribespeople are stricken with tuberculosis. The sanatorium at Hwalien (above) is one of three built in the foothills along the coast; at Sin-Khang sanatorium (below), Lil talks with two mountain girls trained by Mustard Seed as nurses' aides for tuberculosis patients.

At one of the five "Rooms for Mary," Lil and a mountain mother stand beneath a painting symbolic of Mustard Seed's concern for mothers and babies. Five such clinics have cut down the high infant mortality rate among the mountain tribes. The painting is by a billboard artist named "Frank," a cured leper who was converted in the leprosarium and now serves the church with his brush and palette.

味王
THE MUSTA
SEED. INC.
大慶貨運
15-10963

At the busy Mustard Seed headquarters building, supplies are moved out quickly to the point of greatest need (opposite, top). The Mercy's Door Night Clinic in the same building always opens to a long line of Taipei's poor and sick (bottom).

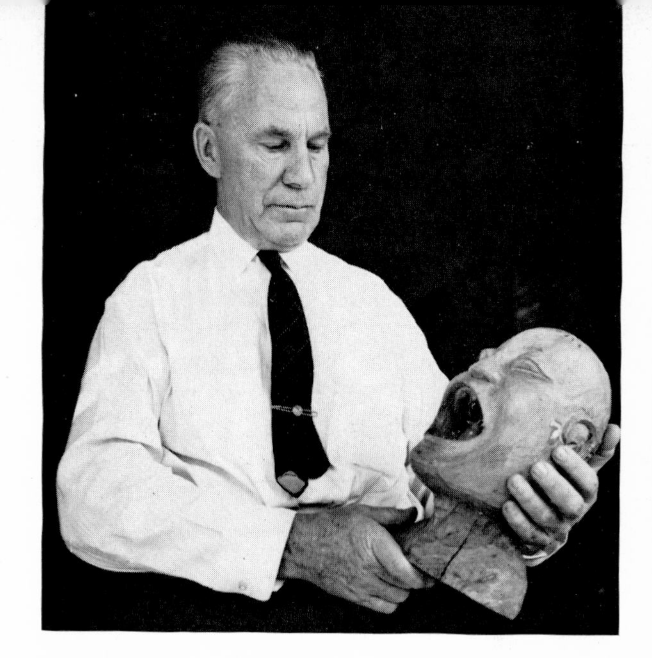

Jim Dickson, missionary on Taiwan since 1927, is president of Taiwan Theological College. His leadership opened new frontiers of Christian service: above, he holds one of the wooden heads used to train former headhunters to become dentists for their tribes; below, he baptizes a leper in the church built through his wife's efforts.

A hand to hold, a love to trust: orphans cling to Lil Dickson on every visit.

"But now we have freedom of religion, too," Lil said. "We didn't have that under the Japanese."

"Go to it," Jim said, with an encouraging smile.

For her meetings she would need a musical instrument that she could carry easily. A pump organ was too cumbersome. Iok-chong, a friend of the Dicksons, pointed out that accordions were more portable and sounded like an organ. Iok-chong was not exactly unbiased since he was an accordion teacher, but he was also a photographer, which gave him considerable standing with Jim, himself an avid cameraman.

One day Iok-chong showed up at the Dicksons' house at the mission compound with an accordion. "It's for sale," he said to Lil. "The owner says I may leave it with you so that you may try it out."

Strapping it on, she stood in front of a mirror, trying to make sense of the bass chord fingering. "What should I do?" she asked Jim.

Jim put down a camera he was loading. "I don't think you'll ever learn to play it, Lil," he said. "Besides, it costs too much." He picked up the camera again.

When Iok-chong returned for a decision, Lil looked at Jim and gave the bad news to the accordion teacher.

Iok-chong patted the instrument and said pointedly to Jim, "This accordion costs about as much as a good camera. It will not necessarily be of less help to the church and God's work."

Lil got her accordion. She learned to play it at forty-six.

She and Jim were a study in contrasts. She was short and stocky; he, rawboned, tall, rangy, his six-foot height towering over Lil by a good twelve inches. Lil spoke slowly; Jim's words tumbled over each other and were often prefaced by "I'll tell you what you should do," though not everyone, even Lil, invariably took such direct instruction. "I often ask Jim's advice," Lil once said to a close friend, "and sometimes I take it, but not *necessarily*."

She did take it on her idea of outdoor meetings.

But outdoor religious activity was a new idea in Taipei and not all pastors favored it. Finally, Lil persuaded one church to allow the young people to go out with her and announce evangelistic meetings that were being held in the church. She said to the pastor, "When a fisherman wants to fish, he doesn't just sit in a boat and hope the fish will jump in. He goes after them. We at least ought to do that, when we are trying to get people to believe in Christ."

The next Sunday evening, Lil shouldered her accordion, met the young people and pastor at the church, and they started around the block. "I will play and we will sing, and then you announce that all are welcome at the meeting," Lil suggested. Stopping at the first corner, she played and they sang, "What a Friend We Have in Jesus."

Hardly had they begun, when a policeman hurried up. "You're under arrest," he declared to Lil. The young people, terrified, ran. Only the pastor stayed.

Jim had briefed her, "If you should get into trouble with the police, don't be too humble!"

So when the officer told her that she would have to report to the main city police station the next day, she replied, "I'll be there —and I'll bring the American consul with me! This will be reported *straight* to Washington, D.C." The American vice-consul, who lived at the mission compound, had mentioned to her that the United States government would want to know of any incidents involving Americans, so that the attitude of the new government of Taiwan might be determined.

When she visited the police station the next day, a staff member from the consulate accompanied her. "It's all a mistake," the police said to Lil. "It was a new policeman from the mainland. He thought you were a Communist."

"Imagine!" Lil snorted to the consular representative. "A Communist singing, 'What a Friend We Have in Jesus!' "

Her child-evangelism plans moved slowly.

She wrote to her friends: "The native church has for years thought only of caring for the children of the flock. To make them consider that in the eyes of God they have a responsibility toward all children has been like pulling teeth. Often I find a town with only one church in it, about forty children in the Sunday school and ten thousand in the public schools. 'We have a nice little Sunday school,' the pastor tells me. 'Just enough to keep in good order easily, and not too many to be able to treat at Christmas time. So don't come out here with your accordion—some outside children may follow you into church.'

"I remonstrate, 'But you are the only light God has in this town! He is depending on you to shine into the hearts of ten thousand children, not just forty.' Nine out of ten times, I fail to rouse him. Even so, we have about fifty outdoor Sunday schools on the island now, and in strategic places we have two libraries of visual Sunday-school materials to lend." The work gained impetus when Lil was invited to hold a Child Evangelism Conference in each Presbytery (three in the north and four in the south, the latter sponsored by the English Presbyterian Church).

"In Taipei," she wrote her friends in 1948, "where I am anchored a good deal of the time because of teaching in the College and other regular Bible classes, I have a busy Sunday. I collect the Sunday-school children and outside children for several Sunday schools, by going out with the accordion. We have also started two new Sunday schools where none was before. One place is in the slums of the city. I used to pass it on my way from one Sunday school to another and always it saddened me. People there were living in tight, close quarters, packed in solidly as thick as ants in an anthill. The streets were narrow alleys. Any rooms you could see into were like dark, smoky caverns. There was no place for children to play, not a church or any Christian witness, and I was told there were about twenty thousand people there."

Lil asked a deacon and a pastor in the nearest church if they would try to find a room that she could rent to start a children's meeting. They tried several times, but said there was no hope—the people were packed into that part of the city so tightly. So one windy, rainy day as she passed, she felt impelled to go and search for herself. The streets were unbelievably narrow; she knew no street meeting would be possible for it would block traffic and incur the ire of the police.

"After twisting about through narrow lanes," she continued, "I came suddenly to a brick wall, enclosing, of all things in this dark place, a garden. Above the wall, I could see a tree with leaves outlined against the sky. I found the owner and rented it for about fifty cents a Sunday. There, hundreds of laborers' children now hear the Gospel every Sunday. They had never heard it before and neither had their parents who come often also and stand on the outside of the crowd, listening wistfully."

Sunday was always Lil's busiest day. She had nine or ten regular stops, helping with the children's work in many churches, taking care of her "garden" and another new place in a settlement house, and teaching young people's Bible classes in three locations. Her great problem was getting quickly from one place to another with her flannelgraph, child-evangelism material, and accordion. A bicycle was impossible and a rickshaw was far too slow for all the work she wanted to accomplish on the Lord's Day.

"Teaching keeps me very busy during the week also," she wrote. "I have several weekly Bible classes. Every Tuesday and Thursday night we have outdoor evangelistic meetings in crowded parts of the city, sometimes using a loudspeaker Jim has set up. We take theological students with us and nearby preachers and pastors. Last Thursday we borrowed a jeep and used the hood of it for a platform. Standing on it, I played the accordion to a thousand people. Many outside people have started coming to church as a result of the outdoor meetings."

As Jim and Lil sat down to breakfast one morning, she observed, "There are still thousands of children I am not reaching."

"And there are still hundreds of villages in the mountains where the Gospel has never been taken," he replied.

"Reminds me of a story I read somewhere," Lil said. "A shipwreck had occurred in a fog and hundreds of people were drowning. There were two small boats nearby. The man in one boat, seeing the confusion, felt that if he tried to do anything at all, his boat would be overloaded and they might all be lost. So he rowed away in the darkness alone. The other man filled his boat with women and children and then left, sad that those who could not be taken would be lost."

"Then what—?" Jim asked.

"It became known that two boats had been on the scene, but only one attempted to save lives. When the first man was found, someone asked him, 'You rowed away alone! Are you not ashamed of what you did?' The man answered, 'I will be ashamed of it as long as I live.'

"The second man was asked, 'What did you say when you filled your boat and had to leave because you could not save more?'

"The man answered, 'I prayed, *O God, for a bigger boat!*' "

Jim unfolded his napkin and the two of them bowed their heads for the breakfast blessing. "O God," Jim prayed, "for a bigger boat!"

"Amen," Lil fervently echoed.

In a report sent to the mission board in Canada, Lil noted, "We have one hundred fifty open-air Sunday schools. Once a month, the children come to the nearby churches for an evangelistic meeting."

Back came the terse reply, "We believe that children are the lambs of the fold."

"They should see my lambs!" Lil told Jim grimly. "I sometimes have to stop in the middle of everything to break up a crap game!"

Her experiences convinced her of the worth of outdoor evangelism. Far over on the east coast at Taitung, Lil came to take part in a church service, arriving early to practice on her accordion. A young man sitting near the front listened and watched her intently. After a while he came forward and spoke to her. "About two years ago," he said, "you came and had an outdoor meeting and played the accordion. I heard the Gospel for the first time. Now I've become a Christian and I have a church in my house."

Another time Lil was invited to Hsinchu, an hour by train south of Taipei, to take part in the Sunday evening church service. When she arrived, she was dismayed. Although it was a big church, only about fifteen people were there.

"Let me go out with my accordion and invite people to come in," Lil urged the pastor.

"People aren't used to that sort of thing in Hsinchu," he said.

The next time she went to that church, again there were only a few people present. And again she pleaded, "Let me go out and call people in." This time the pastor didn't answer, but his son said, "I'll go with you."

So they went down the street, Lil playing the accordion and the young man announcing the meeting in the church. Because it was so unusual, many people followed and went into the church until it was crowded. The experience completely convinced the pastor. To Lil it was only one of many such meetings, and she soon forgot it.

Two or three years later, when she was about to speak at a little church in another part of the island, a policeman announced that the service had to be translated into Mandarin. Lil was in a quandary until a man came forward and said, "I speak Mandarin. I can translate for you from Taiwanese to Mandarin."

Afterward he said to Lil, "I first saw you in Hsinchu. You were playing the accordion and walking through the streets. I followed you into the church—the first time I had ever entered one. I became interested and went there regularly. Now I have led twenty-three of my classmates to the Lord."

Sometimes her outdoor activities attracted other than the potentially devout. Once, when Lil was playing for a street meeting, she asked a fellow missionary to watch her purse. During a prayer, the missionary closed her eyes. When she looked up, the purse was gone. There was not much money in it, but it did contain Lil's passport. When Lil went to the consulate for a replacement, she was informed, "We will have to take it up with the State Department in Washington, and I will have to tell them the circumstances. I will not report that you were negligent, but," the official added with a twinkle, "I think that you were just a little bit negligent. Doesn't your own Bible say, 'Watch and pray'?"

"Always at our outdoor meetings we had music first," Lil recalls. "Of course, we used my accordion, a drum, anything else that we could muster that made a big noise—a musical noise, if possible. One night we had competition across the way. *They* had a saxophone, and were selling medicine. Jim went over for a look. He came back shaking his head. 'Either you'll have to get better music,' he said, 'or more beautiful girls.'

"After the music the pastor would have prayer and perhaps we would sing a song. Then he would usually have me give a flannel-graph lesson to the children—a foreign woman speaking in their language was an attraction—then we distributed old Christmas cards. We'd sing a song and we'd tell the children, 'Now, if you can sing this, we'll give you five Christmas cards.' We'd get the children up on the platform, singing. That would draw a bigger crowd. Then finally the evangelist gave the message, and always an invitation."

That was the start of Lil's use of Christmas cards. In her letters and in magazine articles about her work, the need was mentioned, and packages of used cards began arriving by the hundreds.

At the post office, the man handling her mail informed her that she would have to pay duty on the cards.

"But they are *used* cards," she protested. "They have no commercial value."

"Duty," the man insisted.

She realized that if she were required to pay duty, the amount of money involved would be tremendous, for there were so many parcels. And if the supply were cut off, thousands of children would be deprived of one of the few bits of brightness likely to come into their lives.

K. C. Wu, then provincial governor, was one of the influential friends she has always seemed to have available at strategic times. Lil went to him.

"Governor Wu," she said, "you are an educated man. You know that a used Christmas card like this"—she showed him one—"has no commercial value. Now, that man in the post office has never had the opportunities you have had. He doesn't know that these cards have no commercial value, or that they can make a child's heart happy. Would you be so kind as to write to him and explain this?"

Governor Wu did just that. The next time Lil went to the post office, knowing that the letter had been written, she could not restrain a triumphant smile.

"The packages," she said. "I'll take them now."

The postal official reached under the counter and took out Governor Wu's letter, which he read through silently and deliberately. Three times he read it, as if seeking for some flaw in the argument, some loophole, in which he could take satisfaction.

Finally, a gleam in his eye, he looked up over the top of his glasses. "It doesn't say *forever*."

11. Typhoon!

Since her return to Formosa, Lil had become a familiar figure in the foothill villages of east and west that were portals to craggy mountain vastnesses where always, just beyond, was another village not yet visited by a missionary. At times she went with Jim, at times with native women, at times with Formosan pastors, at times with missionary women, at times with the Mobile Medical Unit, at times alone.

"I promised the people at Mikasa Yama I would come back for another visit," Lil said to Jim one day. Mikasa Yama, in the mountains of the east coast, was one of the aboriginal villages that Chi-oang had evangelized. Lil had been there previously on a trip with Jim.

"I wish I could get away to go again, too, Lil," said Jim, "but school will be opening in two weeks."

"That's just it," Lil told him. "If I don't go now, it may be ever so long. I have to be back to teach my classes. And I won't have to go alone. Eugenia MacIllwaine will go with me."

Eugenia would be a good one to have along, for she had been a trained nurse before her marriage to Heber MacIllwaine, a missionary to Japan. Girlish-looking at thirty-five because of her slimness and the way her dark hair curled around her face despite her efforts to part it primly, she was no clinging-vine type; Eugenia would be competent in the mountains or anywhere else.

"And take a pastor with you. How about Ng Bun-khim?" Jim suggested. Ng was a Formosan Chinese pastor much interested in the evangelization of the mountain people.

"I'll be back for the start of school," Lil promised, as she began packing her battered suitcase.

From Taipei, the three went by bus north and east over the mountains to I-Lan, which lies on a small coastal plain. There they boarded an equally decrepit bus for Hwalien, some fifty hair-raising miles to the south. Below I-Lan, the bus left the flatland and climbed to the coast road scratched from a wall of rock that rose almost perpendicularly out of the sea, a road so narrow it was one-way with the traffic flow periodically reversed. Stone blocks looking like massive teeth formed the only barrier between the road and sheer space. Here and there, some of the "teeth" were ominously missing.

"Makes you wonder," Lil said, eying them calculatingly whenever the bus lurched around a sharp curve.

Eugenia tried not to lean toward the seaward side as the bus roared on, its driver radiating confidence.

"See, Genie, how beautiful it is, out over the ocean!" Lil said consolingly. Eugenia looked. The green of her face harmonized beautifully with the green of the water.

From Hwalien, the rest of the trip would be by railroad down a coastal valley between the high mountains and a low-lying ridge paralleling the sea. At the station, Ng Bun-khim cast a worried look at the sky. Rain had begun falling gently. "In late summer like this—" he muttered. "Mrs. Dickson, do you think—"

"There have been no typhoon warnings." Lil replied, "I don't believe we need to worry."

The narrow-gauge, hundred-mile single track rail line from Hwalien to Taitung may have lacked some amenities of luxurious travel, but not tea service. Hardly had the train pulled out of the station when a boy came along the aisle, filling, from a teakettle, a tea jar for each passenger; these fitted into brackets under each window. Tea—drunk hot without sugar, lemon, or milk, tea leaf shreds invariably floating in the brew—is in Taiwan at once a drink and ritual. The moment the level went down in the jars, the boy with the teakettle was there to replenish the supply.

Lil pointed out white blossoms along the right of way. "Wild ginger," she said. "Very fragrant." Everywhere were the ricefields, in terraced succession, each field leveled with perfect accuracy so that the low mud bank around the edges would hold water essential for the rice plant's rooting and growing period. The ricefields climbed the slopes as high as terraces could be leveled.

The roadbed passed on trestles over many river deltas—wide, bouldered flats, dry now save for a narrow channel in the center. Huge wire bolsters filled with rocks were draped over earthen dykes built to protect railroad bridges and causeways from rushing water in time of heavy rain. Shattered abutments of previously washed-out bridges were frequently to be seen, testimony to the convulsive power of water gone wild. Lil remembered Pastor Ng's worried look. A typhoon could bring ten to twenty inches of rainfall; the water had nowhere to go but down the mountain valleys in torrents that swept all before them. In several of the deltas, gardens had been planted to the water's edge. They would be assuredly washed out if rains came. "They gamble," commented Ng Bun-khim. "Sometimes they lose."

The rain was coming down more heavily now. The opaque blue-gray waters of the mountain streams were swirling higher as the train sped over them.

Lil was looking out the window at the ricefields. The terraces were a series of waterfalls. "It must have rained hard down here!"

The train reached Giok-li, their rail destination. When they left the station, the wind was already blowing rain in horizontal gusts—the classic pattern. They reached the small Japanese inn where they were to spend the night before the fury of the storm struck. It was as if someone had drawn down a great window shade in the sky, shutting out the light. Life seemed to stand still; the little town of Giok-li held its breath, waiting for the full impact of the typhoon.

"No use of our sitting up all night," Lil said. "Whatever happens tomorrow, we'll be better able to face it if we're rested."

The next morning, it appeared they would have a good deal to face. "Genie, look," Lil called from the window.

The streets were swirling rivers. The water had risen to within scant inches of the floor of the inn. Already, houses on lower ground were flooded.

"Water everywhere," Eugenia said, peering out.

"As if we're in a boat that isn't moving," Lil added.

"We won't be going to Mikasa Yama today," Ng Bun-khim said solemnly as they considered the situation.

"But we won't be hungry," Lil reported. "Fortunately, we brought some food along." Lil had learned through experience that although the mountain people were always hospitable and freely shared what they had, their food did not always sit well in Western stomachs. She had found it was strategic to have something in reserve.

She was content to sit out the day, for she had the habit of bringing one or two books on her trips—"books I should read but never seem to have time for." Eugenia and Pastor Ng monitored the progress of the water. That evening three drenched, doleful villagers made their way to the inn through the water.

"Giok-li will be lost!" one of them wailed, while the others wrung their hands.

"How can you say that?" Lil asked. "The water is no longer rising."

"Only because a dam above the village is holding it back. It is an old dam and hasn't been repaired for years. Never have we had as much rain as this. The dam may break at any minute."

Another of the visitors nodded agreement. "We are getting boards ready so that we can tie our children to them when the water comes. If they float, perhaps they will live."

"Why wait?" Lil inquired. "Why not escape now?"

"We cannot escape," they said. "There is no way out."

As they left, one of them looked appraisingly around the room. "This inn would go quickly."

"Well," observed Lil to her companions, "since we have no boards and no ropes, we'll have to depend upon the Heavenly Father. Besides," she said, looking down at her chunky frame, "I would need a *very* big board."

The dam held; but a week passed before the water went down. With the help of the pastor, Lil spent her enforced idleness translating a child-evangelism book into Taiwanese.

After a few days reports reached them that the railroad tracks and bridges had been washed out both north and south of Giok-li. One old man predicted, "You'll be here for months. Maybe for a year." But already Lil felt that time was running out. School would soon be starting in Taipei, and she was determined to be there somehow. But first she must visit Mikasa Yama.

Couriers came three times during the week—twice to tell them that the way was impassable, the third time to say, "We will lead you."

The guides went ahead, followed by Lil and Eugenia, then Pastor Ng. Here and there a narrower gorge had been temporarily bridged by a tree, cut so that it dropped across the chasm. Suspension footpaths looking like delicate spiderwebs still hung in place over others, but many of the boards that formed the walking surface were missing, having been torn away by the wind. In places, one had to creep along the bare cable that had supported the floor, holding onto the cable railing, while the whole thing bobbed up and down and at the same time swung from side to side.

One of the most challenging of the crossings came at a point where the road suddenly ended at the water's edge. The guide pointed. The iron bridge that stood here had been swept downstream by the high water, then, its ends snagged by trees, it had tilted on its side until its floor stood perpendicular.

The mountain men explained that it was necessary to climb up to what was now the top of the bridge, then work one's way across.

"Why, that must be twenty feet straight up!" Eugenia exclaimed.

"And they suggest we'd do better barefoot when we get up there," Lil said.

"To think that a trained nurse would come to this," Eugenia grumbled good-naturedly. "Lead the way, Lil!"

"Do you suppose my dress will ever come clean?" Lil wondered.

"If not, you've got others just like it," Eugenia said with a laugh, since she was acquainted with Lil's wardrobe technique. Lil had once found a dress pattern that she liked. To save trouble—decisions were for more important things than choosing clothes—she turned it over to a dressmaker. Any time she found material she liked, she bought enough for a dress, which was made to this same pattern. Always neat-appearing, except perhaps on such a trip as this, she was not and had no wish to be so style-conscious that she seemed to be wasting valuable time or thought on herself.

Grasping such handholds as she could find, Lil climbed up the jagged end of the bridge, Eugenia behind her. At the top, she slipped off her shoes; an ever-present mountain man took them and watched carefully as she began to edge her way across.

"Look over there," Eugenia said. At the far end, a group of aborigines watched their progress intently.

"They're either praying for us or laying bets," Lil whispered. They finally made it to the other end.

So they came to Mikasa Yama, keeping a promise. Tired, dirty, hot though they were, they had to begin the church service immediately, for the people expectantly assembled.

After the service, the local pastor, Toh Bok-su, said quietly, "Mrs. Dickson, we are arranging things so that you and Mrs. MacIllwaine may have a bath."

Nothing at the moment could have sounded more attractive. "But how—?" Lil asked. Mountain homes are small and crowded, with no privacy; the people had built a bamboo bedroom next to the church for their two women guests and even that much attention was unusual.

Pastor Toh simply smiled and hurried off. Presently he reappeared. "This way, please."

When he showed them the place that had been prepared for them, Eugenia remonstrated, "This is a pigpen!"

"But the pig was moved into the next stall," Pastor Toh said with dignity, "and they have thrown down a clean board for you to stand on." Moving off, he added, "The women are heating water in the butchering kettle."

Presently the mountain women handed in pails of hot water and soap.

"Eugenia! Aren't we fortunate?" Lil exclaimed, luxuriating in the unexpected privilege.

In the adjoining pen, the dispossessed pig grunted disapproval.

"Well," admitted Eugenia, "everything is relative."

They had two days of meetings, Lil telling Bible stories and illustrating them with the flannelgraph, Eugenia holding clinics. Eugenia could bandage the ulcers and administer simple remedies. But often she could only shake her head and tell Lil in an aside, "Tuberculosis."

The second evening Lil asked in the church meeting if the people had any questions about health and sickness. After a while the chief rose. "We would rather hear about God," he said. "If we are right with God, other things will follow."

Lil's eyes filled with sudden tears. Other things would follow if Christians in other parts of the world who had more of this world's goods would make such things happen.

From Mikasa Yama they went on to Yamaseito and then to Roposan, making their way on foot along awesome mountain trails. Roposan was Tyal, but adjoining it was a settlement of the Bunan tribe, where there were only three Christian families. When the visitors arrived, the Tyal pastor suggested that they call upon the Bunan chief and invite the whole village to church that night. The chief himself led his villagers through the streets to the service, Lil with her accordion providing the processional. The Tyals gave all their seats to their Bunan guests, and stood outside the windows of their own building, looking in.

At Roposan the next afternoon, a messenger arrived breathless.

He brought a note from the pastor at Giok-li: "Do not try to walk to Hwalien. The road is not open."

Lil handed the note to Eugenia: "I *have* to get back for the opening of school." She scribbbled a note which she handed to the messenger: "I will open the road."

Eugenia shrugged. Surely it couldn't be any worse than what they had already encountered.

"I'll hire eight men to go with us," Lil decided. "Good mountain men. If there is any way to return to Hwalien, the mountain men will find it."

The next morning, they started out, coming down to the valley where they rejoined what was left of the railbed. Just two weeks before they had sped so swiftly along these same tracks by train. Now they moved so slowly, a straggling line that bunched up at rivers and streams where decisions had to be made on how to get across. Sometimes they had to go far upstream to detour around a wide river delta. Sometimes the men took council and then, with an encouraging gesture, waded boldly into the water, somehow knowing where the shallows were. Sometimes they swung on hanging vines.

"If Jim were here, I know he'd say, 'Me Tarzan, you Jane,' " Lil said with a laugh to Eugenia. Jim liked movies. He could recount in detail pictures he had seen ten years before that had struck his fancy. Lil's personal convictions did not allow her to attend motion pictures. Jim had no such compunction.

At one point the guides steered them unflinchingly to an abutment where one end of a trestle had once rested. Now there was no trestle, only drooping twin bands of steel track, joined precariously by wooden ties that instead of supporting the rails, hung from them by the spikeheads.

"We go across *that?*" Eugenia asked in disbelief.

One of the Tyal men took Lil's hand firmly and urged her forward.

"Can I do it?" Lil wondered. Then she remembered lines that had given her strength, steadied her steps, so many times:

When He says, "Follow Me,"
I am no longer small,
But suddenly as tall
As He is, and my stride
Extends at His command . . .

Carefully, she placed one foot out on the first tie beyond the abutment. It seemed firm enough. The Tyal guide nodded approvingly and stepped with her. If the spikes pulled out of the ties under their combined weight— Well, her ministry would be ended. Not finished, just ended. But God had somehow managed before she came into the world, and she presumed He would somehow manage after she left it. She took the next step. And the next.

As they left behind the firmness of the stone abutment, the rails began to tremble and then to sway with each step. She was conscious of the roaring gray water far beneath, the thunder of the boulders being swept along in the current.

But one did not cross a river in one bound. Always it was one step at a time. Anyone could take one step, then another and another. She concentrated on placing her feet on the ties. The Tyal gave a mutter of satisfaction, squeezed her hand and released it. Lil looked up. They were across! She turned to watch the progress of Eugenia and then Pastor Ng as each came nimbly alone.

"Am I ever glad *that's* over," Eugenia said as Lil took her hand for the last boost.

But there was more to come.

Where the mountains seemed to close in ahead of them, the man in the lead stopped short. The women moved wearily ahead to see what was the matter and found themselves looking into a pitch-black tunnel. Water dripped from the arched entrance.

One of the men glanced upward, his eyes seeking a way around. Then they noticed a farmer's bamboo and plaster house on the hillside. Attracted by the group, the farmer walked down to them.

"How long will it take us to walk through the tunnel?" Lil asked him.

"Half hour," said the farmer.

"How long to walk over the mountain?"

"Three-four hours."

"That settles it," Lil said. "We go through." At her signal, the lead man moved ahead, although with no enthusiasm. The rest followed him in, stumbling along the tracks.

"One other thing," the farmer called after them. "Watch out for snakes!"

At that, Lil vigorously struck up a hymn. When the first drop of icy water hit her cheek, she recoiled, then sang louder than ever. The rest joined in, quaveringly, then with a gusto that apparently struck terror to the cold hearts of any lurking snakes that had been enjoying peace and quiet since the trains stopped running. It was too dark to see anything but the needle's eye of daylight that marked the other end of the tunnel, the goal toward which they sang their way. Much too slowly, it seemed, the spot of light grew larger and larger, although probably never before nor since have any eleven people on foot made better time through that dripping tunnel.

It took them three days to cover the sixty typhoon-wracked miles to Hwalien. The bus trip the rest of the way to Taipei seemed positively sumptuous.

"I told you I'd be home for the start of school, didn't I?" Lil asked sweetly when she walked in on a dumbfounded Jim, who had heard disturbing radio reports from the east coast.

12. "I Must Take Out My Bucketful"

Upon her return, almost before she had put down her battered accordion, Lil called in a number of Formosan Christian women. "I've learned that in the mountains, sixty per cent of the babies die, partly because they have no adequate clothes. Can't we let these two mountain men who have returned with me from Mikasa Yama take back with them clothes for at least a few little ones?"

They sent out a hurried call to other women and among them they made five dozen baby garments for the men to divide among the three villages she had visited. These, plus medicines Lil pestered the doctors at Mackay Hospital into giving her, were sent off.

A plan was stirring in Lil's heart—a plan that had come to her on one of her first trips into the mountains with the Mobile Clinic, to the village of Mantai. One morning before sunup she had been awakened by voices calling the doctor: relatives of a woman who had been in labor since the day before had come for help. Although the clinic did not at that time offer obstetric care, this was clearly an emergency. The doctor asked Lil to go with him to the hut where the mother lay.

The house had a dirt floor and no windows; light came from a wood fire. The woman was lying on a grass mat on a bamboo platform. Lil and the doctor stood by the bed but they could do nothing but wait—and pray. They asked God to guard and bless this little mother in this primitive house hidden away in the mountains, and the wee life struggling to come into the world. Dawn outlined the doorway of the hut. As the light streamed in and the fire became red coals and then gray ashes, the baby was born, a boy. Someone had heated water in a tin. "You bathe the baby," the doctor said, handing the infant to Lil. Her eyes went round the room, looking for a utensil big enough to hold the child. She saw nothing. Then her eyes fell upon a large frying pan; it would have to do. Gently, she bathed the baby. There was nothing in which to wrap the child, not a shred of cloth. "We'll have to use gauze," she said to the doctor, "for his swaddling clothes."

What a miracle is the birth of a baby, any baby, anywhere, she thought. When she handed the child to his mother, the smile on the woman's face, the luminous mother love in her eyes, the tender possessiveness in her mother arms, brought a mist to Lil's own eyes. If someone had asked her, "Why did you ever become a missionary?" she could at that moment have answered, "So that I might put this baby into his mother's arms!"

But, she thought, suppose there had been no Mobile Clinic? What of all the babies born in the mountains without proper care? What of the humble homes not ready to receive them? How many babies were themselves the only brightness in mountain homes that had not even a blanket to warm their tiny bodies? The baby she bathed in the skillet and wrapped in gauze—and the other babies who had not even this much—weighed heavily on Lil's conscience. Was there, even after two thousand years, still no room for Mary?

From that early trip to the mountains she had brought back this burden—and another: What could she do about tuberculosis? On every trip made by the Mobile Clinic, the doctors found dozens of cases. Only rest, proper hygiene, and good nutrition could help, and these were beyond the means of the mountain people. There were tuberculosis sanatoriums for those who could afford the care, but nothing for those who could not. Lil went to the American Aid office for guidance. "The problem is as big as the sea," she was told. "Anything you can do would be like taking out only a bucketful."

"But because I am a Christian," she said, "I must take out my bucketful."

She bared her heart to her correspondents at home. "If you walked into a mountain village with Christ and found more than 80 per cent of the people sick with tuberculosis, the bright-eyed children all in danger, would you walk out again, saying, 'Too bad!'? Would you try to forget it, to crowd out the memory with trivial things, to crush down all thoughts of silent suffering? I know you wouldn't! You would try to plan somehow to separate out the sick ones, protect the little ones.

"Sometimes I try to get aid from large organizations, and I think they do for the moment consider it. But they are too far removed from the shabby little grass-thatched bamboo huts on the far east coast of Taiwan or from little villages which dot the mountaintops where gaunt faces spell out the doom that the dread T.B. has already placed upon them. Nobody seems to care. The aborigines live so far away in such wild and inconvenient places. 'I have a plan,' I explain patiently to people I try to interest in this task. 'We have places chosen, one for each main tribe. We could build wards to take care of two hundred T.B. patients at a time, with a Christian doctor nearby in each place to take charge.' "

This was the plan—but where was the money for such an ambitious project to come from?

"Why are you so still?" a friend asked Lil one day.

"I'm feeling sad because my wings are not wide enough."

Not until January, 1956, would she have a tuberculosis ward at the Christian Center she was by then developing on a plateau above Po-li in central Formosa; and in March of the following year, modest sanatoriums at Sin-Khang, overlooking the blue ocean on the southeast coast, and at Koan-san, in the mountain foothills, farther north. Never would her wings be wide enough to let her feel comfortable.

The mountains always left their mark upon Lil, and she upon them. In 1950, when Jim, who could not get away to see for himself how the mountain churches were faring, was bemoaning that he had no one to send whom he could trust to report to him with complete candor, Lil looked at him quietly. "How about sending me?" she asked. And so, with Pastor Tiu, a slim, earnest, bespectacled evangelist, she visited seventy churches over a period of four months. At each place they held regular church services and met with the Session, the ruling board of the church. Taiwanese do not take kindly to women speaking out—that was one reason why Pastor Tiu had come along. When Lil had an idea, she had to phrase it diplomatically. "Now this is just a suggestion," she would say diffidently, "probably not a very good one—" and before long, the idea would penetrate the consciousness of someone who would promote it, often as his own. "You can do anything you want to do if you don't care who gets the credit for it," she frequently said.

One suggestion she often made had to do with the construction of the mountain churches. They were usually good for only a few years, because they were built of bamboo. In time the typhoons and heavy rains would smash them flat and they would have to be replaced.

"But how else can we build?" said the mountain people. They utilized bamboo for everything, even for "disposable" communion cups—cutting off short lengths of bamboo just below and above each joint, discarding them after one use.

"Why, building stones are all around you!" Lil wanted to exclaim. "Every riverbed is full of them." But she didn't put it that way.

"In the river are stones," she said. "You are fortunate to have them."

"But the river is down there," they would say, "and we are up here. Stones are heavy."

"Suppose," Lil said gently, "each family would be responsible for carrying up just four stones a day to where the church will be built. It wouldn't take long. "And," she added, "I think we could get people to provide the cement."

As a result of this idea, she would see, within a decade, stone churches rising all over the mountains, many of them built to a pattern designed by Jim, the cost of the cement, three hundred dollars U.S., paid by churches and individuals in America and Canada.

In one village when she was walking to the house where she had been invited to spend the night, three of the church leaders hurried along the path to catch up with her. "There is a chief in this district who has been persecuting Christians," one said. "When he hears that someone has become a Christian, he gets a group together in the middle of the night and—" his face saddened.

"And what—?"

"They go and beat that one. Sometimes it's a widow or an old men. If they don't beat them, they defraud them some way."

Lil's lips tightened. "Where does this chief live?"

The man pointed. "Down that valley and up the other side."

"Let's go," Lil said grimly.

"But the chief will be asleep by now!" the man protested.

"We'll wake him then."

So they tramped along a dark trail with only the moonlight to show them the way.

At the chief's house, their talking roused a woman. "I must see the chief," Lil announced.

"He is asleep."

"It is important!"

The woman turned away. Presently the chief came sleepily to the door, smelling of liquor. He tried to focus his bleary eyes on the visitors standing before him, the stocky white woman in the forefront.

"I hear you've been making trouble for Christians," Lil snapped. "Well, I can make trouble for you—big trouble. And I *will* if I hear that you've hurt just one more Christian!"

Then she turned and marched off. No more trouble for the Christians came from that quarter.

Lil often went into the hills to take part in the dedication of new churches. On one trip, she attended seven of them, all resulting from the work of a layman named Lau. Lau Sian-si (Mr. Lau) had been such an undesirable for most of his life that when his child died, no one came to help him. (Ordinarily, the whole village stops work on such an occasion.) He loaded the little body on a water buffalo cart and went out alone to bury his child. Then his wife died, and again his neighbors ignored him. After this, he became a Christian and his life was transformed. In his own community—the hardest test of all—he began preaching, bringing a change to the whole village. Here was built the first church among the Bunan people. From the east coast he came to the west, and in six months these seven new churches had been built and were awaiting dedication. In two of the places every last adult in the village had become Christian.

The change was a source of bewilderment to the schoolteachers and police. One policeman was completely baffled. "The Japanese government tried for years to cure these people of drinking and other bad habits," he said, "and they failed. Then our government tried and it failed. Now Christianity comes along and almost overnight the people are completely transformed! For Christianity to do what the government could not do, I call disrespect for the government!"

The government to which he was so determinedly loyal now represented more than the provincial administration of Taiwan. Defeated by Communist forces on the mainland of China, the Nationalist government moved to Taiwan in 1949, establishing the capital of the Republic in Taipei. The government of the United States paid new attention to the island, though uncertainty regarding America's intention to defend Taiwan, if attacked, led to considerable uneasiness, which reached into mission compounds. By 1950 many missionaries had returned home. The Dicksons stayed.

One day in June Lil spoke to Jim about her concern. "This is something we ought to pray about and ask all the churches to pray about—that God will intervene and keep the Communists away."

"I'm all for prayer," Jim said, smiling, "but I suspect you've got something in mind."

"I just thought somebody should send out a letter to the churches—somebody official. It ought to be signed by a church council or by some prominent people, calling for a day of prayer."

"Fine," Jim agreed. "You get the people to sign it."

But she couldn't get any signers.

"Why?" she asked one man who declined. "Don't you think it's a good idea?"

"Splendid idea," he said, "but if we sign, we are writing our death warrants. When the Communists come, they will hunt us down."

"Then I'll sign it myself," she retorted. And she did, and sent out the letter.

The following week, on June 27, 1950, President Truman ordered the United States Seventh Fleet into the Taiwan Strait to interpose its force between the Communists on the mainland and the Nationalists on Taiwan.

Lil was not surprised. She said to Jim, "Now we have to send out another letter urging the churches to hold a day of thanksgiving for deliverance. God was responsible, not America. America is changeable. God isn't."

This time there was no problem about signers.

Not long after this, Lil had a caller. As the visitor came in and sat down in the Dickson living room, Lil studied her. In her thirties, she had a brassy sophistication about her, even to the dark glasses she affected.

"You are from Minnesota?" Lil's caller asked.

"You seem to know something about me," said Lil, looking at her very directly.

"We—I—know a good deal about you. Why didn't you go home, as the other missionaries did?"

"Because my work is here."

The woman took off her dark glasses and looked toward the window. Then she put them on again to stare at Lil, as if the glasses offered some protection against this mild little missionary whose feet tended to lift off the floor when she sat in a deep chair. "What would you do if the Communists came?"

Lil chuckled. "I would go on praying and working."

Again the woman doffed her dark glasses, looked away, put them on and looked back. "Did you send out a letter?"

"Yes, I sent out a letter. I think I know which one you mean."

The woman stood up to leave. "That was dangerous," she said softly. "When the Communists come, they will know."

Later that evening, Lil asked Jim, "Why does the world always seem to get into a fight right where I'm standing?"

13. Three Suicides a Week

"Don't look now, Lil," said Jim one day, the corners of his wide mouth turning up in a smile, "but isn't that your angel coming up the front walk?"

Lil discreetly tugged at the curtain and looked out. "Pastor Chhoa! *Again!* He's not my angel!"

Jim's blue eyes twinkled. "Oh, I don't know. You say that your angel gives you a nudge now and then. Pastor Chhoa's not only nudging—he's pushing."

"But how can I do what he wants me to do?" Lil demanded. "How can I get involved at the government leprosarium? I have open-air meetings every night and almost every day. I told him that!"

Jim sighed. "A pity God gave you only two hands." He took those two hands in his big ones. "But He gave you a great heart!" And then he slipped out as the pastor from the leprosarium was shown in.

Pastor Chhoa spoke as a man overburdened and desperate.

"You must come. We had three suicides last week. We had three the week before that. Four the week before that. And nobody comes."

Lil closed her eyes.

"You must come," the preacher said insistently. "You must come."

What if he *is* God's angel? thought Lil. What if the insistent words of this harried little man were God's words? Lil felt as if heaven were backing her into a corner.

"Very well, Pastor Chhoa," she said to her caller. "I will come."

When he had gone, Lil told herself, I don't know anything about leprosy! I am not a doctor. I don't know the proper treatment to give. I'm not even a nurse. Then she thought of how Jesus had put it: "I was sick, and ye visited me." Nothing there about complex medical skill, only about simple friendly concern. Somebody cared enough to come and it was the caring that counted and that offered its own therapy. Pastor Chhoa had said of the government leprosarium, "Nobody comes."

It wouldn't be easy, Lil knew. She often remembered the Christmas dinner she had helped to serve at the leprosy clinic across the road twenty years before. The shock of that experience was still vivid in her mind. Dr. G. Gushue-Taylor of Mackay Hospital, who had established the clinic, had later started a leprosy colony near Tamsui, by the sea; Lil had visited it a few times. He called it Happy Mount, trying even with the name to ease some of the tragedy and heartbreak that leprosy brought with it. And certainly the lot of patients there was far happier than that of most victims of the disease who, ostracized by relatives and friends, had to make their living as best they could, more alone than those ministering in the name of Christ had any right to let them be.

"How did you get into leprosy work?" Lil once asked Dr. Gushue-Taylor.

His bushy eyebrows came together as his face sobered and the lines in his forehead deepened. "I was then superintendent of Mackay Hospital. One day a nurse hurried to me in great excitement to say that a leper was waiting who wanted to talk with me.

When I went out, he made no attempt to come close but stood at a distance of several paces. 'Stood,' did I say? He slumped, one of the most pitiable sights I have seen in this world. His hands were stumps. The cartilage structure of the nose had caved in. His eyebrows had fallen off. His eyes were wide, but not sad. Sadness is a memory of better days, a hope for happiness to come. This man was beyond sadness, beyond remembering, beyond hoping.

"And do you know what he asked me? It was such a small request. He did not ask for healing—he was beyond that, too. He asked permission to lie down under a tree on the hospital grounds —and die." Though a medical man walks often with death, there was a tremor in Dr. Gushue-Taylor's voice as he spoke. "I had to tell him to move on, because if he stayed there, all the patients would leave the hospital."

The incident weighed so heavily on the doctor's mind that he decided he had to begin leprosy work. He could not bring leprosy patients to the hospital grounds, and so he set up a clinic, and later a little church, across the road. This was not the complete solution, however. Coming to his clinic were a baker, a practicing dentist, and other individuals who by the nature of their work should have been isolated. He made a nuisance of himself among the Japanese by urging, at every opportunity, that a leprosarium be established. As a result of his interest, he was asked by the Japanese to go around the world to learn all he could about the way leprosy was treated and patients hospitalized. When he came back with the determination to start a leprosarium himself, his friends in government said, "Look around, find the right location, and the government will give you the land."

By rickshaw, by train, by taxi, he scoured the countryside within a ten-mile radius of Taipei. Finally, to the south, he found the perfect spot—a hillside within easy reach of the city but away from settled areas.

Dr. Gushue-Taylor invited the government welfare head to visit the spot with him. "See the many advantages," the missionary doctor pointed out. "Isolated yet accessible. Too hilly for farming, not too hilly for a hospital. Too high to be flooded in high water. And look out over the valley!" They turned and the splendor of the far view caught up their thoughts. "It will be just right for my Happy Mount Leprosarium," he concluded.

The official did not turn. *"Arigato, gozaimus."* He politely hissed the final *s* of his thank-you. "It will be just right—for the *government* leprosarium."

Dr. Gushue-Taylor was shocked at this betrayal. "The government can choose anywhere," he said. "I am limited to a location convenient to the Mackay Hospital."

The official patted the doctor's arm. "This is the right place for us. We must have it. But I will help you to find another site."

So it was that here the government built its leprosarium, later called Happy Life, and near Tamsui Dr. Gushue-Taylor was provided land for Happy Mount, where Lil became an occasional visitor. She and Jim even contributed a couple of goats to the doctor's leprosarium, though Lil never regarded that as a sacrificial offering. It happened this way:

After Japan went to war against China, food was rationed, then more strictly rationed. Japanese soldiers were fed first, and if anything was left over, it went to the civilian population. The normal minimum of three bowls of rice a day fell to one bowl; the people were advised to supplement their diet with anything else they could find. Newspapers said that snakes were good to eat, and gave what purported to be tasty, kitchen-tested recipes. Other recipes showed how to whip up various kinds of grass into succulent dishes.

There were tears in Lil's eyes when she told Jim of a Christian family in which the son and his wife and children sickened, one after the other, because of too little to eat. One day the old father and mother took their own lives, hoping that now there would be enough for the rest. "We've lived our lives," they wrote, "but yours are just beginning."

Lil said to Jim, "That's the way it is all over Formosa. People are dying for want of food, babies are dying because mothers can't nurse them."

"There must be something—" Jim mused, "some way to get

milk—" He punched a fist into his cupped palm. "I've got it! I'll tell you what we'll do. Goats! We'll import goats from Japan and have goat's milk for babies. If we show them how to do it, Lil, then other people will get goats and the milk can save many lives."

Lil held up a restraining hand. "This won't be *my* department. I have never studied goats and I'll have nothing to do with goats."

"I'll take care of them," Jim assured her when he sent off the order. "You don't have a thing to worry about."

Weeks later Lil was home alone in the big three-story red-brick house on the mission compound when she heard a commotion on the front porch. There were crates and crates of white goats! "Not at the front door!" Lil cried when the delivery men pried open the crates and the goats stepped out and began exploring their new home. Because they had come by ship and then by truck, they were still a bit seasick and swayed drunkenly about. Lil wagged her counting finger. "Four-five-six-*seven* little ones." The big ones were already out of counting range.

The kids were baaing hungrily. Shooing out one that had gone into the house, Lil advised it helpfully, "Your mother is out on the lawn. Go out there if you want something to eat!" When that didn't work, she tried Japanese—after all, they were Japanese goats. That didn't work either. In desperation, she picked up one of the little goats and carried it out to the yard and set it down hopefully beside a big goat. The mother goat was completely uninterested.

"You've got a problem," she told Jim when he finally arrived. "These little goats must be somebody else's kids. The big ones don't act as if they are their mothers. What happens now? How do the little ones eat?"

"They have to be fed from bottles, I guess," Jim said. "That's it—bottles, the kind that babies use."

Lil looked accusingly at Jim.

"Now, Lil," he said, "I don't know anything about bottles. Would you—?" He looked so contrite that Lil chuckled and replied, "All right."

At an exhorbitant price she was able to buy canned milk at one of the few grocery stores that had any left. Mixing hot water with the milk, she prepared seven bottles of "formula" every morning. By now the goats were quartered near the theological college across the road. Each morning, Lil went over with her pailful of bottles.

"If you have seven goats, you should have seven hands," she reported despairingly to Jim. "They're *very* impatient."

"I'll get Ronny to do it," Jim said. "By the way, I've got to visit a few of the mountain churches for the next couple of weeks."

Ronny did the job faithfully for two mornings. Then he turned in his bottles. "I've been washing my hands all day, Mother," he said. "I can't get the smell off."

So it was Lil, who had never studied goats, who brought up the seven kids, and unnumbered others. She learned more about goats than she wanted to know. Happenstance or not, Jim was invariably away when a goat was having a blessed event. Goats were by now all around the big mission house, eating the grass and the leaves off the trees as high as they could reach by standing on their hind legs.

When the wind was unfavorable, Lil had the distinct impression that her missionary neighbors veered away from the Dickson house. Dr. Gushue-Taylor, who by now was giving most of his time to his leprosarium, at first chided Lil and Jim. "Goats won't live on Formosa. I know goats. I used to take care of them when I was a boy."

But when he saw how well the goats adapted, he changed his mind. "This is a good thing. With goats, people won't starve." By now, the goat output was such that pastors were picking up pairs to take into needy areas. Goats from the mission compound eventually appeared all over the island. Their milk helped to save lives.

"I think we could use a pair at the leprosarium," the doctor one day conceded.

"How are you going to get them there?" Lil asked.

"Taxi," he said, as if he did it all the time. Walking out into the street, he summoned a taxi and had the driver swing into the compound. At the Dickson house, he said to the taximan casually, "You don't mind if I take along a couple of goats, do you?"

"How big?"

While Lil held her breath, the doctor shrugged. "Oh, ordinary."

The taximan in turn shrugged.

Quickly rounding up two goats, Dr. Gushue-Taylor pushed one into the back seat ahead of him. He climbed in next and pulled in the other goat as Lil herded it into position. The door slammed and the taxi, with the doctor and the two goats in the back seat, drove off. Lil waved a cheery good-by to the three faces looking out of the rear window at her. When she saw Dr. Gushue-Taylor the next time, she told him, "I knew that the one who waved back was you!"

Lil realized that the government leprosarium near Taipei with six hundred and fifty patients would be different from Dr. Gushue-Taylor's colony which had only sixty-five. How much different, she would soon learn.

The first problem was transportation. Mrs. Hogan of the Assemblies of God had a car and could drive. Furthermore, she also played the accordion. "Will you go with me once a month?" Lil asked. Her friend agreed.

"We'll have a meeting," Lil planned it out, "the way we do in child-evangelism work, and then afterward we can give them a treat of cookies or candy. When I go up to the mountains, I know what it is to live without sweets for a long time. You get hungry for them. It would be the same way with those people shut away at the leprosarium. I'll buy lots of cookies."

So the next day the two of them started out. Down the south valley Mrs. Hogan drove, and then near a Buddhist temple they turned off the main road onto a narrow lane that led up the hill into the colony. One of the patients called Pastor Chhoa, who was there to meet them, smiling with pleasure at their coming. "The lepers have no church," he said, "but there is a big public hall where we can meet."

Following their open-air routine, the two women strapped on their accordions and, accompanied by a few of the Christian patients and the pastor, they walked along the dirt paths, singing, playing, and announcing the meeting. Most of the patients were in their homes—shacks they had thrown together with bamboo and whatever materials they could find and their own physical limitations permitted. They stood in the doorways as the procession passed. Lil was glad she had to concentrate on her playing, though now and then she stole quick glances at the swollen faces, the blotched and discolored skin. Some of the patients shuffled along behind, others hobbled on makeshift crutches. An old man, attracted by the music, walked with his clawed hand on the shoulder of a friend in front of him. He was sightless.

At the dismal auditorium the women led in song and Lil told a Bible story with the aid of the flannelgraph. Then it was time to distribute the cookies.

She had planned this carefully, too, saying to Mrs. Hogan, "If I were a leper, the thing that would hurt me most would be having people draw back from me." She had resolved to go among the patients and pass them out with the personal touch of Christian love. Smiling determinedly, she picked up the big bag of cookies and stepped down from the platform to the first row.

She had not planned carefully enough. The horror of her mistake struck her: How do you give cookies to a man who has no hands?

Lil's eyes blurred.

The next time, she brought squares of paper on which to put the sweets. But that, too, was awkward.

Cookies were of course no adequate answer to the needs of the patients. Neither was a visit to one who was sick. In fact, Lil soon began to suspect, the harmless-looking statement of Jesus was psychologically loaded. The visiting, the seeing with one's own eyes, the touching with one's own fingers, the feeling with one's own heart—these came first. Compassion cannot operate even at arm's length. Before she knew what was happening to her, she was involved utterly, because God had made her responsive to need.

One of the first things she did was find out more about leprosy.

Also known as Hansen's Disease, it was caused by the *Bacillus leprae,* she learned, and was most prevalent in hot, damp climates. That would certainly apply to Formosa, Lil thought; the island in the summer months was a steaming bath. Leprosy took three forms. First was the nodular, in which normal skin tissue was replaced by lumpy masses of cells similar to those found in syphillis and tuberculosis. Second was the smooth or anesthetic type, which attacked the nerves. The third type was a combination of the other two.

Less infectious than tuberculosis, the disease was transmitted usually only through long and close contact; forty per cent of the infections which had been traced were found to be due to living in the same house with a leper and thirty per cent more to sleeping in the same bed. Children and young adults were most susceptible.

In the nodular form, dark red or coppery patches appeared on the face, backs of the hands and feet or on the body; they came with a feverish attack and faded when the fever subsided, only to reappear. Eventually the skin thickened and the nodules appeared, at first pink, later changing to brown. Eyes degenerated, and the mucous lining of the nose and throat thickened, changing the quality of the voice and impairing breathing; eyebrows fell off; ears and nose became thickened and enlarged. The nodules tended to ulcerate, leaving open sores. The patient, gradually becoming weaker, ultimately died of exhaustion or of some other disease, often tuberculosis, which his ill health encouraged.

The smooth type appeared as patches of dry, slightly discolored skin, the result of deterioration of the nerves. There was a loss of sensitivity over the affected areas. Certain nerve trunks thickened. Muscular power diminished, tendons contracted, nails became hard and clawed, open ulcers of the feet were common, fingers and toes died and dropped off, paralysis affected the muscles of the face and limbs. The disease in this form could take twenty or thirty years to run its course, if not arrested.

Some stages of the disease, particularly of the nerve type, were not infectious at all. Yet, from Bible times, leprosy had been one of the most dreaded diseases and those who contracted it were shunned and segregated.

The fear factor in leprosy was twofold, Lil suspected: that it could not be cured; that it could not be hidden. Modern medicines —at first the old Indian drug chaulmoogra oil, and then the new and more efficient sulfones—have made clean the "unclean," and in children, especially, may clear up symptoms of the disease. But when the physical appearance of longtime patients is irreparably altered—when fingers, nose, eyebrows are gone—medicines cannot restore features, though surgery has been used with some success to graft small patches of scalp to provide new eyebrows. When the marks of leprosy remain after the disease itself has been arrested, the old suspicions are excited, often making the cured patient unacceptable to society, even to his family—though he may be less of a threat than many people thought to be healthy but who harbor some other disease. Furthermore, when fingers or their usefulness are gone, skills and the means of making a living have gone with them.

At the government leprosarium, the patients had to endure not only their private heartbreak, but many physical privations. On her next trip, Lil heard about them—humbly and sometimes inadvertently told, because those who did the telling did not always know that their situation could be any different.

As she and Mrs. Hogan walked the rough paths one day, Lil's attention was drawn to a tall young man who kept pace only at great effort. "It is my foot," he apologized.

"What's wrong with your foot?" Lil asked.

"An open sore," the man replied, wincing as he walked.

"What is the doctor doing for it?"

"The doctor?" he said, puzzled.

"Doesn't the doctor give you medicines?" Lil asked, stopping short.

"I have never seen a doctor since I have been here."

Another patient explained, "I have heard there is a doctor, but I cannot say from personal experience."

Lil's blood began to simmer.

When the woman walking on crutches by Lil's side stumbled, Lil shot out a hand to steady her. "I am sorry for my clumsiness," the woman apologized, "but the paths are rough." A few moments later when she turned an ankle on a loose stone and almost went down herself, Lil had to agree. She muttered to Mrs. Hogan, "You would think the paths would be paved, when so many of the patients have such difficulty walking!"

Lil eyed another patient walking with them. His cheeks were hollow and he swung his hands awkwardly as he shuffled along. His eyes lighted when he saw her looking at him. "Thank you for the sweets you bring to us," he said impulsively. *"Do-si-ah."*

The sweets were so little that Lil felt embarrassed. They had by now solved the distribution problem: they used paper bags. Even a stump of hand could somehow manage to press a small bag close to one's body for safe carrying.

"How do you like the meals here?" Lil asked him.

"The meals?"

"Your food—is it good?"

The man's eyes looked troubled. "I should not complain," he said, "but it is hard to cook when—" He held up his awkward hands.

"You cook for yourself?"

He nodded. "Each does his own cooking. I can manage better than some. Many of the others have no hands. How can you take a pan from a fire when you have no hands?"

So that explained the burns she had seen! Two arms had to clamp around a hot utensil to pull or lift it from the fire. Lack of feeling would prevent the patient's knowing he had been badly burned, and the deep sores, constantly aggravated, never had a chance to heal.

Other patients reported that the superintendent kept for himself a large share of the food money. Those who had no relatives or friends had no one to supplement their food. And with the cloth money the government provided, the superintendent bought the cheapest, shoddiest material he could get, pocketing the surplus. Because of his indifference and corruption, the doctors did not make rounds or provide medicines.

Lil's blood boiled. It was just after the war and many government officials, thrust into office without preparation, were incompetent; that was to be expected. But corruption—for which others suffered—was something else again.

She went home that day deeply troubled. Perhaps by their next regular monthly visit, she would have a plan.

A week later, she was still baffled. Early in the afternoon as she thought about it, she suddenly felt a strong compulsion: *Go to the leprosarium—now!*

Lil called Mrs. Hogan to find out if she could go along, only to learn that her friend was unable to go.

Was this a sign that Lil had her signals wrong? The compulsion remained. She had told Mrs. Hogan, "I have the strangest feeling about this—I call it the angel at my shoulder, giving me a push in the direction I should go."

Forty minutes later, a little bewildered and embarrassed about the whole thing, Lil arrived by taxi at the leprosarium. I can have a meeting as usual, she consoled herself, for she had remembered to bring her accordion. She strapped it on and began walking and playing.

"Mrs. Dickson!" some of the leaders among the patients greeted her in surprise. "We did not expect you."

One of them added tersely, "You'd better have your meeting early. We have another one scheduled for five o'clock."

The atmosphere was electric with tension. "What is this other meeting?" Lil asked.

"A protest meeting."

"What are you protesting about?"

"Everything! Lack of food, lack of clothes, lack of medicines, lack of doctors and nurses—"

"The superintendent," one said, "never comes among us. He is afraid of us. We will go to him! We will make him listen!"

Another revolution, thought Lil, and as usual, I'm right in the middle of it. She motioned to three of the top leaders, and led them over a little hill out of sight of the others. "I am only a woman," she said, "and you know more about these things than I do. But I am saddened to think of what may happen because of this meeting you're talking about. Someone may be killed. They are likely to put barbed wire around the colony, and soldiers with bayonets. They will say it is too dangerous for foreigners to come here, and I may not be able to reach you again." She added sadly, "You will not get what you are asking this way."

The leaders remained silent.

Lil took a deep breath, drew herself up to her full five-foot height, and faced the three leaders as confidently as if she had a blank check in her pocketbook. "If you call off your meeting, I promise you that I will bring you all that you have asked."

The three leaders, at first unwilling, gave their reluctant agreement. "We will talk to the others," they said without enthusiasm.

The protest meeting was not held. Lil went home that evening scared but determined. Now she knew why God had sent her.

14. Church of the Lepers

That same evening, after her visit to the leprosarium, Lil called on Dr. Signe Berg, who was helping in the mission hospital. A small bundle of energy, Dr. Berg was a devoted and warmhearted Christian. Her husband, also a medical doctor, had been one of the first missionaries killed by the Communists in China. Far from embittering her, the experience had given her greater identity with those who suffered.

"I've promised you to the lepers," Lil greeted her. Then she launched into the story of what she had seen. "Will you go with me?" she asked when she had finished. Dr. Berg replied promptly, "Of course."

"We will need drugs," Lil said. "You make a list, and I'll get them." The next morning, Lil spent all the money she had for medicines that filled two large baskets.

"It's not much for so many," Lil said with a sigh.

Dr. Berg moved her glasses up on her nose. "Neither were five loaves and two fishes."

The two of them started out in a taxi for the leper colony. Having delivered them, the taxi wheeled away in a cloud of dust.

They stood self-consciously in the driveway, their two baskets of medicines at their feet. "Where do we start?" Dr. Berg asked.

Lil picked up her basket. "Let's begin with the most advanced cases—I call it the Ward Nearest Heaven's Door."

Those who could walk spread the happy news that a doctor had come, and other patients crowded in. Lil interpreted, for the patients spoke Taiwanese and Dr. Berg spoke Mandarin. Every patient needed care. Busy as she was, Lil despaired. How would they ever cover the whole colony? As she assisted Dr. Berg, she became aware that a group of men were watching intently from the corridor.

They were the leaders of the day before. But now the tenseness had gone out of them. They were cool, objective. "You and the doctor cannot possibly go from bed to bed to see each patient," their spokesman protested. "We will organize a clinic. Everyone who is able can come to the clinic for treatment. We will find out ahead of time which patients who are confined to bed need the doctor, and after the clinic each day, we will take the doctor to them."

The clinic was set up in a public hall which the Buddhists used for their meetings. Each morning Lil and Dr. Berg came with their medicines and their concern—curative powers in both. Lil had sent out letters to her friends back home, not begging for money but simply telling of the need and leaving their response to their consciences. As money came, it was used. "God will give us only what He can trust us to give away," she quoted to Dr. Berg and to anybody else who would listen. If Lil could not be a great giver, at least she could be a great giver-away of what others channeled through her. She would not burden Jim with projects and responsibilities of her own; his responsibility was to support her and their family, and that he did it on $200 Canadian a month was a small miracle in itself.

For a while, Lil and Dr. Berg came every day, then every other day. Often the clinic lasted from eight-thirty in the morning until four in the afternoon. Always it began with a short period of worship. "The drugs are bought with God's money, and you must know Him in order to thank Him," Lil said to the patients. Then those in the long lines were given medicines—the serious cases handled by the doctor, and the light, "motherly" cases by Lil, the headaches, stomachaches, ointment for wounds, and all the minor ailments that a mother might care for in a home. The patients, when their turn came, slipped into the chairs in front of the missionaries to tell what they needed. Now and then a woman would wait in line to say shyly, "I did not come to ask for anything. I just came to say thank you."

Lil described the procedure in one of her letters: "When a leper patient sits before me, I know that a thousand doctors are not competing to get him. There is no one who wants to care for him but the dear Lord and His willing but not too clever servants. With each patient we begin with the trite formula used here in the leprosarium: 'Have you any pain?' Foolish question! They come on crutches, feet bandaged because they are ulcerated and often amputated, hands useless or sometimes gone, their faces ashen or blotched and twisted. 'Have you any pain?' Their lives are one long torture!"

All the patients were undernourished. Lil got some milk powder, then she hired two men to rise early and make hot milk. At dawn, a large pail of it would be brought into each ward, and every patient had a bowlful to drink.

A central kitchen was needed. The room used for this purpose during Japanese days had been mostly partitioned off into cubicles for extra patients. However, one large room remained intact and in it were the big concrete Chinese stoves for cooking—a place underneath for wood to be fed into the fire, round holes on top to accommodate huge kettles of rice. The superintendent gladly turned over the room to Lil. In one corner of the kitchen she built a food storage locker. Former cooks were recruited from among the patients. The meager rations provided by the superintendent had to be supplemented. But, far from objecting to Lil's innovations, he stayed out of her way; anything that made the patients happier made them less troublesome to him; therefore, his administration would be less likely to be called to account.

"When Jesus fed the five thousand," Lil pointed out, "that was just one meal. Now there are six hundred and fifty to eat three times a day and every day—but it is still the Lord who is feeding them." Every day the money came, "manna from heaven," just enough for every need and none left over.

Lil had told the grievance committee of the lepers, "I promise you I will bring you all you have asked." But there was so much to do, and not all of it could be done with money.

Among the patients was one who had an old trombone. When Lil walked along the garden paths playing her accordion before church service, this man would be waiting with his instrument to join the procession. When she would finally play "Down at the Cross Where the Saviour Died," a look of deep pleasure would come over his face and he would lift his trombone to his lips to join in this one tune that he could play. Lil often repeated the song many times just to keep the light going in his eyes.

One day, when Lil paused in front of his house to play "Down at the Cross," he came out of the door empty-handed. "Where is your trombone?" Lil asked.

He lowered his eyes. "I can't play it any more—my fingers are gone."

That night Lil said to Jim, "He knew just one song and he played it well. I'm sure he played it all the way through just before he put his trombone away forever." She looked at her own capable hands. "The last line of that song is, 'Glory to His name!' With his last touch," she said, "he praised the Lord. I hope I may do as well."

"You will," Jim said. Later on, he mentioned, "The mission council has provided me with a jeep. I'll be glad to turn it over to you, if you want it for getting out to the leper colony and back. There's just one thing—"

Lil looked up expectantly.

"The reason I *think* they gave me the use of it, and the reason I *know* I'm glad to give you the use of it, is that nobody can get it to go."

"I'll get it to go," Lil said grimly.

She found a driver who wanted work and told him he had a job if he could get the jeep going and keep it running. Under this powerful incentive, he soon had the jeep in working order. But not even the driver could do anything about the car's weatherworthiness. The torrential rains came in through all the cracks. Driver, Lil, and any other passengers always arrived safely, but often drenched.

The jeep bravely carried everything that was crowded into it. Sometimes the nondescript load was clothing of all sizes and conditions. Anything of Jim's left hanging in his closet for more than a week was likely to wind up at the leprosarium. "Lil," Jim grumbled once, "can you find a pair of pants to fit me?"

"I did have a pair exactly your size," she said with a straight face, "but I found somebody who needed them worse."

"There's a point when nobody can need them 'worse,'" Jim muttered. "And I've reached it!"

One day while the clinic was in progress, Lil became aware of a commotion outside. Voices rose and fell, there were hurrying footsteps, exclamations of delight.

Some of the patients came running to Lil. "The Catholics have brought us clothes—ten pounds for each person!" They had never seen so many clothes before; if they received one garment a year, they were grateful.

The patients who brought the word did not hurry away, but stood in front of Lil, wondering what she would say to someone else's concern for those she had come to think of as her brood. "What shall we do?" they asked hesitantly.

Lil looked up from the cut she was bandaging. "We will thank God for the clothes!"

When another organization brought blankets, they thanked God for the blankets, too. "God's love comes through many routes," she said to them.

Still there were suicides at the leprosarium. Often a telephone call would come in the night, "Bring a doctor quickly! So-and-so has tried to kill himself." And Lil would call for her driver and dash out in the jeep, picking up a doctor on the way. Sometimes they were in time, sometimes not. Once it was a young soldier, born on the mainland and who had contracted leprosy somewhere in the South Seas.

"Why did you do it?" Lil asked, bending low over his bed, as a mother might gently rebuke a son.

"I'll tell you why," the youth said bitterly. "Because I have a terrible disease for which there is no cure. Because I am in this dreadful place and there is no chance of getting out. And most of all, because nobody cares."

"Somebody does care," Lil said softly. "This will not always be a dreadful place. And someday there will be a cure."

On another day, there had been three suicides. Lil stopped at the bedside of Ui Sian-si, a patient in the Ward Nearest Heaven's Door. He had been a school administrator and once a skilled pianist. Now his hands were gone, one foot amputated, and his face disfigured. "*Why* do they do it?" Lil asked him.

Ui Sian-si was thoughtful. "Perhaps because they have nothing to occupy their minds," he replied. "We have no touch with the outside world—no newspapers, no magazines, no radio, no educational movies."

This gave Lil something new to think about—and to act on. She wondered why it had never occurred to her before.

Getting the newspapers and magazines was easy. Lil looked over the colony and found a building used as a storeroom that would make a good library. Then she went to the superintendent. "We will build a storeroom for you if you will let us have this building as a library for the patients."

Bowing and rubbing his hands together, he immediately agreed. Things had progressed to the point where when shingles blew off or the lighting system failed or something else went wrong, he would ask, "I wonder what Mrs. Dickson is going to do about *that?*"

The library was set up, and the International Women's Club furnished it with tables, benches, bookcases, and provided numbers of picture magazines.

Getting a radio wouldn't be difficult, either. But Lil had another plan for improving morale. Remembering the lilt of bright music that always had cheered her in discouraged moments, she hoped to make use of a record player that had been given to her. "Can't we put a loudspeaker horn on this so that we can play gay music several times a day?" she asked an electrician.

"We can do more than that," he said, catching her enthusiasm. "We can fix it so that *every* ward has a speaker and even patients who are in bed all the time can hear the music. Not only that, but we can fix it so that the system can be hooked up to receive radio news and music, too."

This would mean that a music room would have to be provided and someone put in charge of it all. What had started out as a simple, spontaneous notion had developed into a complex project, but the extra money came. When all was in readiness and the loudspeakers filled the wards with cheering music for the first time, the expressions of surprise and contentment on the faces of patients who could never again leave their beds was completely rewarding.

Educational movies were something else. Lil took that problem to the office of the United States Information Service. "I've heard that you have movies and slides about life in America that you're showing all over the island wherever there is a call for them," she said.

"That's right," the man in charge nodded. "Do you know of a group that would like to see them?"

"Indeed I do," Lil said. "Would it be possible to show an educational movie once a week to six hundred fifty patients out at the leprosarium?"

The official toyed with his pencil a moment before answering. "This may sound brutal, Mrs. Dickson," he said, "but the lepers are not a politically important group. We are here for politics only."

Lil got up. "I guess I wouldn't make a very good politician." She went home feeling rebuffed and discouraged.

Lil shared her rebuff with the growing list of interested people in America to whom she was sending her newsletter. She wrote:

"No, the lepers are not 'politically important.' They are not rich, not powerful, not persons with authority. They are humble people who are unfortunate. It remains for those of the free world with Christ as their Saviour and example—in His short life here He so often stopped to care for lepers and heal them—to show mercy and compassion."

A Sunday-school class in New York dashed off a letter to the State Department. Very soon a chastened official came to Lil's home and said, "We will be glad to make available to you all the motion pictures you want for the lepers."

Before long there were more than a hundred Christians in the colony; but they still had no worthy place in which to worship. Their services were held in the Buddhist meeting place, but there was an embarrassment about it. "We don't like to have those Buddhist gods staring at us when we are praying to the true Father in heaven," one of the Christians put it. "We need a curtain to curtain off the gods." Lil dutifully measured the front of the room, bought the cloth, and made the curtain. Her account book, every page of which she headed, as a sober reminder, "In Account with God," bears the entry, "Cloth for curtain to shut out the Buddhist gods."

"Would you come for Easter and arrange for Communion?" the Christians asked Lil. Gladly, she took it up with the pastor. Communion was never more sacredly received. It was also served to those unable to be present at the service. In some cases, the sip of wine had to be poured gently into a mouth that could scarcely move and which there were no hands to serve, and the bit of bread placed on the tongue. As Lil made the rounds with the pastor, she saw that patients had tacked over their beds reminders of days that were kinder and homes that once were carefree. There were photos of children they would never see again, and photos of themselves—young and beautiful and whole—as they would never be again, this side of heaven. The pictures brought an infinite gentleness to Lil's touch, an infinite compassion to her voice as she greeted those she had learned to know and to love.

Encouraged by the change of heart of the USIS, Lil visited the American Aid headquarters. "I need help at the leprosarium—"

"Leprosy work—Hansen's Disease—you should see our medical department."

Lil went to the medical department. "Things are in bad condition at the leprosarium here. It's too big for me to handle. Can you help?"

"We're not *charity,* Mrs. Dickson!" The man was still shaking his head when she walked out.

A few months later, a caller came to the mission compound house. "You visited our office some time ago requesting help for a leprosarium," he began.

"You're not the man I talked with," Lil said.

"I know. He was transferred. I'm in charge now. I have a few minutes, and I'd like to know more about the leper colony."

Lil cast an anxious eye at the sky. "We're going to get some rain." As they sat down in the living room, the downpour started—a cloudburst. Ordinarily, people were coming and going and there were all sorts of interruptions, but the heavy rain provided a curtain of privacy. For an hour it continued, keeping away other visitors and holding this one. Lil shared her heartbreak. "The *big* thing the colony needs is adequate housing; bamboo and mud are no good. When I go out there after this rain, probably some of the shacks that patients are living in will be flattened." Then she launched into her ideas about politics. "This is really a war of ideologies. The free world maintains that it treats ordinary people better than the Communists do. We know the Communists destroy lepers. Just recently, I heard how the Communists asked all the lepers in one section of the mainland to make themselves known so that they could be given a place where they would be isolated and allowed to live in peace. The lepers believed them. The Communists set aside a special hilltop and gave the lepers grass and wood with which to build houses. After the houses were built, soldiers surrounded the place and set them on fire. Those who ran out were shot. This is what the Communists did. We of the free world neglect the lepers—so they kill themselves."

And then the rain stopped and sunlight sparkled on the wet leaves and grass.

The next day, Lil's visitor went with her to the colony. She took him all over it, and in the process, saw one place even she had never seen before. They were in the library room, and somehow, the two of them happened to look together through a window and into a dungeon below. It was empty except for a few rags.

Lil asked, "What is this?"

Someone behind her replied, "The leper's prison."

Lil gasped. "No wonder there have been suicides," she whispered, shaken. Perhaps the sight impressed the American Aid man, too, for again he came back, and this time began making plans. Before he was finished, he had channeled three hundred thousand dollars into the construction of seven beautiful dormitories.

But the little things—and sometimes not so little—were left to Lil's ingenuity and concern. Concrete paths, for one. Almost all the patients had bad feet and many of them had imperfect hands that could not properly hold crutches. Uneven footing caused them to fall and injure themselves. With a group of patients who knew where the serious cases were housed and the routes such patients would ordinarily have to take, Lil decided where the concrete walks should go. "What better use for God's money," Lil asked, "than to make crooked paths straight?" One of the main routes—the path from the entrance gate up to a knoll overlooking the valley—the patients in their gratitude named "Lillian Walk."

The contractor avoided a too-smooth finish on the paths. When Lil asked why he had done this, he explained that crutches could slip on smooth concrete; when there was a little roughness, walking was easier. Is that why God makes *our* paths a little rough? Lil wondered. If the way is too smooth, too easy, perhaps we would slip.

When she was called to the colony for an emergency one night, Lil found that the paths were in total darkness. Again she and the leaders of the patients made the rounds, deciding where electric lights should be installed so that the patients could walk safely at night.

Still, there was something lacking—a worthy church. Lil wanted the Christians to have a place of beauty for their worship services, a place of dignity for funeral services. One day in early 1952 she confided to Jim, "They have waited too long. I am going to try to build that church for them this year, God willing."

Someone gave one hundred dollars toward it. The lepers themselves had made about six hundred dollars by raising chickens. Dr. G. Gushue-Taylor returned from Canada bringing fifteen hundred dollars, for the church had been one of his desires, too.

Lil and he went to the colony to search out a location. On a rise overlooking the valley, below the dormitories that were built farther up the hillside, they found the perfect spot. With some of the patients gathered around them, they asked God's blessing. Lil described the scene in a letter: "A leper prayed, 'Father, we have longed for a church and waited. Now it begins to look as if You are going to allow us to have it.' I knew it was not that the Father had not allowed it, but that we Christians had been so slow, years and years too slow, in love and awareness, to provide it for them."

Lil did not wait any longer; she began building step by step as the money came. One morning when Lil went out to the colony a group of lepers were waiting for her. One of them stepped forward and presented her with a small package. "This is a gift of money toward the church," he said. "Here also is a gold ring someone wishes to give. The money has been disinfected. We know this is not much, but we want to do our part."

Lil said gently, "The church is being built by God for you, for in the beginning we had no money at all. It has all come as a gift from Him through those who love Him." That night she entered in her account book the money so humbly disinfected and presented, and "one gold ring." Pondering that so many of the patients had no fingers, she gazed at the ring thoughtfully. What was its history?

There was excitement and renewed hope now among the

Christian patients. Lil's eyes were reflecting the good spirit when she stopped by Ui Sian-si's bed. "We will soon have the church," she said joyfully.

"I will never see it," said Ui Sian-si, turning his face to the wall. "I will never have a chance to take part in the services. If only I could walk!"

"You'll get to the church—I promise you!" she said.

At home, she put the problem to the young people who helped her: "I need something like a low cart that will have a chair in it and that can be pushed on the cement paths, so that we can take to church those who cannot walk." Together they worked out plans for the contrivance.

One Sunday morning in October, 1952, the bell of the Church of the Lepers rang out across the valley for the first time. The lame and the halt and the blind and the maimed slowly and reverently filed up the hill and into their church. The platform was crowded with visiting missionaries; leper choirs sang joyful songs. Ui Sian-si was there, in his cart, his face shining. Those who could not come were able to enjoy it, too. The electrician had installed a microphone at the pulpit so that the services would go out to every ward through the loudspeakers.

But beneath the ground, a dragon was sleeping.

On the highway below the Church of the Lepers a Buddhist temple stood. Lil had heard mutterings that perhaps the Buddhists would oppose the building of a church so near, but nothing happened until a smaller, outside building was under construction.

Buddhist nuns sent a message to the church leaders: "Our head men have been here and they have told us that a dragon lies under the ground. You are making a building right on top of the dragon's neck. This is disrespectful to him and will cause trouble. Please remove it."

The contractor and the Christians were dismayed. "It will cost much money to move it now," said the contractor. The Christians declared, "We do not believe in dragons, and we should not be bound by their traditions."

Lil hushed them. "We will try to do it God's way. If it costs us more money doing it His way, He can easily help us get the money. He wants us to live nicely with all our neighbors with never a bit of ill will among us. Now, see what you think of this—" and she presented her plan.

So it was that on an appointed day, Lil and the Christian leaders met with the Buddhists. Lil said to them, "We will be glad to move the building, but you must tell us where it will suit you to have it."

Their opposition melted. "We will let you know," they said, as if it were no longer important. "Sometimes we will come to your church to listen," they added, "and sometimes you must come to see us."

A little later they sent up another message. "We have consulted our head men again, and they say it is all right. You do not need to move the building." They sent blossoming shrubs to plant around the church, and one more friendly message: "We like to hear your people singing."

One day when Lil returned from the leprosarium in her jeep—it had so long been unclaimed by anyone else that she regarded it as hers—Jim reminded her, "The mission council meets in our house tomorrow." As the hostess she would have to be there.

"Lil," Jim went on, "I've got wind of something. I don't think they like your using the jeep for nonmission work."

"But it wouldn't run for anyone else—not even for you!" Lil exclaimed.

"I'm on *your* side," Jim said with a smile. "But the hard, cold fact is that it's not your jeep."

The meeting the next day had barely begun when Lil was called out of the room to receive a cable. "A station wagon is being given to you by World Vision," she read with elation. The Rev. Dr. Bob Pierce, president of the Pasadena, California, organization that had grown up around his interest in helping the needy and those who serve them, had been to Taiwan and was drenched in that jeep.

When she returned to the meeting, one of the council members said, "Mrs. Dickson, it has just been decided that you may no longer use the jeep."

"I don't mind one bit," Lil answered them sweetly, while Jim listened in surprise.

Later she sidled by Jim, flashed the cable, and whispered, "Wasn't it nice of God to let me have the good news first?"

Jim grinned widely. "You know," he said to the council, "if anyone can get that jeep to go, it will surprise me very much."

Even though some of the needs were being met at the leprosarium, there was still much to do. When one ministers to hundreds of patients, they have hundreds of needs—errands to be run, supplies of various kinds to be bought, and most of all, personal attention. As Lil went from bed to bed and ward to ward, she gathered up all kinds of requests, some wistful, some heartbreaking. One day she took out brightly colored oilcloth covers for the patients' drab tables. A little girl about fourteen, pretty as a flower but with her hands already twisted from the disease, approached Lil and said shyly, "I have no table or desk or cupboard, nothing but a bed. I have asked for a table; they said there are no more. But could I please have a small piece of oilcloth, so if I ever *did* have a table, I would have something to put on it?"

Lil saw to it that she was given both a table and oilcloth to put on it.

On her rounds Lil stopped by the bedside of Ui Sian-si, and had prayer with him. "You seem sad!" said Lil. "And you're the one who has done so much to change things around here. The newspapers and magazines and radio and movies were your idea, and the carts that help not only you but others get to the church service—"

"I guess I'll have to tell you," he said reluctantly. "Every night I am considering suicide. I know it is wrong, but the temptation is very strong."

"But, Ui Sian-si, what is the matter? You are one of my best advisers!"

"It is so little that I hate to speak of it," he said, "but I cannot bear it any longer. The boards of my bed are broken and I cannot fix them. I have reported it many times, but the hospital people do not send anyone to repair it. And now the rats come up and bite me at night."

Lil had never paid much attention to the beds before, but she looked carefully. It was as Ui Sian-si had said. The bed was only bare boards, full of slivers and wide cracks, and now the boards had broken.

"We will see about *this!*" As she charged off to her car, she left orders: "I want Ui Sian-si's bed mended by the time I get back here—and I will be back *very* soon!" Never did she go faster into the city. At a shop she bought a thick tatami mat, the Japanese-type mattress woven of springy fibers, lightweight and clean smelling. The cost was so little—just one dollar, U.S.

On the way back to the colony, Lil had a sobering thought. Ui Sian-si was not the only one. All the patients should have bed mats. When one is sick and spends much time in bed, that bed is very important. But where would she get the money? She was spending all that came in for food, drugs, clothes.

At least Ui Sian-si was taken care of. His bed had been mended and she watched as he put his new mat into place and then lay down upon it. A happy smile twisted his face. "Now you can sleep tonight," Lil tried to say gruffly.

A few days later Dr. Henrietta Mears and Miss Esther Ellinghusen of Los Angeles came to Taiwan for a visit. Lil took them to the leprosarium and to the Ward Nearest Heaven's Door and told them of the bed "crisis." They left a gift to buy tatami mats for all the others in that ward.

But what about the rest of the patients? A name, a face that she had forgotten, flashed through Lil's mind. A pastor had come from America for a visit and stayed at the Dickson home. When he left he said, "If you ever have a project that you think would interest my young people, let me know."

She had it! "WOULD EACH OF YOUR YOUNG PEOPLE BE INTERESTED IN GIVING A LEPER A BED AS A CHRISTMAS GIFT? BED COSTS ONE DOLLAR. HAVE 650 PATIENTS," she cabled. The young people responded wholeheartedly. By Christmas all the patients had comfortable beds and the knowledge that somewhere, someone cared.

There were big things, too. Miss Alma Drucks—Sister Alma—a deaconess of the Lutheran church with nurses' training, came to give full time to the leprosarium. There was no place for her to live and she took up housekeeping in the little vestry of the Church of the Lepers so that she would be available to the patients day and night. Sister Alma's black uniform and white cap became a familiar sight in the colony. Her coming resulted in improved health among the patients, because of the expert and loving care which she provided. As she and Lil paused by the bedside of one of the Christians, he said, "Look, my wounds are all healed. When I go home to Heaven, I will tell the Father that you came."

Lil related the incident in her newsletter and explained, "He meant that Christian compassion came, the compassion that reached all the way from America to this dark place, with medicine, a bed, some comforts and loving care. He meant Christian friends in America, for we come to them with nothing in our hands, and only as it is sent to us to give to them, do we have it to pass on."

The beds, the chairs, the church, the radio—all testified to the worth of the individual. The suicides diminished. When a man, even a leper, had some sense of his dignity as a person, he did not carelessly throw his life away. Even funerals—and there were many—could show that a man was worth much or worth little. At the leprosarium there had been little dignity in death. When a patient died he was tied up for easy cremation. The patients protested and were grudgingly provided with a shabby crate.

At the first death after the completion of the church, Lil asked the Christian leaders, "Did you have the funeral service in the church?"

"No," they answered.

"Why not?" she demanded. "A service in the church helps to show that when a Christian dies, we give him back to the Lord."

"The box they gave us is not good enough to put in the church," they said.

Lil went home thoughtfully, and by the time she drove up to the big mission house, she had a plan. Calling Everlasting Life, one of the young men involved in many of her projects, she outlined the plan to him.

"I want a large box, beautifully carved, lined with tin so that it is washable, and on wheels so that it can be taken easily up to the church. Then we will put the shabby box of the lepers into the big beautiful coffin, and they will be glad to have the funeral service in the church, and it will give them extra comfort."

Coffins were made in special coffin shops by specialists; nobody else would do that kind of work. But Lil wanted something better than an ordinary coffin. She and Everlasting Life went to a furniture store. "We want a large chest," Lil said, "with a cross carved on top and flowers carved on the sides, tin lined—"

The man looked at the two of them suspiciously. "*Where* is this to be used?"

Everlasting Life spoke up. "In the church."

"And *what* are you going to put in it?"

Before Lil could answer, her helper said, "*Many* things."

The furniture man, satisfied, made notes of the specifications, and in due time the "chest" was delivered. Someone had given Lil a beautiful piece of yellow silk—"It looked just like glory incarnate." With it she made a cover for the coffin, as is the custom on the island.

Lil went along for the first service. On top of the coffin was the cross and a profusion of flowers. Wheeled into the church with its burden, it was placed before the altar. The Christians gathered and sang hymns, the pastor gave a message, and then, still singing, the Christians went out to give their brother back to the Lord.

"We would like to sign up for the coffin," some of the Buddhists later told the church leaders.

"You are not Christian!" they said. "It has a cross on top—"

"But," they replied, "it is such a nice coffin!"

15. "Save My Baby!"

Lil picked up the crying jet-haired baby girl and cradled her in mother-hungry arms. The child squirmed restlessly. One sick baby in one orphanage in Taipei, and there were so many sick babies all over the island—hundreds, thousands, who knew how many? Mainlanders had begun their exodus to Taiwan as soon as it was permissible at the end of World War II. The stream grew to a flood when the Nationalist government itself took refuge on the island. In the confusion, families often were separated and food and resources always were scant. In 1950 every orphanage was crowded.

One institution where babies were dying at the rate of five to seven a week had been called to Lil's attention. It was not equipped to take care of babies and did not want them. The babies were dying from lack of care, lack of cleanliness, lack of, as Lil saw it, "everything." On one of her frequent visits, she grew concerned especially about one, crying and tossing in her crib.

"Won't last long," an attendant said disapprovingly, as if it were all the baby's fault.

But she might last, if—Lil patted the child's head tenderly, put her down gently in the crib, and hurried out to a telephone. Coming back, she sponged the fevered face, found a chair, took the baby into her arms, and sat down to wait.

Within an hour a slight Chinese woman, wearing a high-collared dress with skirt slit to above the knee, came hurrying in. *"Peng-an,"* said the woman, bowing.

Lil returned the greeting. "I want you to take care of this baby *full time*. I will pay you. See that she is fed and kept clean."

The woman looked around questioningly.

"They won't bother you. They'll be glad not to have to worry about the baby." Lil reached into her purse and took out money.

A few days later when Lil returned, she could hear the child crying even while she was walking down the corridor. "I tried everything," the hired woman said.

Lil felt the tiny forehead. "Still sick." She wondered what to do, and then the baby settled the matter. Whether in an involuntary baby gesture, whether out of a need of love, the little one held up her arms to Lil.

She said to the hired woman, "I'll take her home with me."

After months of loving care, the child became completely well. Properly nourished, she was growing into a beautiful little girl.

"You need a name," Lil said to the child one day. "How about Bi-lian?" That was the Taiwanese equivalent of Mei-ling, the given name of Madame Chiang Kai-shek, the courageous woman to whom Lil had once listened on the contraband radio station, and with whom she had since become acquainted.

The little girl smiled, black button eyes sparkling.

"Bi-lian it is!"

When Lil caught Jim dandling Bi-lian on his knee, she said, "Jim, I've been thinking."

"You usually are." He grinned. "And usually I wind up right in the middle of something."

"*You!* What about the goats?"

"Well, you see— What was it you were thinking about?"

"Jim, I *can't* take Bi-lian back to that orphanage. She'd die. The other little ones there are dying."

"Then we'll keep her," Jim said. That was exactly what Lil had in mind.

They adopted Bi-lian under Chinese law. Later, Lil pointed out to Jim, "The Communists may come and foreigners have to leave. If we left Bi-lian, the Communists would kill her for having lived with us—" So on Lil's next trip to the States, Bi-lian went along, and was adopted and naturalized by American law so that the Dicksons could keep her safe forever.

There were other babies, too, that aroused Lil's concern. One of them she discovered—"by accident," some would have said—when she was returning from the boys' prison on the edge of Taipei with a doctor she had drafted to give medical treatment to the boys.

"Dr. Dale," said Lil, "I have a strange feeling about that orphanage where so many babies died—the one where I found Bi-lian."

Dr. Dale replied politely but noncommittally, "Oh—"

"I just have a *feeling*—" Lil explained.

Tiu Sian-si, the driver, threaded Lil's car through the crowded streets, using the horn with great skill. If there is anything that puts a car utterly and immediately out of operating condition in Taiwan, it is horn failure. The streets were crowded with pedestrians, many of them carrying something staggeringly heavy. With their burdens suspended in baskets slung from either end of shoulder yokes, the bearers jogged along in a half-trot. Bicycles and three-wheel bicycle trucks, themselves regulated by openings in pedestrian traffic, slowed fast vehicles to their own pace. In the open country and rural sections, there was always the supreme obstacle—the ubiquitous oxcart, turning back the speedometers of everything behind it a thousand years.

"I wonder about that orphanage—" Lil said, worrying.

Tiu Sian-si, approaching three cyclists, gave the horn three brisk, evenly spaced toots—one for each, as cyclists expected. They would no more respond to a toot intended for someone else than they would bother to look for oncoming traffic when they swung out of side streets.

"It's just that sometimes I feel as if I'm being *pushed*—sometimes into trouble, sometimes out of trouble," Lil went on.

"Woman's intuition," said Dr. Dale genially.

"Or an angel at my shoulder," said Lil, looking out of the window.

Tiu Sian-si slowed the car to a quick stop when four small school-crossing guards suddenly lifted a traffic barrier of two bright red plastic cords forming a safety lane through which a bevy of diminutive, uniformed pupils chattered their way across the street. The children across, the guards let the cords fall to the ground and traffic resumed.

Lil turned to Dr. Dale. "*Can* you spare just a few more minutes? Do you mind if we stop at the orphanage?"

"Of course not," said the doctor.

Lil gave the new directions to Tiu Sian-si.

The orphanage was as dismal as ever. The children looked up at them warily as they walked through the silent corridors. "This is not a happy place," Lil said. "The children are too quiet; there is no laughter." A tiny girl in a soiled white kindergartener's apron shrank back behind a door as they approached.

The doctor noted the listlessness of many of the children and shook his head. "They're sick," he muttered.

"No wonder," said Lil wrathily. "Did you ever see a dirtier place? Or dirtier children?"

"Children are made to get dirty," said the doctor soothingly.

"And mothers are made to scrub them clean! What I could do with a bucket and brush in here!"

"Well, Mrs. Dickson," said Dr. Dale presently, "I'll admit it's a discouraging picture, but it's what a doctor would call a chronic situation, not an acute one. They're all somewhat sick—and you could say the same thing of a large percentage of the people of the world. They'll die someday—before their time—but not today. It's a job for a nutritionist, a welfare expert, a farmer—and, yes," he said with a slow smile, "a scrubwoman. But not for a doctor."

"But surely—" began Lil, then stopped. "We're about to be

welcomed—or thrown out," she whispered. "Here comes the woman in charge."

The woman approached, her slippers making prim slaps on the dirty floor, equaling in primness the high tight collar of her red-flowered dress but belied by its rumpled state. She stopped before the two visitors and bowed coldly. "May I help you?"

"Do you have any other children here?" Lil asked quietly.

The woman's manner softened just a bit. "We have a few babies in the back."

Dr. Dale had already turned to go, but paused when Lil asked, "May we see them?"

The woman motioned them on, then slipped ahead to open a closed door. They moved past her and silently entered the crib-lined room. Some light came through a dirty window glass. A dim naked electric bulb seemed to emit darkness rather than light. Tears stung Lil's eyes at what she saw. The doctor went from bed to bed, gently manipulating small pipestem legs, shaking his head at the wide staring eyes of undernourishment, touching his cool fingers to hot baby foreheads, applying his stethoscope to small, convulsive chests.

He paused at one crib, unhooked the ear pieces of his instrument and let them rest behind his neck. "This one's very sick. She won't live through the night."

The woman at the door showed no interest.

Lil came over and stood by the doctor's side, looking down at the tiny figure. The baby did not look up; she seemed hardly to be there at all. "I'd pay for her in the hospital," Lil said, "but they always say they're filled up."

"I'll telephone them to have a bed ready."

When Lil explained to the woman at the door what they were about to do, she showed her first sign of interest. Sick babies were a problem, and if they died, they were even more of a problem. There was a special gleam in her eye, too, that Lil did not see. "That one? Yes, take that one!"

In the car, Dr. Dale looked at Lil, holding the sick baby. "I guess it wasn't a false alarm."

At Mackay Hospital a bed was in readiness. Lil waited until the waif no one else wanted to mother lay sleeping, little more than a fitful breath of life on the white crib sheet.

"How is she?" Lil asked the next day, and the next, and the next. And finally a doctor said, "She will get well." Lil hardly needed the word of a doctor. The baby had become alert, had taken on weight, had become beautiful with the perfect beauty of babyhood. One day the doctor told her, "She'll be ready to leave tomorrow."

Lil walked across the compound to her home, the weight of the day's burdens feeling light as a feather. At the house, Jim, who had arrived before her, looked up from the color transparencies he was holding to a lamp. "I brought the mail over from the post office," he said. "Some letters for you."

Lil ran through the envelopes. Most of them were from the States, a few from Canada, some blue air-mail letters, some letters in regular envelopes. She thought of the times when contributors or just plain letter writers enclosed a stamped return envelope—as if an American stamp would take a letter from Taiwan! There was one letter addressed with Chinese characters. She opened that one first, passing it to Jim to translate. She could speak Taiwanese fluently, and remembered some of her Japanese, but reading either was something else again.

"It's from that orphanage where we got Bi-lian," Jim said. "Did you get another baby there not long ago?"

Lil nodded happily. "She'll be ready to leave the hospital tomorrow."

Jim turned to the letter. "They say they don't want her back. It's a leper's child."

Lil's happiness left her.

The baby couldn't stay in the hospital. No other orphanage would accept her, knowing the background. "We'll just have to bring her here," said Lil. "The cook's wife can take care of her. She's good at doing unexpected things."

The woman welcomed the opportunity to earn something extra, and the baby delighted her. "She is beautiful," she smiled. "But we can't always call her 'she.' You must give her a name."

Lil looked at the happy infant, small arms waving in sudden vigorous movements that seemed to startle even the baby to wide-eyed surprise and then to pleased gurgles. "Let's call her Joy."

"Sun Bok-su niu, what is the spot on the back of the baby's neck?" the cook's wife asked Lil a few days later. Lil carefully examined the small red blotch. At the first opportunity she had Dr. Dale take a look. With relief, Lil reported, "The doctor says it's nothing to be worried about—just a birthmark that probably will disappear in time."

Meanwhile, Lil's work at the leper colony went on. One day as Lil was making her rounds, noting what was needed to make the place more attractive and the lives of the patients more comfortable, a woman approached her carrying a baby. The flower-like faces of the babies and children of the leper parents, among the disfigurement of the adults, was a disparity she had often noted.

The woman was close enough now for Lil to see the tears streaming down her face. Desperately, she held out the girl to Lil. "Save my baby! Save my baby!" she pleaded.

"Is she sick?" Lil asked.

"She is not sick. I am sick," the woman said. "Is she not a beautiful baby?" She held the little head forward. "Do you not think she is beautiful?"

"My, *yes,*" Lil agreed.

"If she must stay here, someday she will not be beautiful."

The children should not be here at all! Lil thought. Living in the midst of these advanced cases, they would probably get the disease. Taken away at an early enough age, they would be untouched. But where could Lil put another leper's child? No orphanage would take it in—any more than they would take Joy. No private home would board a child that came from the leprosarium. There was her own home—but that was not the final answer. There were dozens of babies here, and she could not take them all.

"I will try to plan what to do," she assured the mother gently, and turned away. That was the hardest part of life—the turning away when you could not do what needed to be done. That evening, Lil, utterly depressed, ate dinner in silence.

A few days later, Lil and her young helper, Everlasting Life, were in the Ward Nearest Heaven's Door tacking up large pictures from Sunday-school picture rolls, to provide color and meaning.

"Sun Bok-su niu!" The urgency of a man's voice caused her to wheel. One of the patients stood there apologetically, given strength only by his anxiety. "Sun Bok-su niu, my wife and I have twin baby boys. She has no hands, and my hands have lost their strength. We can no longer feed them, bathe them, dress them, even—" his eyes welled with tears—"hold them. Another patient is trying to help, but we cannot go on—"

Lil could not retreat this time. There was no time to wait for a plan. "Do you want me to take them?" Lil asked gently.

The face before her registered vast relief and yet vast love. Lil, looking at the scarred features that for a moment became radiant, thought of Another who loved so much that He gave a son.

She and Everlasting Life took the twins back to the mission compound. A missionary nurse gave them personal care the first week; they were so tiny that no one thought they could live. Meanwhile, Lil began praying desperate prayers for guidance. There were three babies now—Joy and the twins.

"Where are you going to put them?" a friend inquired of Lil, and Lil thought how nice of her it was to ask. Then another wondered, "Where are you going to put them?" and another. Beginning to feel somewhat harried, Lil explained that she could not keep them in her home, which was mission property and not intended to be used as an orphanage.

Lil relayed the question higher. "Where are You going to put them?" she prayed.

The next night the answer walked up to Lil's front door.

He didn't look like an answer to prayer; an answer seldom does. He looked like an American tourist. His name meant nothing to Lil. When he knocked on the door at nine o'clock, no hour to be making a social call in Taipei, it would have been easy to turn him away. But answers to prayer do not keep regular hours. You're likely to run into one any time of day or night.

He had heard of Mrs. Dickson's work, he said, and could he talk to her? She was polite and tried to answer his questions. Before long, she was telling him of the three babies she was sheltering and how she was being pressed to remove them from the mission compound. "I need a home for the babies of leper parents," she sighed. On that note, he thanked Lil for her courtesy and went on his way.

Two weeks later a cable arrived from the "tourist"; he was the Rev. William F. Roberts of the Far East Broadcasting Company. He had gone home to America and put Lil's question on the air. Listeners had responded. "SENDING $2500. START YOUR BABY HOME," his cable read.

"An-Lok, we'll call it," said Lil. "Peace and Happiness."

Lil found the perfect plot outside the city in a ricefield. No houses were in sight, only the blue-misted mountains in the distance and the graceful nodding rice stalks at her feet.

Do I dare to do it? she asked herself. Her heart replied, You do not dare not to dare!

The land was purchased, and a building started. She shared the story in her monthly newsletter, and finally was able to tell her friends at home, "An-Lok will be open in a few weeks."

At the same time she was sharing another anxiety with Jim. "I had a letter from a doctor in England who knows about leprosy," she said one evening. "He writes that if we take not only the new babies, but all under a year old, the chances are they won't get it. We also need a home for older small children who have been exposed—children up to about five years old—where they can be kept under observation, not mixed with the untainted babies."

"Now, I'll tell you what you should do," Jim began. Then he stopped. "No," he decided, throwing up his hands, "I don't think I could!"

"The Saviour said long ago," Lil pointed out, " 'I would have you without carefulness.' It is a blanket of blessed forgetfulness and love to draw over us at night, so we can sleeep."

16. Candlelight and Compassion

A few months after Lil brought baby Joy into her home, she was making her rounds one afternoon at the leprosarium. One of the patients fell into step with her. A slight, pretty girl, she had entered the colony soon after Lil began her "housekeeping" work there. On the mainland she had been a schoolteacher; her alertness helped her to pick up the Taiwanese language quickly. She seemed more refined and cultured than some of the others, and she and Lil were friends from the start.

This day, they walked along the concrete paths, chatting together. "You speak Taiwanese very well," Lil observed.

"So I can talk to you," said the young woman. "You are my friend."

"And God is your friend, too."

"Yes, God is my friend because He is your friend and you are my friend." The girl paused, as if summoning courage to say what she wanted to say. "Do you know what it is to lose something?"

"Two of my babies died," said Lil softly.

"Then you do know. I lost only one." Tears filled her dark eyes. "My husband and I escaped the Communists on the mainland. Taiwan was a place of refuge, and we came here as did so many others. Here our baby was born. A beautiful baby! The doctor noticed a black spot on my body. He said it was leprosy. I had hardly any time with my baby—just enough to see how beautiful she was!"

"Where is your husband?" Lil asked gently.

"Gone—who knows where? He was afraid."

"And the baby—?" Lil asked. "You know, we hope soon to have a home for babies of the patients."

The young woman wept. "They took her away when I was brought here. To an orphanage, they said." She shook her head wonderingly. "Such a perfect baby. No spot on her—except a small red birthmark on the back of her neck, and it will no doubt go away as she grows older—"

Lil felt a tingle of excitement. "What orphanage—?"

"One in Taipei. They told me the name. A woman here said it is one of the worst."

"How old would your baby be?" Lil asked hesitantly. She was almost afraid to ask.

"She was born six months ago."

Lil could hardly speak for the wonder of it. "I have your baby right in my own house."

The woman looked at Lil, wanting to believe it but hardly daring. "My baby—?"

"I've had her for weeks! We call her Joy. I will bring her," Lil promised. "You *will* see your baby! And when you are cured, your baby will go with you."

That evening, she had a phone call to make. "Dr. Dale," she began, "you remember the day I felt we should stop at the orphanage where we got Bi-lian—?"

Little Joy and the twins were the first babies moved into An-Lok.

Besides this home for the untainted babies of leprosy patients,

Lil in desperation started her Observation Home for the babies who had been with their parents for longer periods and so were susceptible. Dr. Gushue-Taylor offered her a house at the Happy Mount Christian Leprosy Colony, a house which had not been used for years and which stood apart from the others and could be fenced off. Lil had the little home redecorated and made pretty and livable.

Some of the parents were reluctant to give up their children. Lil described the problem in a newsletter: "There was heartbreak in each interview. 'Will you bring them back sometimes so we can see them?' asked one mother. In all that sordid, grim place to which she was confined for life, her baby was her one bright spot of happiness. It meant sacrifice of all her present happiness so that her baby might have a chance. It is anguish for them to give up their babies and it is anguish for me to have to ask them to do so, and yet with what love and care we will surround them, with cleanliness and good food and green grass to play on, with missionary doctors and nurses carefully observant."

Four sets of parents promised to put their babies in the Observation Home, but at the last moment only two were willing to give them up. The mothers brought the babies to Lil's car. There she had prayer with them to the Father who knows aching hearts, and took the babies in her arms.

As the car moved off, Lil looked back. One mother had turned away sobbing, reaching out to friends. The second mother stood alone, her face inexpressibly desolate, as she poured the remaining milk out of the baby's bottle onto the ground.

One of the babies cried all the way, a full hour's ride. His mother had been terribly disfigured, and yet to this tiny one, she was the most desirable person in the whole world. The other baby, too young to be heartbroken, slept throughout the journey.

The number of babies entrusted to Lil increased. As money came in beyond current needs, she used it to expand facilities. The Observation Home was provided with its own building near An-Lok.

One mother said, "If only you could take a picture of my baby and give it to me, I would hold it against my cheek at night and then perhaps I would sleep without crying so much."

Lil wondered why she had not thought of that sooner. The next day she took a photographer out to where the blue-misted mountains formed a backdrop, and the ricefields the foreground, and had him make a picture of each child.

Harder even than taking the children away was bringing them back every three months for the parents to see. She was afraid at first there would be so much pent-up emotion that the parents would sweep up the children in their arms. "You do not need to fear that," one of the patients told her wistfully. "The parents love them too much."

In the Church of the Lepers, the children sat on the railed-off platform, each in turn held up for the parents to see. Most of the children were too young to understand; they gazed with innocent wonder down at the sea of upturned faces where mothers and fathers watched with yearning love lest they miss any moment of the experience. One little six-year-old girl did understand. When she recognized her father coming down the church aisle and saw him smile at her, she burst into tears. To look at someone beloved and to know that she could not be cuddled in his arms was too much for her to bear. The father went to the side of the church at the opposite end of the platform and took a seat where his face would be shielded, for he, too, was weeping.

The motherly woman in charge of the children, knowing that all the details of each child's life would be important to the parents, told about each one, his or her characteristics, likes and dislikes. Thinking to encourage some parent, she pointed out one little girl and said, "This child every night at bedtime calls her mother, over and over again." She did not know which one was the mother, but Lil knew. The mother turned her head, her eyes overflowing. Lil shared that mother's emotion in her own heart and knew that every evening that mother's thoughts and heart would go over the mountain to where a child was calling, "Mother, Mother."

As Lil gathered up the children to take them back and the parents waved *"Peng-an,"* there was a sob in their hearts that must have caused angels to weep.

When there were fifteen babies in the Babies' Home and twenty-five in the Observation Home, Lil was buying clothes, shoes, and outfits in quantity. "Dear Lord, don't get tired of my coming so often and with so many requests, please," she prayed. "You got us into it and now we cannot stop at a halfway point. We just have to keep on coming to You—baby shoes and pajamas are a part of it!"

One night when the house at the mission compound was dark and the noises of the city were muted and Lil lay awake, warmed by the peaceful silence, she said quietly, "Jim, suppose the Communists come?"

"That's not likely, with the Seventh Fleet on patrol."

"But it could happen?"

"Anything could happen. If they came, we would have to leave very suddenly—if we could."

"Jim, I'm worried about the lepers. Every time I leave them I wonder, suppose I couldn't come back again? What would they do? What would become of them?"

"Don't underestimate God, Lil. It may seem at times as if we are carrying the world on our backs. We're not. We're His agents—not the other way around."

How close to danger she and Jim had been so often, Lil thought, yet God had taken care of them. Could not—did not—God take care of all His children without favoritism, the lepers, too? She drifted off to sleep.

At the next meeting at the Church of the Lepers, she told the people, "We're going to learn a new song. Every time I come to visit you, it will be the last song we sing together." With her accordion leading, they sang:

> Be not afraid whate'er betide,
> God will take care of you;
> Beneath His wings of faith abide,

God will take care of you.
God will take care of you
Through every day, o'er all the way;
He will take care of you,
God will take care of you.

After the service, as Lil went to her car, the patients gathered around and began singing, "God Will Take Care of You." So began a tradition that continues to this day. "God Will Take Care of You" is the last ringing assurance any visitor has as he drives away from the Church of the Lepers, and which the patients have as they wave good-by.

Sometimes courage and happiness came from small things so ordinary that they would scarcely be regarded as "missionary" work. When, for example, Lil discovered that the patients did not have chairs to sit on—nothing but the edge of the bed in their room and a rock or the ground when they went outdoors to sun themselves—she enlisted the support of her correspondents; every leper was given the dignity and comfort of a chair of his own. When she saw the battered rice bowls they were using, she campaigned again, until every patient had two new ones. "Things that a mother would think of," she explained.

When she saw that the Communion service was held in the bright glare of fluorescent lights, Lil rebelled. She took one of her own white tablecloths, and bought a silver-plated Communion set, flowers, and candles for the next service, establishing a gracious custom. "In the candlelight they cannot see one another's disfigured faces," she explained to Jim.

It would take a woman to think of that. And it would take a woman to think of anything as happily impractical as costume jewelry. "Every woman in America has costume jewelry which she never wears," Lil wrote her friends back home. "A few of those pieces would make women over here very happy."

The discarded jewelry began arriving, earrings separated, chains twisted, sets missing. "A lot of people must think our women have only one ear!" Lil grumbled, finding earrings that could not possibly match. Lil decided she would have an "earring party" in her home. Calling in two or three of the girls who assisted her, they made up packets from the tangle—a pair of earrings, a necklace, and perhaps a brooch in each—in readiness for distribution at Christmas or some other special time.

Some strange specimens turned up, sent with good intentions but, like the stamped return envelopes, unusable—everything from National Honor Society pins, to lapel buttons bearing such insignia as:

30 Years Loyal Service—Standard Coated Products
P.S. 115—'31
CHS, '05—LABORE ET HONORE

Then there was the sunburst medal with a typewriter embossed in the center and the words *Speed, Accuracy*. "If it just had a headhunter's knife on it instead of a typewriter—" Jim laughed.

The utterly impossible ones were simply discarded. The rest were passed along to brighten the long days of women who had so little of beauty in their lives.

It was not all one-way. The patients learned to give, as well as to take. "Happiness comes from doing something for others," Lil said to them. "People have done something for you. Pass it on! That is your gift for God."

A few days later one of the women came to Lil and said, "At first we didn't know what we could do for anyone. Then we thought of something. Once a week those of us who have hands will wash the hair of the women patients who have no hands. Would this be, do you think, a gift for God?"

"A beautiful gift!" Lil replied.

Meantime, there were projects that needed big answers. Sulfones were proving more effective than the old leprosy drugs, but not even miracle drugs could restore missing fingers. There needed to be a place where patients could learn new vocations, adapt themselves to their limitations. This would give them enough independence to strike out on their own after the disease had been arrested.

"We need an occupational therapy room," Lil said to Jim.

She was thinking of that on a visit to America in the Fall of 1953. She had met Dr. Daniel A. Poling of New York, editor of *Christian Herald* magazine, on his earlier visits to the Orient. She knew of his interest in children; *Christian Herald* had operated a large orphanage and industrial training school in Foochow, mainland China, until the Communists appropriated it. Some of the children with a leader made their way to Hong Kong, where a new orphanage was set up. Additional orphanages were established in Taiwan, and later in Korea. Dr. Poling, Lil felt, would be able to help her with the big plan she had for the leprosarium—the Occupational Therapy Room and a halfway house for women patients who had been cured but who, coming straight from the colony, would not be accepted into society.

He listened intently to her story and seemed as disappointed as she when he had to say, "We just can't take on any new kind of work; we are already overcommitted. I wish I had the eighteen thousand dollars you need." He spread his palms despairingly flat on the top of the big table in the office board room, his bushy eyebrows drawn together.

"Well," said Lil, standing up to go, "if you ever get any money designated for leprosy work, will you keep this in mind?"

Dr. Poling readily agreed. "But I must in all fairness point out that we don't receive gifts of that sort—designated for kinds of work in which we are not already doing something." He took her hands in his. "If we do, it's yours."

A few days later, he let out one of his rare exclamations, as he sat at his desk looking at the mail. "By George!" It was a check for eighteen thousand dollars, marked *"for leprosy work."*

"That woman has the Lord working for her," he said, passing the word to his associates and shaking his head wonderingly. The Christian Herald Occupational Therapy Room and the Home for Women became a reality in 1954.

The therapy building rose just below the Church of the Lepers. It was a bright, airy room, with wide windows overlooking the valley. There was a fireplace for cold, gloomy days, and work to do so that suffering and loneliness could for a little while be forgotten. It became a social center, sewing center, all-purpose room. Here Christmas parties were held, and gifts distributed around a Christmas tree. Here Lil arranged teas for the women to help them feel like women again—with candlelight and table linens. Here clothing and the bits of costume jewelry were distributed.

Of one such party, Lil wrote to her friends at home: "I went early with much brightly colored crepe paper and flowers to make the tables ready. We had ordered especially nice cakes and candies and had carefully ironed the dresses sent from America, second-hand but not noticeably so. Each dress had been folded and wrapped in colored tissue paper and tied with ribbon. After worship and special singing, they had their refreshments and then we presented each guest with a beautifully wrapped parcel as a gift—not an old dress flung contemptuously to a leper patient who must accept bitter charity because she has need. Such happiness they had in opening the parcels, comparing their dresses, trying them on."

At the leprosarium, the Chinese New Year, which usually falls in February and is the most important family holiday of the year in Taiwan, was always a sad and often a tragic day. For this is homecoming time—something like Christmas in America. The patients could not return home, except in their thoughts—and sometimes these were too crushing to endure. Remembering the joys they had once had with their families, several usually took their lives at this season meant for happiness.

To brighten the day, Lil planned a New Year's party in the spacious Therapy Room. First there was a service of worship, in which the soldier's choir sang, "Jesus Is All the World to Me." Most of these Christian soldiers had met the Lord in the leprosarium. After the worship part of the program, refreshments were readied. As Lil played the accordion to create a background of music and gaiety, she noticed many of the women patients slipping up to the front of the room to look at the pictures tacked to a bulletin board on the wall. The pictures were of their children, taken at Christmas time. The mothers were reassuring themselves that their children were well and happy.

When Lil announced that Dr. Poling was coming out for another visit, the patients immediately began wondering how to thank him, and through him the donor.

Then they had an idea. Out of the now eight hundred patients there was one who had skill enough to make a worthy gift. Chhoa—his name was the same as that of the pastor who had first appealed to Lil to visit the leprosarium—once had been a talented wood carver, but for twenty years he had not touched a chisel. Though his fingers had nearly wasted away, the others told him, "You must make the gift."

Lil brought him a block of camphor wood and the tools he needed. With the chisel strapped to the stump of one hand and the mallet strapped to the other, he roughed out the figure of a water buffalo—the beast of burden of Taiwan. Gradually it took shape.

The mallet sometimes clumsily missed its mark and blood flowed from Chhoa's finger stumps and mixed with the fragrant wood chips. He wrapped bandages around the stumps and went on with his work. Out of the persistent strokes, the water buffalo emerged. The gift was ready when Dr. Poling came.

This was the start of a new career for Chhoa. He soon lost count of the number of carvings he made for presentation to visitors and for sale. In a showcase at the Therapy Room, along with samples of his work, were displayed beautifully and intricately embroidered towels and scarves worked by the women. Sister Alma, hovering over the patients like a mother hen, her white starched deaconess' hat, white collar, and black gown always immaculate, emphasized to visitors that all were carefully disinfected—the washable pieces by Sister Alma herself, a personal labor of love.

Always Lil's was a bitter-sweet life. Through some blunder, the milk sold in Taipei became contaminated. Hundreds of babies died, including several at An-Lok. Each time, a little coffin would have to be made and Lil would go sadly to the leprosarium to face parents with the news, "The baby I carried away to take care of for you is dead." She would rather have died herself. Her own griefs she could bear; to share the grief of another was almost unbearable.

After the funeral of one baby in the Church of the Lepers, the mother of another came to Lil and said shyly, "My husband and I know that our baby is ill. We have prepared our hearts for the worst. If our baby dies, we don't want you to grieve." Their utter unselfishness fell on Lil's bruised heart like a benediction.

"God Will Take Care of You," Lil and the patients sang to each other.

Something could be learned from almost every experience. In the church one morning Lil was presented with a bill. "What's this?" she said.

"We held a funeral in the Therapy Room," the leaders told her. "We didn't want you to know."

It was the funeral of a boy who once had been a patient and whose father was still a patient. The boy had responded to sulfones and was cured. From the leprosarium he went to Observation Home for several months. When his disease did not return, relatives were allowed to take him to their home; his mother had run away.

They told Lil the rest of the story. At school, the boy had been taunted, "Your father is a leper!" The taunts made him so miserable he committed suicide—at the age of eleven.

"We made a mistake," Lil said to her assistants. "We shouldn't have let him go where anyone knew about his father or that he had been in the leprosarium."

When the mother of baby Joy became negative, she went to the Christian Herald Home for Women, the baby with her. After six months, still negative, she was ready to leave.

Lil gave her a piece of motherly advice. "Don't ever go to the leprosarium again," she said. "Don't talk about it. Don't even come to see me. Don't do anything to connect your life with leprosy, not only for your sake, but for your child's sake."

Lil lifted Joy to her lap and held her close. You could not take a baby into your heart and let her slip out again without feeling an emptiness.

The woman married a Christian and had a happy home, Lil learned, when she came back once for a quick visit. Lil saw her occasionally on the street, Joy with her, now toddling along. But there was no sign of recognition. This, too, was the price of love.

17. A Grain of Mustard Seed

"Be sure to write!" Lil's relatives and friends said to her when she and Jim had first sailed to the far Pacific in 1927. The request was really not necessary. Writing was in Lil's blood, transfused in part by Glenn Clark. Communicating ideas, and particularly communicating emotions, was something she not only enjoyed doing but felt the compulsion to do.

"At first," she says, "I wrote just to relatives and friends. Then sometimes they would ask me to send letters to someone else. I added those names to the list." She made carbon copies; then, as the list grew, she mimeographed the letters on an old Japanese duplicator. There was no regular schedule; they were sent as she had something to say and money for postage.

The letters were pounded out on her typewriter usually late at night in the little study where she kept her best-loved books. Every morning also she was there early, for a "quiet time" before the day's onslaught.

She had another reason for writing: "Among the missionaries, nobody seemed to have my ideas, and I was thought a little odd.

Outdoor meetings were not usual, and neither were outdoor Sunday schools. In fact, all the things I did seemed to be different. When I first wrote, I had no thought of anyone's sending money. I was pouring out my heart, telling what I thought of things I saw happen. But money did come in. I tried to use it carefully, but I used it all. It was a gift from God and I used it just as it came, trying to alleviate suffering."

In 1951, she began sending out monthly mimeographed letters, partly as a thank-you to people who wrote in response to an article about her work which appeared in *Christian Herald* magazine, partly for the sake of her own morale. "To have a wide circle of friends I can write to once a month is a wonderful safety valve, for I can share my problems with you," she wrote. "It keeps us from getting that terribly alone feeling that we often used to get here on the island. Students mimeograph the letter for me after school. I could send out more if you know people who would be interested—"

Every letter had in it somewhere a bit of verse—perhaps some of the same ones that had been pasted in the lids of food jars in British Guiana. Every letter shared the vignettes of her life that others in their own lives might have passed by as being commonplace, but which made her readers feel that they were personally involved.

She told her readers one month, "My report letter is not laboriously composed as some seem to think. It is just a slice out of my life, a cross-section of what happens in our little world. Every day is exciting, interesting, tantalizing in its terrific challenge; every night I am spent emotionally, physically, and mentally, but satisfied, because it is for the Lord. It does not matter that our work consists of fulfilling humble, homely needs of the common people, for they are aching needs, and it was once the common people who heard Him gladly."

Always, making her rounds—and the circle of her "rounds" grew larger and larger—she carried a notebook, jotting down not only the needs to be met, but impressions, incidents, that she wanted to pass on to others who would never themselves walk among lepers or headhunters or visit an island of need halfway around the world.

The number grew from fifty letters a month to the hundreds, to the thousands. When Marilyn returned to Taiwan from college in 1954, she was appalled by her mother's haphazard mailing list and promptly and neatly organized the names in alphabetical order in card file drawers. Lil had just never had time. Mimeographing eventually had to give way to offset duplication. Finally, the addressing of envelopes—five thousand every month for airmail, and twenty thousand every two months for surface mail—and other clerical chores required full-time help. Lil refused to use an addressing machine lest the personal touch be lost. As the list grew and as the volume of contributions increased, a California friend, Eleanor Doan, who was visiting Formosa, suggested to Lil, "You ought to incorporate."

"I don't want to be a corporation," Lil protested. "I'm just me!"

"It's not fair to people who contribute if they can't get income tax deduction for their gifts just because you don't want to do anything to help them!"

Maybe Miss Doan had something there, Lil conceded; maybe it was possible to think too exclusively of the needs close at hand. If anyone on Formosa came to her and asked for help, she would of course give it. When Americans asked for help—

A "treasure hunt" finished off the process of convincing Lil. It wasn't altogether as unlikely as it sounded. There was just enough sense to it to make it interesting—as with fishing, which is done with no positive assurance, only the possibility, that fish are to be had. Lil had explained with gusto all about buried treasure to a Norwegian doctor in Ping-tung, a thriving city near Kaohsiung and the Great Salt Coast, in the southwest of the island. The doctor had a hospital in a fine old Japanese house.

"The Japanese had to leave Taiwan hurriedly," Lil said, "and empty-handed. Some of them were quite wealthy. They couldn't take their wealth with them, so what would they do with it?"

"Give it to someone?"

"Probably not. Their feeling toward the Taiwanese was bitter."

"Leave it here somewhere?"

"Exactly! Only the rich would have anything to leave, and so we can narrow down the possibilities to the nicer houses that were here in the days of the occupation." She looked around at the ornate hall in which they were standing; the large rooms had been converted into wards and even the corridors had beds here and there for the overflow. "A house like this one, for example."

The doctor stroked his chin thoughtfully. "So. A house like this one—" He looked speculatively at the walls.

"But I do not think a rich man would hide his treasure in his house, for fear the house might burn down." She walked slowly toward the door leading to a garden; the doctor followed. "The Japanese are lovers of gardens and can do more with a small plot than any other people in the world." This garden still showed the care that once had been lavished upon it, though now it was a functional place in which recuperating patients sat and walked in the cool of the day.

"I think," said Lil, her eyes wandering around the garden, "a Japanese would hide his treasure outdoors, in his own little garden. He would have to hide it under some specific object, so that he could tell his grandson, 'It's under that large boulder, or—" she saw a heavy stone seat between two trees, so heavy it looked as if it had never been moved—"under that seat. That's a likely spot for treasure to be buried."

The next time Lil visited the Ping-tung hospital, a member of the staff asked her, "*What* did you tell the doctor? As soon as you left, he moved that heavy stone seat in the garden, called for a shovel, and began to dig furiously."

"Did he get anything?" Lil asked.

"Blisters!"

Jim's friendship with the Taiwanese who had been unwilling vassals to the Japanese overlords brought him many "tips" about buried treasure. And just often enough to keep interest aroused, stories appeared in the newspapers about treasure troves.

"Another find in the Philippines," Lil noted one morning at the breakfast table.

"The government always gets most of it," Jim observed. "By the way, they say there's gold buried over there under a Japanese admiral's house—in Baguio."

Lil had an idea. "Jim, you need to get away for a rest. You've been looking tired. Why don't you go to the Philippines for a few weeks?" The Philippine Islands to the south and east were only a short, inexpensive hop by plane. "And maybe Phil Hogan would like to go along." Phil was Jim's close friend, and was living with them at the time.

"I don't see how I could get away," Jim said.

"What about weaving looms?" Lil asked. "Didn't you want to get one of the kind the Filipino mountain people use, so that you could have some made for the mountain people here?"

Jim's eyes lighted. "You're right! Looms! I believe I'll do it!" He smiled. "Maybe we *could* go to Baguio, too." He rushed off to invite Phil Hogan.

Two weeks later, Jim sent Lil a light-hearted cable from Manila: "TRIP SUCCESSFUL. YOU'RE WORTH A MILLION."

Glen Graber of the Mennonite Mobile Unit had dropped in at the Dickson home in Taipei the morning the cable arrived. The Mobile Unit was going back to the mountains; Glen had been rendering invaluable service at the leprosarium, in prisons, wherever he was needed. His wife, a trained nurse, had been running the An-Lok Baby Home. Glen, thinking Lil was receiving bad news, read the cable over her shoulder. When Lil chuckled and turned around, Glen, towering over her, gave her a strange look, smiled politely and excused himself.

Lil said one day to Glen, "Suppose it had been true—that we had a million dollars and I could have some of it. I've been trying to plan the kind of mission board I'd like to have. Not a big board—just a few people who would be willing to help, sort of the love-of-God-in-action type. We would just do the work we saw to do, believe the Bible, do exactly as it says. That's the kind of board I'd like."

She picked up a book and turned to a page.

"What's that?" Glen asked. "One of your daily devotional reading books?" He smiled, for Lil was forever calling someone's attention to particular readings which had impressed her and which often she underlined in red.

"This one is *Gathered Gold* by Julia Grange," Lil said. "Listen: 'There is a solution to every problem, whatever you may think to the contrary. Never say despairingly, "There is no way out." The difficulty is within yourself. You are biased by prejudice, custom and an orthodox way of looking at things.' " She handed the book to Glen. The words "an orthodox way of looking at things" were underlined in red.

"That's the trouble with so many mission boards," she said. "They begin doing certain things a certain way, and then they never can do anything else or do them any other way."

Glen smiled. "You're as orthodox as they come."

"I don't mean theologically. You can be unorthodox theologically and terribly orthodox in method. I'd rather have it the other way around. When there's a job to be done, let's do it. More things are left undone than this world dreams of, because somebody called a committee meeting. First you have to meet the glaring need, and then you can meet the real need—the deep-down problem."

Glen said quietly, "Why wait for the million dollars? Let's set up a board anyway. Even if there isn't any money."

"It would have to be a board," Lil dreamed out loud, "that allowed flexibility. When someone comes along with a problem a little out of the ordinary, we don't want to say, 'Sorry, we can't handle that because it's not our kind of work.' *People* will be our kind of work, the humble people who have no one to stand up for them, no one to care for them—"

Glen, dressed in his usual black suit, and Lil, dressed in her usual blue dress, thought it out.

"Too many churches have 'mission work' because it's a part of the church costume," Lil continued, "the way a girl carries a pocketbook, whether she has anything in it or not. Mission work has to be a passion, not a profession. And when it's a passion, you don't go by the book—except by the one Book." She paused.

"You've got to have a name for your board," Glen pointed out.

"It will take faith," Lil went on. "Faith as a grain of mustard seed—how about 'Mustard Seed' for a name?" She leafed through a Bible to Matthew 17:20: " 'If ye have faith as a grain of mustard seed, ye shall say unto this mountain, Remove hence to yonder place; and it shall remove; and nothing shall be impossible unto you.' "

And so, on January 4, 1954, Mustard Seed, Inc., was set up as a nonprofit corporation under the laws of California, with Harold LeVesconte, Lil's brother who was an attorney, as treasurer. Contributors now could claim United States income tax deduction.

"It must be the first time a Bible verse was ever incorporated!" Glen commented.

Corporate status did not of itself provide income; always Lil's work had been and would continue to be a work of faith. The Mustard Seed office in its early days was in the Dicksons' mission compound home. "I started it in the study," Lil says, "then later we took the upstairs bedroom and all the rooms out back. Behind every door you could find a secretary or somebody working." Again, the other missionaries on the compound wondered at Mrs. Dickson's "unorthodoxy," though they were becoming accustomed to almost anything sitting on or baaing from or hurrying in or out of the Dickson end of the property. Lil had to close in a section of the second-story veranda to make an extra room to accommodate a homeless mother and child, and this architectural transgression, though neatly done, also raised a number of eyebrows.

Preparing the monthly letter became a sizable chore. It had to be duplicated, folded by hand, inserted in envelopes which had been addressed, stamped, sealed, and taken to the post office. Taiwan is blessed with a postal administration which delights in new stamp issues; Lil early found that her letters were more attractive when mailed with stamps of several smaller denominations than with one stamp for the whole amount, and when the combination was as different as possible each time. This would not have been a particular problem, except that Taiwanese stamps are ungummed because of the island's humidity. Each Taiwanese post office has a paste pot and brush for the use of patrons in sticking stamps on their letters. Lil's mailings, with thousands of letters and three or four stamps to a lettter, became an assembly-line operation. A wide, flat paintbrush was used for applying paste to whole strips of stamps at one swipe, then they had to be torn apart and stuck on the envelopes before the paste dried. Envelopes, also ungummed, had to be sealed in the same manner.

This particular month, the letter had been mimeographed, folded, sealed in the envelopes. Then the whole house seemed to come to a standstill.

Catherine, a Taiwanese girl—one of Lil's "young people," as she affectionately calls her assistants—came to Lil's desk and said cheerfully, "Mrs. Dickson, we're ready to put on the stamps."

"There's no money for stamps," Lil replied. "We just can't send out the lettter."

Catherine's cheer did not falter. She was accustomed to money crises at Mustard Seed. Mrs. Dickson was the despair of some of her assistants with business backgrounds who were accustomed to orderly, predictable ways of doing things. Often, on the day before a payday—Lil herself has never received a salary—there would not be nearly enough in bank accounts in Taipei or California. But if some other need arose that could be met, a genuine need, Lil would promptly write a check and hand it over, depleting the funds by that much. "God can fill only an empty vessel," she would tell her assistants.

"And He can always count on you to empty it!" they sometimes felt like answering.

She wrote in her journal: "What if one of the disciples, instead of passing out the loaves and fishes to the hungry and needy, had thought, 'I will keep them a little while, save them, then I will pass them out later'—and suddenly the Saviour should stand beside him with a searching, reproving look. Could the disciple stand that gaze, I wonder? 'I gave these to you to pass out to the hungry,' the Saviour might say. 'Why have you kept them? Do you not know that God will give to you all that He can trust you to give away?' "

Her young people had seen modern miracles of loaves and fishes. They remembered the day at the end of the month, when at twenty minutes to noon there was no money and when at ten minutes to noon it had taken four men to carry in the baskets of money; someone who owed a sum to Mustard Seed had made a deposit to their account. Not that the amount involved was so tremendous—though when you do not have it, any amount is tremendous—but the exchange rate then was much inflated. At one time shortly after the war it had cost more than eighty thousand dollars in local currency to send a first-class airmail letter to a foreign country. That dipped eventually to ten New Taiwanese dollars, equivalent of twenty-five cents U.S., with a stabilized exchange rate of forty to one.

On another morning, one of the young people said, "We have to send a great deal of money out to the clinics today. What are we going to do? We don't have the money."

Lil answered blithely, "The day is not yet done!"

The money came in the afternoon mail.

Not long after this, Lil herself grew uneasy about money. The same young man turned to her and said, "The day is not yet done!" Before the day was done, the need had been met.

Even the clerk in the postal station used by Mustard Seed had a hopeful manner of speaking. When he checked Lil's box and found it empty, he never said, "You have no letter," but always, "Your letter has not yet arrived."

So Catherine was not unduly dismayed by the lack of twenty thousand dollars—five hundred dollars U.S.—for stamps. But it did mean that the young people working on the mailing would have to do something else to fill in the time.

An older woman who helped with the housekeeping wandered out of the kitchen and was surprised by the lack of bustling activity so typical of the office.

"No money for stamps," Catherine explained to her.

"But there *is* money," the woman said, drying her hands on her apron. She walked over to Lil. "You have the money, Mrs. Dickson. It's wrapped in a towel in the linen closet!"

"Linen closet?" Lil went with her. The woman reached her arm as high as she could, searched with her fingers, brought down a towel-wrapped hard-cornered parcel. Lil pulled back the towel, revealing two large blocks of crisp Taiwanese bills.

"Now I remember!" Lil gasped. "Three or four weeks ago I thought I had too much cash on hand. Where can I put it? I wondered. Then I thought of wrapping it in a towel, thinking it would never occur to a thief to look in the linen closet."

The amount was just enough to send out the newsletter.

But not all Lil's problems were resolved so painlessly. Separated for long periods from her own children, she waited for their letters anxiously. On every furlough she and Jim spent as much time as possible with them. Marilyn had been back to Formosa when she was sixteen, but Ronny had never returned since leaving in 1940. When Lil saw the uniformed special messenger coming up the walk one day in July, 1952, she had a premonition that this one was for her, not for the office. The cable handed her read, "RONNY HAS POLIO."

18. Boys Behind Bars

Never had America seemed so far away to Lil. "Shall I go to Ronny?" she asked Jim.

"You will have to make the decision," he said gently. "Our furlough is due next year . . ."

Lil spent a sleepless night. She knew as well as Jim that there was no money now for a trip. She knew too that Ronny's wife would be with him; how hard it was for a mother to relinquish her priority. If she somehow managed to go, all she could do for Ronny would be to see him, and to pray for him. She could pray, with all her mother love, right where she was. And in her mind's eye, she could see him, too—the baby she so desperately wanted; the toddler to whose crib she crept anxiously in the night; the lad who excitedly watched the bombing planes go out across the Taiwan Strait; the boy who at first grudgingly and then happily practiced piano in a jungle village; the tall young man . . .

Ronny had fourteen years with his mother and father—nine of them in Formosa and five in British Guiana. Like his father, Ronny grew husky, big-boned. Like his mother, he developed a love of music, poetry, and literature, inheriting also his grandmother's gift for painting, which had apparently skipped one generation. Ronny's insatiable appetite for reading spurred not only his writing, in which he was a perfectionist, but his thinking, in which he was highly independent. Never satisfied with "pat" answers, he chose always to think things out for himself; and when he had done so, he could explain his views articulately.

After staying with his uncle, Lester LeVesconte, for three years while he attended high school in Elmhurst, Illinois, Ronny entered Park College in Kansas in 1948. Though brainy, Ronny was by no means an academic recluse; he got along well with people—"always rich in friends," his mother puts it. In his junior year he married Lois Forrey, daughter of missionaries. The future looked bright for the alert twenty-year-old six-footer and his pretty wife.

Following graduation from college in June, 1952, he tackled his master's degree at the University of Kansas City, in Missouri, studying during the day, working at night. Insurance for poliomyelitis was popular; both Ronny and Lois took out five-thousand-dollar policies. A month later, the dreaded paralysis struck him.

After a year in the hospital, doctors told him he would have to spend the rest of his life in bed. Ronny, still refusing to accept pontifical pronouncements, not only fought his way up into a wheelchair, but went back to school, completing his master's in 1956. The next year he entered the University of Chicago to work on his doctorate. After he had completed all requirements but his dissertation, his advising professor moved to England; the new professor asked him to select another subject. Ronny wrote to his parents: "I'm not going to spend the rest of my life working on a Ph.D.!" In 1960, he and Lois moved to San Francisco. Lois took a position in a travel agency, and Ronny's talent with words found ready acceptance in advertising. He's still an advertising man, still uses the wheelchair for the most part, but can get around with a crutch and drives his own car. They have no children.

Part of the cost of being a missionary, Lil had known all along, was that one's own children were so far away, so soon. She had her own son with her for a comparatively few years, but there had been other boys, close at hand, who needed mothering . . .

A girl who helped with the outdoor Sunday-school work had

brought some of these boys to Lil's attention as she was packing up her accordion after a Taipei street-corner meeting one Sunday evening. It was 1950, during the tense time of transition in Taiwan. No one knew whether the Communists would attack, only that they were boasting on their radio broadcasts, "When we take Taiwan, one million people will die!"

The girl was saying, "There are twenty-five little boys—maybe more—in a police station in the city. I know the man in charge and I can get you in. She added, "I think you should talk to those boys."

"I'll let you know," Lil said to her, picking up the heavy accordion case and looking for a taxi.

Lil talked to Jim that evening about the boys. "I'm not anxious to do it," she admitted. "With martial law, you get into trouble if you look sideways."

"Trouble," Jim sagely observed, "doesn't seem to be something you work hard at avoiding."

"But to walk right into the lion's mouth—right into a police station—I don't know about that."

"But, you see," Jim reminded her, "you're not visiting the police—you're visiting twenty-five little boys."

"Well—" For once, Lil had no answer.

When the girl asked her a second time, Lil felt she could not resist the invitation. With Everlasting Life, she went to the police station and was admitted. The boys—heads shaved, shabbily dressed, barefooted—were allowed to come to one small room and crouch on the floor, while Lil, with her accordion, taught them to sing, gave them a Bible lesson, and had prayer.

After that, she came every week. When the service was over, many of the boys crowded around her, talking, sharing confidences. Perhaps something in my face reminds them of their mothers, Lil thought.

"I'm not bad, I'm not," one little lad of ten kept saying to her softly, during one visit.

"They're so hungry for mother-love," Lil said to Jim one day, "hungry for anything at all that is good and clean and decent.

Society pushes them into jail and forgets them, and thinks it has dealt with the problem!"

A few weeks later she heard of a larger prison just outside of Taipei, where there were many boys. This time she felt courageous enough to take the initiative in visiting it. Piling a big bundle of used Christmas cards into a taxi with her, she set out. At the prison, she gave the guards generous bunches of the cards, and they smiled and let her go in.

Inside, she found about a hundred and fifty very dirty boys, thrown together with older men, some of whom were senile, or deranged, and derelicts of all kinds. The ancient buildings adjoining a prison factory were located on low ground and the floors had not been adequately elevated; Lil could see high-water mud marks on the walls. "Why are you so *dirty?*" Lil asked one of the boys. Surely, anyone could keep *clean.*

"No water for baths," he replied, shattering her indignation and substituting anger of a different kind. When she saw some of the prisoners taking water for cooking their rice from a trench into which others had urinated, she was seething.

Lil confronted an official. "I would like to come each week and hold Sunday school."

He consulted a chart. "Sunday morning at seven-thirty would do," he decided. "Before the boys go to work at the looms."

"I'll be here," she said grimly. Using her own money for taxi fare, she returned not only that Sunday, but week after week. As at the police station, the Bible lesson was the preface to getting acquainted. While the boys clustered around, Lil and her helper would find out where they came from, why they were there, how long they had been there, and all the other things that small boys would like to be able to tell their mothers if they could.

"Do you know, Jim," she reported to her husband after one of her visits, "a lot of them are there not because they stole or anything like that, but simply because they didn't have a residential permit!"

"Residential permits are important," Jim said. "If the police didn't have some check, the Communists could infiltrate."

"But *little boys!*" Lil scoffed. "Perhaps they changed their pants and forgot to move the permit from one pair to the other. And some of them came over from the mainland with the soldiers or with relatives and never had permits in the first place. They're just little street boys with no home at all. The police arrest them as *vagrants!* Once they're put into prison, they're forgotten."

To be arrested without a residential permit on one's person, Lil found, meant a three-month term. After the time was up, unless an adult sponsored the boy, he had to stay on in prison. Because the police were too busy to contact the parents, many of them had no idea what had become of their boy. Lil talked to one youngster, sentenced to three months, who had been there for seven years. By then, he had no one left in the world to come for him; he was an orphan.

Lil concluded there were two things she could do: she could be the sponsor for boys ready to come out, and try to help them get back to their homes; and she could do something about the prison housekeeping.

Again she sought out a prison official. "You have boys here who could leave if they had a sponsor. Is that correct?" Lil asked.

"That is correct," he admitted.

"Then I will be their sponsor."

The official looked up from the papers on his desk, studied Lil through his heavy glasses, and asked the question that, more readily than any other, identifies the dimensions of a man's heart. *"Why?"*

"Someone must do it."

"You understand there is much work and time involved in processing the boys out. There are many papers—"

"I have time," said Lil.

So the wheels were set turning. Lil helped get the boys out, sending them back to their homes with various of her helpers.

In one case, a father who, it turned out, was wealthy, had mourned his son for over a year. Thinking him dead, he had adopted another boy. Now, happily, he had two sons.

Because a rickshaw coolie knew the district another boy came from, Lil asked him to escort the boy to his home in the mountains above west-coast Tainan. The coolie was not a Christian but he was an honest man and Lil knew he would do his best to find the boy's parents. When he returned, he said, "When I got there with this boy, the whole village gathered round. They asked, 'Who found him? Who took him out?' I told them this is what Christians do."

At the same time Lil began "housekeeping." The officials, as at the leprosarium, were willing to let her do anything that made them look good, as long as it didn't cost them any money, effort, or worry. One of the first things she did was to have concrete walks built from building to building, to lift the boys out of the dirt and mud. "I never heard of people using money like that, but it's my own money, so I guess it's all right," she said to Jim.

Next, Lil repaired the beds. Then she and her helpers painted the inside of the entire prison.

Clean clothes were something else they needed—but before that, baths. "I'd like to take the boys out tomorrow," she said to the official.

"For what?" he asked.

"Baths!"

He threw up his hands.

Miss Marjorie Bly, a missionary nurse, was with Lil that day. "We marched them to a duck pond," Lil remembers, "soaped them down, then let them go swimming. We had to repeat the process about five times, until we got down to the skin."

She enlisted Dr. Dale to give them medical attention; most of the boys had scabies, and no wonder. Many suffered from trachoma.

Lil was full of "unorthodox" methods to secure her objectives—in this case, piped-in water and better conditions generally. When she could get them to go, she took American Aid personnel along with her to the prison, always pointedly introducing her visitors to the officials, and emphasizing that they were "very big men with American Aid." She brought along some of the American military to help with the painting; this object lesson, too, was not lost on the embarrassed officials. One day, the painter who mixed the colors for her shook his head wonderingly and asked, "Do you know you've painted this prison four times?"

He did not know that she was painting it, if a bit deviously, right into new quarters. Eventually, new children's prisons were built, one in the south of the island, one in the center, one in the north. But these were to come much later.

Early one Sunday, Lil and Everlasting Life arrived for Sunday school and found a small boy tied to a chair. His eyes were so swollen with tears that they were almost closed. "He can't be more than four or five," Lil said indignantly. "Everlasting Life, untie him!"

Turning to a guard standing nearby, she demanded, "Why is this boy tied up?"

The guard shrugged. "He's always trying to run away."

"What crime is he charged with?"

The guard said apologetically, "He's a bank robber."

"A bank robber!" Lil exploded. "That little boy?"

Even the guard knew the strange story: The boy had followed the man who swept the building into the bank; everyone thought the boy belonged to him. The money in the bank was kept in large baskets, tied with string in bundles of ten thousand dollars N.T., which is about two hundred fifty dollars U.S. The child picked up one of these packages and walked out with nobody noticing. As he went down the street, he found that people were interested in what he had. When he took the string off, and started giving the pieces of paper away, he drew quite a crowd. The police came to see why so many people had gathered, and found this boy in the center with what was left of the bills. Quite freely he told where he had got them. The startled police took him to the bank, where the officials had him arrested.

He didn't understand banks and he didn't understand prisons. He was so small, he could go through almost any hole, and had escaped repeatedly.

"We'll look into this," Lil said indignantly to Everlasting Life. "Tomorrow when the regular officials are here, we'll see what can be done."

But when she returned on Monday, the lad—Robin Hood, Lil called him—was gone. He had found another hole. "He doesn't realize," said Lil sadly, shaking her head, "that the outside is simply a larger prison, for they will keep on hunting for him."

More boys were coming in all the time. In two years, Lil sponsored two hundred fifty of them. The fortunate ones had parents or relatives to whom they could be returned. Other boys in prison with no relatives could not be taken out; they had nowhere to go.

"I need a place for those boys," Lil said to Jim one day. "I've tried every denomination under the sun, asking if they would like to start a boys' home. No one can take it on. What shall I tell those boys—'Wait a few more years and maybe somebody will get around to you'?"

Jim sighed. "In a few more years they will no longer be boys!"

When Dr. Bob Pierce came to Taiwan for a visit in 1953, Lil took him out to the prison and explained the problem. "God helping me, *I'll* do it!" he promised. "But you'll have to give me two months, speaking with me in America, to help raise the money."

"I'm not glamorous," said Lil. "I'm just an old missionary."

"An old missionary makes it authentic," urged Dr. Pierce.

Lil looked at the boys who were watching eagerly. There was Hoa-te, resentment written all over his face. Hoa-te had come over from the mainland with the soldiers. He had no home, no place to go, and was one of many such boys. Perhaps if Hoa-te and others had a chance, the bitterness would fade from their eyes.

Lil turned to Dr. Pierce. "You let me know when."

She had long ago decided where she would build her boys' home. It should be south of the city, near the leprosarium, so that Sister Alma could oversee both places. A hilltop a half mile away from the Church of the Lepers would be the perfect spot. There was a knoll on which she could visualize a boys' church standing someday. There was space also for a dormitory and a dining room. If God wanted her to have that land, she would get it. But she couldn't ask God for something she didn't know anything about herself, not even the price.

After visiting the leprosarium one day, she went across to the other hill. An old woman lived there in a dirty house, next to a pigpen in which sprawled the biggest pig Lil had ever seen. Her first thought was, Will we ever get rid of the smell?

The old woman was willing to sell the land at a reasonable price. She had only one stipulation: "You must pay the money in two weeks."

A week passed, and only the normal operating funds came in the mail. Three days before the deadline, the postal clerk passed out several letters to Lil when she appeared. Inside one was a check for one thousand dollars, from someone Lil had never heard of. The letter said, "Use as you think best."

"God has sent us that money to buy the land," she told her staff. She made the required payment and went off to America. Early in 1954 she came back with ten thousand dollars U.S. The first big house, the nucleus of the Boys' Home, was built. Hoa-te was one of the first six boys to move in.

Things did not at first go well. The home was clean, it was beautiful, it was in the open country, and the boys had freedom. But they still had their prison psychology. The first leader was not successful. He had been an officer during the war, and ran the place military-style. "The boys do not need discipline," Lil tried to explain to him. "They need love."

When friends asked, "How are you getting along with your little criminals?" Lil bristled. "They are *not* criminals—they are just little boys."

Despite Lil's efforts at the prison, the boys there were dirty most of the time and were used to being in dirty surroundings. When she took them to the Boys' Home, she had to teach them to be clean. A bath every day and the floors washed every day were the rule—and are the rule in every Mustard Seed home today. Not only the boys but the leaders had to be trained.

"If the boys were *comparatively* clean, the leaders were satisfied," Lil recounts. "One time I went out to the Boys' Home to deliver the food money. The boys were all out playing and having a good time; the leader was sitting comfortably. The place was dirty. It hadn't been cleaned or scrubbed. I took the leader out to the potato patch—in this land you must never rebuke anyone in front of someone else.

"I laid down the law to him: Now, see here, you have thirty boys—big enough to be grown men. I work hard in the office, and I can't come out and scrub the floor for these great big boys. They should keep their own place clean, and it is *not* clean. We are having a *home* for boys, and that means a decent, respectable place."

She waved a wad of bills under his nose. "There will be no food money until this place is clean and those boys clean it! Not only today, but every day!"

She took the food money with her back to the city, and heard afterward that Sister Alma fed them supper that night. "I've never had to say a word about cleaning since then!"

Lil has strong ideas about cleanliness and laziness. "There comes a time in a boy's life when a parent has to do a little stern talking. That happens in any home as well as here. At our place, if a boy has bad marks and must drop out of school, then it is time for him to start working. Somehow, the leaders hate to talk to a boy about this. They bring the boy to me, and I have to talk to him. If that doesn't work, then Jim talks to him. We say, 'Unless you work, you can't eat. God made that rule—we didn't. We've helped you this far, now you have to stand on your own feet.' "

But when the time comes for a boy to hunt a job, and after she has talked to him like a Dutch aunt, Lil is immediately on the telephone, developing leads, smoothing the way ahead of him, finding a place where he can live, and even underwriting his room and board for a while if necessary.

Lil's trips to the prison continued. Glen Graber often accompanied her. His good naturedness was built on the same generous scale as his body. Very seldom was he without a sparkle in his eye and the hint of laughter in his voice. When his eyes did cloud and his voice become stern, he was a formidable opponent.

"You know," Lil said one morning before they set out for the prison, "I see the boys and men in the front rooms, but I have never been in the back rooms of the prison. I wonder what's there?"

"Bluebeard's closet!" Glen suggested.

"That may not be funny," Lil said uneasily. "They have never taken us into those rooms—"

"I'll tell you what we'll do," Glen said. "We'll go out there with the pastor and just blunder right on through."

After they had been with the boys for a while, Glen whispered, "Time to get lost." Off he started, Lil and the pastor in his wake. At the end of a corridor, they came to a door, and went on through. Casually, Glen opened one door after another. In the lead, he was smiling all the way—until he opened the last door. Lil, nearest to him, saw his face suddenly harden. He stood still for a moment as if to bar the way, then his big hands relaxed, and he moved ahead of Lil and the pastor into the room. Several men were lounging in bunks, making incoherent noises, going through odd, repetitive motions; one could see at a glance they were deranged.

But this was not the sight that riveted their attention. At a table sat a boy about four years old. The child had the saddest face Lil had ever seen—wan, wistful, completely defeated. Then she saw his club feet. They were turned in once, then turned in again; he could not possibly walk.

A guard hurried into the room. "You have lost your way! This is not the way out. Come, I will show you."

Perhaps we have found our way, Lil thought, the shock of it still heavy upon her. That night, a sad face appeared before her no matter how she turned nor whether her eyes were open or shut.

In the morning when Glen Graber came, he looked at her strangely. "I can see that you did not sleep either," he said. "The pastor and I will go and get him."

When they returned, the pastor was carrying the boy in his arms. "His name is Peng-Heng. He is an orphan. He cried when we left the prison—it is all the home he remembers."

"How did you get him out?" Lil asked.

Glen explained, "We just picked him up and walked off with him."

The three of them took Peng-Heng to Mackay Hospital. He

was a lonely boy when they left him. A few days later, when Lil approached his bed, he looked up brightly and dry-eyed. "Peng-Heng," she said gently, "do you want to go back to the prison now?"

He smoothed the clean white sheet and gave his shy answer. "This bed is *very* soft."

Lil put her arm around the small shoulders. The lad had never slept on anything but boards before. "We will take care of you," she promised.

The missionary surgeon felt that the misshapen feet could be straightened, "But we can't keep him here during the whole term of treatment."

"He will stay at our house," Lil decided.

"It will take two years," the doctor warned.

"What are two years if they change a boy's life?"

A Bible teacher came to the hospital every day and taught Peng-Heng of God's love. She found him responsive; he could memorize verses and prayers quickly, and she was proud of her pupil. After a series of operations—painful ones between which he stayed with the Dicksons—Peng-Heng could walk and run. By then, the Boys' Home was completed and well organized, and became Peng-Heng's home.

There was a boy in prison whose face in particular attracted Lil—a small earnest face that was always attentive during the Sunday-school lessons. From the records Lil knew that he had no father or mother living; he was the kind of boy she wanted for the Boys' Home. When Lil asked him when his sentence was up, the youngster smiled, and told her, "Two weeks."

"Would you like to come to my Boys' Home?" she asked.

The smile faded. "My grandfather has written that he wants me to come to live with him."

"Oh, you have a grandfather! Well, I will sponsor you out of prison, and see that you are taken to your grandfather's home."

The boy gave her a wistful look, and moved aside to make room for the others who were waiting to talk with this woman who seemed to care what happened to them.

When he was released, Lil arranged for one of her helpers to take the boy home, all the way to the mountains of the east coast. The helper returned with a strange tale.

They had taken the bus part way down the coast. Suddenly, the boy said, "We get off here." It wasn't a regular stop, and there was no road, not even a path. But the bus stopped, and the boy started confidently up the mountain. After much climbing, they came to the home of an old man, his wife, and their blind daughter. They were happy to see the boy.

"He is not really mine," the old man explained as his wife heated water for tea. "One day while I was cutting wood, I heard shrieks of distress and I hurried to where the cries came from. I found a woman trying to push this little boy over the cliff.

" 'Don't do that!' I shouted. 'If you don't want the boy, I'll take him.' And so she gave him to me." The old man sipped his bowl of tea, holding it in both hands as if to give warmth to his fingers and alertness to his memory. "It seems that a man had come from the mainland, bringing with him his second wife, and the child of his first wife. The second wife soon had a son of her own, and she wanted to destroy the first wife's son so that her boy would be heir to all they had. Which," the old man said shrewdly, "was not much. When her husband was away, she took first-wife's child, who was then about nine years old, up to the cliff overlooking the sea, and there she tried to push him over. He was old enough to struggle and I—" he mused, "—I was young enough to hear." The old woman sat respectfully silent and the blind daughter listened raptly to the story she must have heard many times.

"The boy lived with us," the old man said, "and became as dear to us as our own son." His voice broke. "During the war, the American bombing planes came. Our home was destroyed, my own son was killed. Perhaps it was a mistake, for who would bomb a mountain? We had nowhere to go but deeper into the mountains, where we found a cave and there we stayed, trying to find enough to eat. There was no food and we became so weak that we could hardly walk."

The old woman's eyes glistened as she lovingly watched her husband, who went on with the story. "One night I crawled from the cave to a neighbor's garden. With my own hands, I dug up some of his potatoes. They looked so good, there in the moonlight. And then I thought, that is stealing. I put them back, covered them over, and crawled to the cave.

"The boy found a chicken somewhere and brought it to us. For this he was put into prison—they said he stole it. Now these years later you have returned him."

Hearing this, Lil understood. The boy wanted to live in her Boys' Home, but he would not forget the old man who had saved his life.

"I have a plan," Lil happily announced to her staff. "We'll bring them *all* over—the old man, his wife, the blind daughter—and the boy can grow up in Boys' Home with other children his own age. We'll find a little house for the others." The staff approved but didn't quite see how this project could be wholly justified. "Well—" Lil thought a moment. "It *was* an American bomber."

Many of her boys came from prison where they had picked up gambling and other activities she frowned upon. To counteract these influences, she tried to provide them with wholesome recreation. She liked to see boys on horseback, so she bought two horses, which were comparatively cheap.

The boys loved the horses. But the leaders, feeling that a horse ate as much as a man and did nothing but stand around, begrudged every mouthful the horses got. When Lil went to the Boys' Home she found the horses "so lean that you could see just how they were put together!" Not only had they eaten all the grass, but in desperation had taken to eating leaves. As high up as they could reach, all around the place, the leaves were gone.

"What did you do about the horses?" Jim asked, his cowboy solicitude reasserting itself, when Lil returned from the home one evening after dark.

"Shhh!" Lil cautioned. "I brought them with me. They're in the garage. Don't worry," she added hastily, "the door is shut! Nobody will know."

"Lil," Jim said firmly, "you can't have two horses in a garage without people knowing!"

"I couldn't let them starve, could I?" Lil argued. "Besides, it's the rainy season, and not many people will be out."

For a week Lil plied her horses with bran and even cod liver oil, trying to restore them to health. As the rain slacked off and the sun shone, she watched her chance to let them out to eat some grass.

One of the missionaries stopped by the Dicksons' house that evening. "You know," she said, "I looked out today and I thought to myself, Why, that looks like a horse! Well, I knew it *couldn't* be a horse."

"It was a horse," said Lil glumly. She added brightly, "I'm just fattening them up for a couple of days—"

"Fattening horses—for *what?*"

"I mean, well, really, I'm taking them right back."

When Lil returned the horses to Boys' Home, she gave strict orders about what they were to be fed. However, Lil's horses just didn't seem to be under divine protection. For in a few weeks one of the horses died. Undaunted, Lil bought another horse, so that she still would have two. One of them made a considerable contribution to the Christmas Eve pageant put on by the boys. When the Wise Men appeared in quite respectable black beards, Lil noticed the boys nudging each other and laughing. They couldn't keep their secret: They had cut off part of the horses' tails to make the whiskers.

Hoa-te grew up in Boys' Home—Hoa-te, the bitter little rebel from the mainland, without mother, father, home, even homeland. Gradually, the bitterness left him. After he finished school, he went to work for an automobile company. Then he was called for military service.

Just before he left for the army, he was attacked by juvenile hoodlums in Taipei who thought he was the leader of a rival gang. One of them beat Hoa-te while the others held him. The police rounded up the boys and called Hoa-te to the police station to bring charges. He came bandaged, but able to walk. The father of the boy who had beaten him was there, too.

"You must lay your charge against the boy who was responsible," the police told him.

Hoa-te looked at the boy for a long moment.

"This boy is not to blame," he said finally. "He hasn't had Christian training and is not as fortunate as I am. I have no charge to make."

Meanwhile, Lil was making her regular visits to the leprosarium, and when she was away for even a few days at a time, troubles seemed to multiply. She returned home from one short trip to Hong Kong to discover that the man she had put in charge of radio broadcasts over the loudspeaker system had inadvertently tuned in a Communist station—almost the unpardonable sin. Lil made apologies as best she could.

Jim was busy too; he always had some project going on. The enthusiastic reception given a visiting dentist in mountain villages where he pulled teeth from morning to night, convinced Jim that some of the mountain young people ought to be trained to do this kind of work, though he was informed that the government could not set up a school of dentistry. Lil was startled one evening when at the end of a hard day she walked into their living room and saw in the dim light a spooky row of heads on the mantel, all tilted backward, mouths gaping.

Approaching the mantel cautiously, she found they were carvings—twelve of them. When Jim walked in, she asked, "Are you training headhunters?"

"No, dentists," he replied. "I've collected a bucket of teeth from dentists around town. We'll fill the mouths with plaster, put the teeth in where they should go, and let the young people practice pulling them." Under the guidance of a woman missionary dentist, they did just that. For a training period of a month, twenty-four mountain youth practiced on the carved heads. Then for eleven months they practiced on real ones. After that, they returned to their mountain people who were badly in need of elementary dental care.

Jim was spending every possible weekend in the mountains. Returning from one trip, he told Lil casually, "I want bedcovers for the mountain people. I'm getting raw cotton from America and will have it processed here. Can you get cloth to cover them?" Many mountain people had not even one bedcover for the whole family; they crouched around fires at night, trying to keep warm. But there were a hundred and fifty thousand mountain aborigines. How could she put them all to bed warm at night?

"Clothes, too," Jim added. "Some of the children are still stark naked, and almost all are cold."

But because she could not do *everything,* was no reason why she should not do *something.* Bedcovers and clothing bundles went off into the hills by the truckload.

19. "Nothing Shall Be Impossible"

"Our place looks like a warehouse that is breaking out!" Lil said to Jim. Relief goods for his mountain churches were arriving periodically, and because there was no storeroom, they had to be stacked on the veranda. Lil's "office" also was located in the big house on the mission compound even after Mustard Seed was incorporated in 1954. It was convenient, for Lil could run the house, meet guests coming to see Jim, and conduct her own business too. Her "young people"—she never had to go out seeking workers; they came to her—took over room after room.

Finally she declared, "We've got to move this stuff. It's not fair to the other missionaries."

"I'll tell you what you should do," Jim said confidently: "Find an office near the American base. That way, you'll always be safe."

Lil found just the right place, but a few months later, Jim changed his mind. An anti-American riot broke out in that locality, and Jim and Lil would have walked right into it if Jim had not been too busy to keep an appointment at the American embassy that afternoon. The embassy was sacked, employees were beaten, cars overturned and burned.

"I'll tell you what you should do," Jim said anxiously: "Move back to the mission." Which she did—to the chagrin of the rest of the missionaries. "But I don't have any *horses,*" Lil assured them.

When the tension subsided, Lil again began thinking of an office outside the compound. To get the amount of space needed would be expensive. But God surely could work that out, too. He didn't ask for great faith, just for faith the size of the tiniest of all seeds.

One day in the Winter of 1958 God did work it out. It was the time of year when Taipei is cold and damp, following the beautiful, blue weather of October and November, the August-September typhoon season before that, and the sweltering, near-tropical humidity of summer. Sweatered against the chill, Lil was trying to catch up on her correspondence, hindered not by any lack of typing speed, for she was a skilled typist, but by one interruption after another. She had a comforting theory about interruptions: Did not so many of the ministries of Jesus come about because He was interrupted?

Lil was expertly inserting a letterhead in her typewriter when one of her young people announced, "A Taiwanese Christian businessman is on the phone—he wants you to help him with an errand." In spite of her theory, she felt a twinge of annoyance.

"What kind of errand?"

"He doesn't say."

Lil sighed. "Tell him *annie-ho,*" she said, and they both smiled. *Annie-ho* meant "All right."

When the man arrived, Lil could not remember having met him before. As they left, squeezing past drums of relief goods on the veranda, Lil murmured an apology. "When I find office space, maybe our house can look civilized again."

As the businessman's driver swung his car out into city traffic, the man turned to Lil. "I have a big building here in Taipei on North Chungking Road that I'm not using. I'd like you to have it—

the first year without any rent. I can't preach, but maybe I can help in this way to do God's work." He quickly scribbled the address on a piece of paper and handed her a key. Lil managed to stammer her thanks. That was the "errand." He hadn't known quite how to make his offer casually.

When she returned to the mission, she promptly gathered up three of her young people and set out for North Chungking Road to see the building. "It's big!" said one of the girls, looking up at the three-story, block-deep brick and concrete structure. "It's wonderful!" Lil exclaimed.

Adjoining an open-front restaurant on one side, and across an alley from a motion picture theater on the other, the building was located on a wide avenue leading from downtown Taipei toward suburban Yang Ming Shan and Grass Mountain.

When Jim paid a visit, he pointed out certain other characteristics of the location which Lil had not noticed. A radio and hi-fi shop across the street played loud music from morning to night, raucously advertising its wares; and the planes coming from or going to Taipei airport rattled the windows every time they zoomed low overhead. Mustard Seed had not had occupancy long when the staff made another interesting discovery: the building was on a popular funeral route. At certain times of the month when the portents were favorable, several funerals might go by in one day. The status symbols were the number of tall, ornate flower wreaths, each borne by a pedicab; the number of bands, at least one of which would be playing "Auld Lang Syne"; and the number of professional mourners, identified by white headbands. On other occasions the wail of wind instruments and the dull thud of drums accompanied processions of colorfully garbed worshipers from nearby Buddhist shrines, bearing images of their gods. "They're taking the gods out for a walk," was Lil's explanation to visitors.

The office she located on half of the top floor of the walk-up building. The rest of that floor was given over to sorting areas for clothing and bedding. On the second floor, milk powder, multipurpose food, medicines, and used Christmas cards were stored. Sometimes two truckloads of Christmas cards arrived from the post office at one time. The senders' names were recorded, and the parcels dumped into a room, making a glacier that was drawn upon as needed to make up lots of one thousand cards, each stamped with a Bible verse. Iu Sian-si, a tall thin man of about thirty-five, adapted a secondhand post office canceling machine for imprinting the cards at high speed. A former postman himself, he had delivered mail to the mission compound and then to the address where Lil had her first office. He said to Jim one day, "I hear that Mrs. Dickson works with orphans. That is God's work—I'd like to work here." He wasn't long on the job until he became a Christian. "He's invaluable," says Lil, "because he knows all about mailing." The mail is the lifeline that keeps Mustard Seed going. P. O. Box 2131, Taipei, is probably the most widely known address in Taiwan.

The ground floor of the big warehouse-type building provided space for a garage, a carpenter shop, and what would later become Mercy's Door Clinic.

Special gratitude was evident in the office devotional meeting the day the move was made. The day opened then—as it still does—with a half-hour service on "company time" at which Lil's only contribution is helping to accompany the singing of the morning's hymn on her accordion and reading, in her turn, a verse of the day's Bible chapter. The staff members alternate in leading and speaking. A weekly meeting is also held on Thursday afternoon, at which an offering is taken for projects of the staff's own choosing. A unique feature to encourage those who would be timid about praying aloud is a "prayer box." At the proper time in the service, each writes out a prayer on a slip of paper and drops it in the box. The slips are burned without being read—but not without being known to the One to whom all prayers, vocal or written, are addressed.

There was ample space in the Mustard Seed building for incoming supplies of all kinds. Although almost anything eventually finds use, some of the items sent have stretched the imagination to the utmost—and some have been a complete loss.

One day in the basement, Lil and several of the young men who were armed with crowbars gathered around a large wooden crate which had arrived a few days before from Keelung, to which it had been shipped from America. Every crate, every parcel, was an adventure. Iu Sian-si carefully pried up the boards on the top and pulled back the protective paper. Among other things, these items emerged: a doll without a head; an old mailbox; a box of toothpicks. But also there was an Autoharp, trumpet and French horn ("They will use these at the leprosarium," beamed Lil), and three artificial legs ("We can find use for them, too"). Suddenly, Lil let out a scream. Iu Sian-si had shaken a length of cloth near the bottom of the box, and dozens of giant cockroaches fell out and began scurrying across the floor.

Every time one headed in her direction, Lil gasped and beat a quick retreat. Drunken headhunters she could face with equanimity, not cockroaches. The floor grew slippery with their slaughter, and their hard, brittle wings rattled as they tried to fly out of danger. "I didn't know they could fly," said Iu Sian-si.

"You've learned something," Lil said dourly.

Something else was learned, too. Candy had been packed in a glass jar in the crate. The jar had broken, attracting the roaches—probably at Keelung, where the crate had been in storage three months.

A visiting American had been watching the "grand opening." "Why do people send junk?" he wondered. "They go to all the trouble to collect things, pack them, either pay postage, or the U. S. Navy brings it out through 'Operation Handclasp'—and then you get a doll without a head."

" 'Neither will I offer burnt offerings to the Lord my God of that which doth cost me nothing,' " quoted Lil. "That's a good rule to remember. You should see some of the things that have been sent to us. Once we had a shipment of empty tin cans from California. We had to hire trucks to haul them to the mountains and dump them—two truck loads! In another shipment we came upon fish bones!"

When the last of the visible cockroaches had been killed, the group went upstairs to the office floor. Other packages were being opened. Included in one were an upper plate; an obviously second-hand toothbrush; a used can of foot powder; one burned match from a matchbook; three nails; a toothpaste tube cap.

But in other packages were baby blankets; papers of diaper pins; fresh bright garments for layettes; good clothing both new and used. One could imagine the care and love that went into those parcels. Every package had to be acknowledged, and every usable item put in the proper bin. From the clothing bins family bundles were made up—something for everyone—and distributed to the mountain people and others in need.

Drums and sacks of shoes, eventually to be sorted by size and style, occupied a room of the third floor. One day in a frantic search for a pair of wedding slippers—a dress already had been discovered in an incoming package—a drum of scores of pairs was upended in an effort to find two matching shoes.

"If donors only would tie the pairs together before shipping, it would help us a great deal," said Lil. "When you have two or three thousand pairs—"

Two of her girl assistants were meanwhile hunting. "This would do," said Martha, "but there's only one shoe."

Then three identical shoes, but all for left feet, turned up. "That leads to some interesting conjectures—" Lil said with a smile.

A pair of farmer's work shoes tumbled out of another drum—carefully tied together, but with manure still caked on the soles.

"The girl for whom we're hunting shoes," Lil explained, "is a mountain girl, but she studied medicine and has her doctor's degree. She's marrying a young doctor. They have to go where the government sends them, maybe even to different places, for a term that pays back the government for their education. Twenty years ago her people were headhunters."

Eventually, a suitable pair of shoes was found; they were carefully placed by the beautiful dress. One of the staff girls spent her lunch hour making an elbow-length veil to go with the outfit.

At the time of Mustard Seed's move, and helping to precipitate it, Jim was searching for a new campus for his seminary. The school, Taiwan Theological College, was located in downtown Taipei not far from "Sin Alley." Not that Jim had to worry about his young men backsliding, although an unusual number of bars was concentrated in the area, but it was hardly an academic atmosphere.

"I've found a location," said Jim one evening, pacing the living room floor of the mission compound house. "It's perfect—a view that will take your breath—space to grow in—"

"You mean for the seminary?" Lil asked.

"Of course," said Jim, pausing a moment. "What else? The school will sell the old property—we can get a good price for it, perfect business location—and use the money to buy and build up on the hill. We'll build a house there and homes for any other of the missionaries who want to go along—"

"What hill? Where is this place?"

"You go right along the road past your Mustard Seed office, past Shih-lin—where Generalissimo and Madame Chiang have a residence; you know, we've been there, police in front and all—and then on up the hill toward Grass Mountain, and a turnoff on a plateau that looks out over the whole valley."

"I still can't quite picture it—" Lil began.

"Look, you remember Tai-tung Soa—"

"Yes," Lil said weakly. "I remember. If it's there, I want no part of it."

"It's not *there,*" Jim said hastily. "It's just that you can see Tai-tung off in the distance."

"How far off in the distance?" Lil asked.

"*Very* far," Jim assured her. "The place where we will locate is not yet built up. It's still undeveloped—"

"That means no other houses around. And that means—"

"Lil, I know what you're thinking. But you'll find snakes anywhere—even here at the compound during a typhoon."

The new campus turned out to be a wise move; Jim was a genius at real estate and gauging where property values would rise. The other missionaries frowned on the whole idea—why go traipsing off to the wilds of a mountain somewhere with the seminary? Jim's mission board was not wildly enthusiastic at first either, especially over the Oriental chapel that Jim designed. Two facts made the move—and the chapel—acceptable. The first was that Jim really was working for the Taiwanese church, which approved. The second was a travelogue, filmed in Taiwan by an American film company, and highlighting, of all things, the chapel at Taiwan Theological College. The film was shown all over the United States and Canada.

Students flocked to the school. The enrollment grew to one hundred seventy and the number of mountain churches to three hundred eighty-five.

Lil and Jim enjoyed their new home. Though it was a college-owned house on the campus, it wasn't quite so much like living on the town square.

Meanwhile, Ronny was learning to live with his handicap and the direction of Marilyn's life was being set. After graduating from Wheaton College in 1952, she spent two years at Columbia Bible College in South Carolina, before returning to Formosa with her mother the following year. In May, 1956, she went back to Minnesota for a visit, following this with a year at Fuller Theological Seminary in California. In September, 1957, at twenty-five, she returned to Formosa, prepared to spend her life there. Lil *perhaps* unintentionally—*"Seong-te an-pai,"* she would call it ("God has worked it out")—had a hand in what came next.

Noticing the number of American servicemen at loose ends in Taipei, especially on Sundays, Lil rounded up a few of them one Sunday evening for a buffet dinner at the Dickson home. It was so successful it became a weekly affair, with attendance reaching as high as eighty. Marilyn helped with the serving. A young soldier from Neenah, Wisconsin, caught her eye one Sunday evening, and she, his. Vernon Tank, a Lutheran, had ideals much like her own, Marilyn found. He wanted to devote his life deliberately to something significant, not just drift with the current and then someday wonder where he had been, what he had done. They were married in Okinawa in October, 1958. After his military service was completed, Vernon and Marilyn returned to Taiwan, and he went into the work of Mustard Seed. In 1961 they returned to the States so that he could enter Fuller. In April, 1963, he received his B.D. With their family expanded by two adopted babies that year—Marilyn knew she could not have children of her own without complications—they returned to Taiwan to stay.

Bi-lian, Lil's own adopted child, was growing up. Jim enrolled her in the American "public" school, run mainly for the children of servicemen. Lil, stopping by one day to see how she was doing, said to the principal, "I'm Bi-lian Dickson's mother."

He searched the records. "We have no one here by that name," he said, looking at her oddly. "Wait a minute—we have a Dolly Dickson. Could she be your daughter?"

Jim, thinking Bi-lian should have an American-sounding name at school, had entered her on the records as Dolly Dickson without realizing that Lil might just want to know about it. "Well," he explained when Lil charged home, "I thought Dolly Dickson had a nice ring to it!"

Another day when Bi-lian came home from school, she slumped into a chair. "Mother, I cried today," she said.

"What was the matter?" Lil asked.

"Some children teased me. They said I was picked up from a trash can."

Lil sat down by Bi-lian's side. "Everybody knows all about the fathers of other children, who they are, where they come from. But no one knows about you—that makes you the most *interesting* of all. For all we know, *you* may be a lost princess!"

Bi-lian brightened at that.

"Now," said Lil, "see that you act like one!"

One by one, needs that had impressed themselves upon Lil—some of them for years—were met. It took her ten years, for example, to set up the project she had first envisioned when she was present at the birth of a baby in a mountain hut and there was nothing in which to bathe it but an old frying pan. "We must have maternity wards for mountain mothers," she had said to Jim when she returned from that trip. "So many babies die." In one of her devotional books, Lil had written in red pencil at the end of that day's reading: "Pray for maternity wards." It was not only a reminder to herself, but a plea that would go into her newsletter. Ten years later she turned again to that same reading, and wrote over the earlier red-penciled notation, "Thank you, God!" Prayers had been answered.

The first of the maternity wards was built at Hwalien on the east coast, where a narrow strip of land extends between sea and high mountains. In those mountains the Ami and Tyal people live, the latter, descendants of the fierce headhunters of earlier days. Lil spread the word among the women: "Here is a place where you may come to have your babies. Nurses will be on duty, and doctors on call."

"How much does it cost?" one pregnant mountain girl asked timidly.

"It is given in God's name," Lil said. "It will not cost you anything."

And so they came—making the hard journey on foot down from the hills to the place that Lil called "Room for Mary." There were older Tyal women, wearing forever their deep purple and black tribal tattooes, some of whom looked more qualified to be grandmothers than mothers, and younger ones mercifully unmarked by the disappearing custom of tattooing. The long, one-story concrete block building had twenty beds and a hospital-clean delivery room where crisply uniformed nurses were on duty. Says Lil, "So many times, people offer help when help is not wanted, just because they happen to be interested in something particular. The maternity wards, I thought, would be appreciated. This has proved to be true."

Only gifts that came in above needs to which she was already committed could be used. As Lil's projects grew, so also did the monthly income required to support them. Some of her friends worried when she began talking about new projects, for there would be not only the initial cost but the upkeep to consider. "Don't you think things are getting out of hand?" one of them asked.

"Out of my hand, yes," Lil replied. "Not out of God's."

As additional funds became available, Lil established other "Rooms for Mary," so that a mountain woman anywhere would be within a reasonable distance of one. Today five maternity wards are in operation. Farther down the east coast, at Koan-san, a "Room for Mary" serves women of the Bunan tribe, and south of that is another at Taitung. Ping-tung on the west coast takes care of the Paiwans, and Pu-li, in central Taiwan, serves women of several tribes. "All told, we have about two hundred forty babies a month," says Lil.

At the Mustard Seed office, a layette is made up for each mother. There are the usual items: diapers—they were carefully hemmed at first, when few layettes were needed, but now are cut out with hefty blows of Iu Sian-si's sharp machete, many thicknesses at once; little shirts; talcum powder; a bottle of vitamins for the mother. All are done up in a baby blanket, safety-pinned together. There are two other gifts also in each layette, reflecting the tenderness with which Lil thinks of human need: a carefully selected dress and a bit of costume jewelry for the mother. Mother and baby go back to their cheerless mountain homes wearing the precious shared gifts of love.

20. Doors of Mercy

In 1957 the poor of the city of Taipei had no place where they could get free medical care. This burdened Lil. She had been able to do something about medical treatment in the mountains—a need she found on her first trip into the hills when she and Jim had first come to Formosa. The Mobile Clinic did not so much meet that need as show how overwhelming it was. Lil's bamboo-constructed clinic at Pu-li was, like her later "Rooms for Mary," the fruition of long hopes and prayers. In response to Lil's way of simply putting the problem to the conscience of her friends in America, the money came—never enough to do the job wholly, but enough to start it. The clinic at Pu-li turned into a full-fledged Christian hospital, in a fine building, fully supported and operated by World Vision. At Hwalien, Koan-san, Kong-hok, Taitung, Giok-li, Sin-Khang, Ping-tung—it sounds like a roll call of all Taiwan—Lil set up clinics for in-patients and for out-patients; from some of them mobile clinics go out into remote areas once or twice a week. Of course, no charge is made.

In Taipei, nothing had been done. Dr. Tang Tai-seng, Lil's good friend at the University Medical School and her chief medical adviser, had confirmed what she suspected: "There's no free clinic here in the city for the poor people."

Lil knew that in every great city thousands were living on the very edge of destitution. They managed to exist from day to day, but if anyone in the family fell sick, it brought on a major crisis. The money that should be used for food then had to be paid out for the doctor's bills, threatening the health and security of the whole family.

"We've got to start a clinic here in town," Lil said to Jim one day. "We'll call it Mercy's Door."

"The church has been in this area a hundred years," Jim replied, "and still so few Mercy's Doors."

"We can draw upon national Christian doctors," Lil said, "and local nurses who are Christians. We'll need two doctors, a nurse, a dispenser, and the evangelist—that shouldn't be too difficult."

Under Dr. Tang's direction, the clinic opened two evenings a week in the basement of a church in Bang-kah, one of the older, rundown sections of Taipei. Patients began streaming in. The second week the pastor came sadly to Lil. "The church members are furious. They say, 'The idea of letting all those people come into our basement! They might bring in diseases and infect our Sunday-school children! I tried to explain, but they would not listen."

"It's not your fault," Lil said. "We will find another place."

She tried the big missionary hospital. Officials there shook their heads. "Mrs. Dickson, you're letting people come in *free!* They would expect free treatment here, too. We can't run a hospital that way. Sorry, you cannot have your clinic here."

"There's only one place left," Lil said to Jim. "That's the ground floor at Mustard Seed. I thought our place wouldn't be good enough, but at least we'll be near the poor people."

"That's not a bad idea," Jim observed. "You know, when a girl wants to get married, the first rule is, be available. If you want to help the poor people, be available."

Jim's theory must have been valid, for the poor people came by the hundreds. Three evenings a week they began assembling even before the doors were opened. Then they waited quietly in the big room for the doctor to see them and listened to a devotional message while they waited.

Lil could turn her attention now to another nagging worry. Tuberculosis, the scourge of the mountains, was still on her conscience. Her own three small wards in central Taiwan seemed so inadequate. One of the neediest areas was the Tyal mountain country of the north. She complained to a doctor friend, "No one seems to be able to help T.B. sufferers who aren't able to pay."

"It takes money to run a tuberculosis sanatorium," the doctor replied.

"Then we'll get money," Lil said firmly.

Again, presenting the need to readers of her newsletter, she began building at Hwalien as soon as designated funds started coming in.

Patients were accommodated in the tuberculosis clinic at Hwalien for some months, when one day, the police came while Lil was visiting.

"We are putting the patients out!" the police chief announced. "Tomorrow!"

"But why?" Lil wanted to know.

"You are too close to a public school. The germs blow across."

"If you come tomorrow to put the patients out, I will be here tomorrow, too," she said grimly. "With a photographer! This will make a fine story about Free China that magazines in America would just love to publish!"

The police didn't carry out their threat, but pressure was applied so that Lil had to close the clinic and send the patients home until a new one could be built a few miles farther up the coast, away from populated areas. This was done in 1962. Some of the patients, however, were never able to return; the journey to their homes in the hills, the lack of care while there, killed them.

At a mountain leadership conference, one pastor said, "We should have kindergartens in our churches and our own girls trained to be kindergarten teachers."

"At the pastors' request," says Lil, "we rented a place, gathered the brightest girls we could find, gave them examinations, and started training them to be kindergarten teachers. This has been one of our happiest projects. For one thing, the girls are bright, attractive, and wonderful singers. They learn quickly and then go back and do a service for their own people. So if you help one girl, you're helping thirty or forty more children in the village. Now we have over four hundred sometimes, wanting to come to our Hwalien school.

"All over the mountains there's a great awakening. These people have come from a primitive life and all of a sudden modern life has been thrust upon them. They want more education. They want to improve themselves. They don't want to live like primitive savages in this new world. And so they come from every village where the church has young people.

"But it's not easy to get in. The girls have to be recommended by their pastor and the Session of their church. They have to pass an exam. They are very poor and so we don't ask for any money for tuition. We ask only that they sign an agreement that after graduation they will go back to their own church, start a kindergarten, and teach for two years. Of course, they're paid a salary then. Some of them marry before the two years are up, but they go on teaching."

The church provides the furniture for the kindergarten: bamboo stools and tables inside and playground equipment outside. The teachers tell Bible stories to the children and teach them games and singing, and they have milk during the morning. Because mothers and fathers work in the fields or in hilly patches of ground that pass for fields, children would be left pretty much to themselves, doing nothing. When there is a kindergarten, the parents know their children are under the care of a responsible person, and are learning.

Lil has done a good job of interesting her donors in supplying each kindergarten with a pump organ (cost, fifty dollars U.S.) which doubles as the church organ. If the ordinary mountain church should be given an organ, no one could play it. But the kindergarten teacher has learned to play as part of her training, and she can play for her church, too, and have a young people's choir.

Nurses' aid training was added at the Hwalien Girls' School. A Bible training and vocational school, where aboriginal boys are taught farming and animal husbandry, was built two miles away. To enable them to earn money while they study, they are taught how to make baskets, souvenirs carved from wood, and bamboo furniture.

Lil had once said to Jim, "I think I know how a juggler feels when he's trying to keep six balls in the air at the same time." She knew this even better one morning when Tan Sian-si put his hand over the office telephone and said, "It's from the superintendent of the prison."

Tan Sian-si is another of Lil's invaluables. Son of a well-to-do father who owns a hotel in Pei-tou, a resort suburb, he is the cautious one of the staff, the logical business mind who regards any new project as probable catastrophe. Tan Sian-si's proficiency in Mandarin and English as well as in Taiwanese makes him, among other things, chief telephone answerer and caller.

"This is Mrs. Dickson," said Lil, picking up the extension phone. "Will I what? Oh, yes, indeed, I will be right over. *Annie-ho.*"

She looked up, distress in her eyes. "He wants me to come and take the *babies* out of the prison," she told the staff. "I didn't know they had babies in prison!"

As Lil's car turned into a dead-end street, the high, bleak concrete wall of the prison formed a barricade across it. Dead-end street—there was something fitting in that, Lil thought glumly. Built during the Japanese days, the walls, at least, looked as if they would last forever. At a wicket Lil identified herself, and the guard passed her through; the superintendent had given orders. "This way," a waiting khaki-clad woman attendant said. Stopping at a heavy door, the attendant swung back the bolt. This let them into a courtyard where several women clad in black pajamalike garments were sitting on the ground—some of them combing their hair, some cooking over little charcoal fires, some simply enduring the slow passing of time.

On the other side of the courtyard the attendant led Lil through an open door into a large room where rough tables and stools were the only furniture except for a few sewing machines at which women were working. The light was so poor, Lil wondered that they could see what they were doing. The odors of old timbers that for decades had absorbed charcoal smoke and the smells of decaying food and the sharper odors of ineffective sewers assailed Lil's sensibilities. Along a wide corridor leading from the larger room were perfectly plain small rooms with cagelike doors that had smaller sliding doors at the bottom where utensils could be passed in and out. "The cells are empty now," the attendant explained. "It's recreation time."

Lil shuddered at the word.

"Now we go back to the superintendent's office."

There the superintendent said to her, "Mothers who are here may keep any babies under the age of five with them, if they have nowhere else to leave them. But this is no place for babies—I wanted you to see that for yourself. Will you take them?"

"Of course," said Lil. She would decide afterward what to do with them.

He called the mothers together in an assembly area and said, "Give Mrs. Dickson your babies and she will take care of them."

The women turned away, frightened, holding tightly to their little ones. In Taiwan, babies are often sold, girl babies to those who would bring them up from babyhood to be prostitutes.

Lil stepped forward and spoke in their own language. "I am a mother, too, and I understand how you feel. You are afraid that if I take your baby, you'll never see it again. But if you let me take care of your baby for you, I'll bring it back every few weeks."

Eight babies were turned over to her that day. By now she had started a whole new children's compound a few miles from An-Lok, under the appropriate name of Iro-Iro (Japanese for "miscellaneous"). Here she sandwiched in the eight youngsters until Phok-Ai Home—"Great Love"—was set up to care for them on the compound, a motherly woman hired to take charge. Lil began visiting the women's prison early every Sunday morning, taking flowers, playing her accordion, sponsoring a worship service led by a pastor, "so they know I'm here and that their babies are safe."

One of the first mothers to give Lil her child was a young woman who had a smile like sunshine. More intelligent than most, she seemed to have no burden of guilt at all. Not only did she give Lil the child she had with her, but had her husband bring two other children that he was trying to take care of while he worked, too.

Lil inquired at the office as to why this young woman was in prison. They told her a man had come into her house and tried to assault her. She had picked up a knife and killed the man. In Taiwan, killing even in self-defense is punishable. For murder, the sentence is twelve years, for self-defense, six. Because of good behavior, the woman was let out early. Lil was glad to turn the three youngsters back to her, knowing they would be in loving hands.

Lil found self-sacrifice in prison, too. A woman told Lil how her son had been arrested for selling morphine. "He was so young," said the woman wistfully. "All his life was before him. I was already old." She took the blame and went to prison, serving a twelve-year sentence, so that her son might go free.

Lil's visits attracted attention to the women's prison. Some of the Protestants installed fluorescent ceiling lights, the Catholics overhead fans, the Baptists religious pictures. "Provoking one another to good works," Lil put it.

Phok-Ai Annex eventually had to be added to take care of the children of prisoners, some fifty in all. They were coming and going almost weekly, as mothers, released, reclaimed their youngsters.

Along with Lil's major projects, all sorts of minor dramas took place daily—she seemed to attract them. When routine was challenged, she took comfort in a comment that Madame Chiang Kai-shek had found potent:

A prominent woman visiting Taiwan was told she could not go

to Quemoy, the small Nationalist fortress island close to the mainland. Because there was a certain enjoyable bitter-sweet danger in the trip (it was shelled on odd days), visiting Quemoy had become, on even days, one of the things to do when in Taiwan. "But women are not allowed to go there," this tourist was told. Madame Chiang crumbled the routine with one blunt question: *"Why not?"*

Lil often asked herself, "Why not?" when something she hadn't thought of came up.

The blankets were one thing. A worker from Hwalien stopped in the office one day and spoke of the need for blankets to go on top of the tatami mats, to soften the beds of the tuberculosis patients. "They sleep on the bare mats," he explained. "They have a blanket to cover themselves, but no blanket to soften the mats underneath."

Lil mused out loud. "We can't do it for one and not for all." She paused. "So we'll do it for all. We'll start with the Hwalien T.B. clinic, then Koan-san and Sin-Khang, and later, as we're able, the schools."

Don Williams, a young Evangelical Free Church minister who with his wife Betty had come out to work with Lil in 1959, had a list of requests when he came in from Pu-li. One of them involved two widows who had been living together in a little house rented for them by Mustard Seed. "They fight," Don explained. "One of them spends all day gathering wood, working until it is too dark to see. When she comes home, she wakes up the other one—causing trouble. Quite a fighter, too." Don grinned. "The widow's *might!* Is it all right if I rent a second house and separate them?"

Lil nodded agreement. The two dollars U.S. a month required for that purpose seemed to be a modest price to keep two people happy.

Sometimes, Lil's humanitarian impulses led her far afield. One day she was out looking for an orphan boy she had heard was trying to go to school by day and sleep wherever he could at night. She thought a boy like that deserved help. When she found him, she asked, "Where do you sleep?"

"I wait until the teachers have gone home from the dormitory," he answered, "and then I sleep between my friends."

"Well, he has *friends,* anyway," Lil said to Tiu Sian-si. On their way home he turned by mistake onto a one-way road and they found themselves in front of a dilapidated building that seemed to house children. "I want to see this," Lil told Tiu Sian-si, getting out.

It was an old Japanese school building made into an orphanage for two hundred thirty children. Windows were broken, screens torn, dirt was everywhere. The man in charge said, "Our biggest problem is lice—all the children have lice in their hair."

The next day, Lil and "her girls" went out, put DDT on all heads, wrapped heads in towels so the insecticide could do its work, and then shampooed all two hundred and thirty of them.

The archaic wiring of the building struck terror to Lil's heart: bare wires were threaded through paperboard ceilings. The electrician she summoned was paralyzed at what he saw. "It could burn down anytime!" he declared.

Lil reported to Jim, "We could lose a hundred children in one night. I know the danger now. If I didn't do anything about it, and fire came, I would feel like a murderer."

The rewiring was rushed to completion.

In addition, Lil threw out the infested tatami mats on which the children slept, bought new ones, later put in a good floor to replace the dirt floor, and painted everything in bright colors. "We made it so nice that the Welfare Department took part of the building for its own offices," says Lil. "But that was all right, for the children were moved up to a hillside location that was much nicer."

Tan Sian-si tactfully tried to arm Lil against impulsive commitments, but he hadn't made much impression. That was again evident one afternoon when an Ami couple came to the office from Keelung, carrying two tiny undernourished boys.

"They are twins, one year old," began Martha, one of Lil's assistants, who translated their mountain language into Taiwanese. "The parents went to Keelung from the mountains so the father could become a fisherman, but he has no job. They are asking if you will take care of the two children. They can't support them—they have three others. The mother has no milk, and the babies are getting weaker. Someone told them that you would help if they could only get to Taipei to see you."

The mother watched anxiously, her brown dress neat but unbecoming, her black hair combed straight over her forehead toward her eyes. The babies were carefully dressed in hand-me-downs, clean white stockings on their pipestem legs. The father, holding one boy, was fondling the baby's ear, pressing the baby's head close to his.

"What shall we do?" Lil asked her helpers. "If we take them, it means a whole new project, for they are not orphans."

Martha and Eng-cheong—a young radio engineer whose Christian broadcasting Lil helped to support—watched the drama unfold.

"If we keep them for three months—fatten them up—do you think the parents will take them back?" Lil asked.

Martha shook her head doubtfully.

"Ask them."

The woman in the brown dress listened to Martha and then said something very softly in reply.

Martha turned to Lil. "She said, 'How about a year?' "

"Well—" Lil pondered. "*All right*. Tell them we'll take them for a year."

Eng-cheong smiled, as if he had known all along that was what she would do. He had seen her compassion shatter precedents many times.

"Send them over to the doctor to be examined when he can see them," Lil said with resignation. All incoming children were checked by the doctor to make sure they had no communicable disease.

These two were put in Iro-Iro. Their parents were taken out to the pleasant, grassy compound in the suburbs with their children so they could see where they would be living.

Meanwhile, another problem was haunting Lil—a church for the boys at Boys' Home.

World Vision paid for food and schooling for the boys at Boys' Home and Mustard Seed provided clothes and bedding. But still they had no church of their own. Every Friday night the boys prayed for a church. They could see across the valley the lights in the Church of the Lepers for which God had supplied the money. Perhaps He would do as much for them.

"We can't take them to the lepers' church to be baptized," their leader reported to Lil, "so they are going out into the world not baptized."

For four years, in a special prayer service every Friday night, the boys prayed, "Please give us our own church."

Lil finally wrote to an American businessman who had promised help: "The prayers of little boys for four years can no longer be disregarded!"

He sent a check for two thousand dollars. "I had to borrow the money," he wrote.

"Do you think you ought to borrow for this purpose?" Lil wrote back.

"I borrow to buy an automobile. Why not for the Lord's work?"

From World Vision another two thousand dollars came unexpectedly. So the church was built on the crown of the hill, just as Lil had envisioned it from the beginning. "It cost a little more than four thousand dollars," Lil says. "Every month we seem to spend more than we take in, and yet we don't go broke. I don't understand it."

21. The Wild Wind

"When are you coming to the Pescadores to help with the church work there?" The gray-haired Chinese pastor from Makung had journeyed all the way to Taipei in 1950 to ask this one question. He was not satisfied when Lil replied, "Someday. I have my work here."

Five weeks later he was back with the same question, to which he received the same indefinite answer. "I'm not leaving until you set a date," he said firmly, settling down in his chair.

Lil reached for a calendar. God worked in mysterious—even disturbing—ways, His wonders to perform! They agreed on a date.

To Jim she grumbled good-naturedly, "If I have to go, I'd better know where I'm going. Somebody told me once there are *sixty* Pescadore islands. I can't visit all of them!"

"You can mark off about fifty-six of them as good-sized rocks," Jim said. "As to the others—eighty thousand people who are mostly farmers and fishermen, fifty square miles of poverty and coral, Makung the only town of any size. The whole lot are about a third of the way between Taiwan and the mainland. Oh, and one other thing," Jim said. "Wind! Day and night. *Every* day and night. The *kong hong,* they call it—the wild wind."

At the Civil Air Transport (CAT) office—the Nationalist airline that grew out of General Claire Chennault's Flying Tigers—Lil was told that a plane went to Makung every three days. "But getting there is no assurance you'll get back," the clerk warned her. "It depends on the wind."

Lil never felt more lonely than when she stepped down from the plane. She had been the only Westerner aboard—except for the American pilot—and for all she knew was the only one on the entire sixty islands. "I'll be back in three days—I hope," the pilot said to her. With mixed emotions she watched the plane taxi across the grass airfield in a cloud of dust, and then wheel, and hurtle past in a bumpy takeoff for Taiwan.

"Mrs. Dickson!" Lil heard the voice at her elbow, and she no longer felt alone. It was the pastor. "I want you to see the Pescadores," he said. "The Penghu islands, we Chinese call them." He had commandeered a car.

Dominating all Lil's immediate impressions was the barrenness of the landscape. She saw no trees at all until they drove into Makung city. "Too much wind for trees," the pastor explained. "But we have a tree—a big one." Lil had never heard of a place that boasted of having *a* tree. It turned out to be a three-hundred-year-old banyan on the northernmost island of the group.

Jim knew what he was talking about when he spoke of wind, she decided. She saw heavy lead-sheathed telephone cables along a causeway between islands whipping like jump ropes. Farmers had even built coral walls around their gardens, "to keep wind and salt spindrift from ruining the thin soil and their meager crops," the pastor explained. Even crop rows were protected by individual low rattan fences.

Troops were everywhere. While soldiers practiced war games in the fields, sometimes just a few feet away men and women would be absorbedly working, the women with their conical straw hats tied down by scarves. The principal building material was coral, and in the country, the rock walls of houses were left rough and jagged, smoothed only by wind and weather. Houses were scarcely more than dark caves. The stenches of poverty were everywhere.

By comparison, Lil thought, the mountain people of Taiwan were well off.

That night at the pastor's house, as she lay on a tatami mat in the bedroom the pastor and his wife had graciously turned over to her, the wind moaned unceasingly in the eaves and at the windows. Lil lay awake thinking of the opportunity for outdoor Sunday schools and child evangelism. Tomorrow she would make a plan.

A few weeks later, Lil returned to the Pescadores—this time, Everlasting Life and her accordion with her. "They don't know the war's over out there," she had said to Jim. "They're so accustomed to Japanese oppression that they're still huddling behind closed doors with the Gospel." A meeting Lil held on the seashore to encourage the church to begin outdoor Sunday schools was, she was told, the first open-air meeting in fifty years.

Lil went back regularly after that. The Christians lost their timidity and preached boldly. But always Lil was aware of the physical needs of these lonely islands the world had forgotten. The children needed kindergartens. A mobile clinic, with a doctor, nurse, and pastor, would be invaluable. Someday, she promised herself, she would also build an orphanage here.

But she couldn't wait for "someday." (She recalled, with a wry smile, this was the expression she had used when the pastor had first come to Taipei to invite her.) Something had to be done at once.

There was a thin wraith of an eight-year-old girl, for example. Lil's heart reached out to her when she came to the pastor's house. She broke into a big smile when Lil smiled at her, then darted away like a frightened wild thing.

"Who is she?" Lil asked.

The pastor's wife shook her head sadly. "Always she is at church, even for the early morning prayer meetings and the late evening meetings. She has nowhere else to go," and she told Lil the story.

Born in a brothel, the child was of course regarded as an encumbrance by her mother. Passed around to anyone who would take her in, she finally became the burden of a woman member of the local church. This woman would go to church in the morning, stay for a meeting afterward, a prayer meeting after that, and not get home until afternoon. Then she would whip the child because she had stolen food to eat. "That woman might be a good church member," said Lil indignantly, "though I don't see how she could be, and she certainly doesn't have good sense!"

Another Sunday she tied the child to a chair, put the food all ready to eat over on a table, and left her while she went to church, to be gone for six hours. Of course the child worked her way over to the table, and even with her hands tied, managed to get something to eat. This brought on another beating.

"She's a bad girl," Lil was told when she made further inquiry. "She steals."

"She's hungry!" Lil said angrily. "That's all that's the matter with her."

Seizing upon Lil's evident interest in the child, they asked, "Will you take her?"

"She's being beaten all the time here," Lil said. "Nobody has a good word for her. Yes, I'll take her!"

The trip back to Taipei by plane was a source of amazement to the child. Tightly, she held to Lil's arm as the plane took off. At the railroad station at Tainan she studied a train with great interest. "Why is that smoke coming out of the chimney?" she asked. "Are they cooking rice in there?"

The Children's Shelter frightened her at first. One evening she wrapped up her possessions—they were so pitifully few—in a dirty handkerchief and started out to face the world alone again. The matron found her and gently brought her back, to learn to enjoy the strange experience of being wanted.

Through the years, Lil did what she could in the Pescadores.

On one of her visits, the pastor took Lil to what she felt was the most depressing prison she had ever seen. The boys sat motionless, their faces without expression. Sick, diseased, and insane prisoners were shut in with them. One man wore handcuffs and a heavy chain and lived like an animal. What a sight for boys to live with, Lil thought. Forty-one youngsters slept in a space large enough for only half that number, tightly huddled together on the concrete floor.

As in Taipei, Lil began sponsoring boys who had nowhere to go, seventeen in all, and brought them to Boys' Home. "But that isn't the answer," she was saying to Jim by 1961. "Their mothers can't see them here. Usually it's the mother who survives. Many of the men are fishermen and are lost at sea."

Jim smiled. "Now I'll tell you what you should do: you should build an orphanage in the Pescadores."

"I've already told me that's what I should do!" Lil said. "But I haven't had a go-ahead."

In the meantime she interested Pastor Lim, an old friend who had come originally from the Pescadores, to return to help spread the Gospel. Also, she engaged a doctor, nurse, and driver to staff a mobile clinic.

On her next trip to the islands, the nurse said to Lil, "A man died while you were away, leaving his wife and five children. She was so desolate she was going to commit suicide. But the driver of the mobile clinic and I went over to see the mother and told her about Jesus. She decided not to take her life. We returned many times and the pastor also talked to the mother. 'But my two youngest children?' she asked. 'How can I take care of them?' This we could not answer. You must visit this woman," the nurse concluded.

When they met in the field where the woman was working, Lil assured her, "I'll try to make a place for your children."

Standing there in the field, the mother prayed aloud for the first time in her life. It was a beautiful prayer in which not only her gratitude but her love for her children shone through.

"We must take pictures of your children," Lil said, "to see if we can get sponsors for them." They snapped a photograph of the girl. "Where is the boy?" Lil asked.

The mother seemed embarrassed. "He was out in the field with me, and had to get dressed," she explained. Presently he came running, nicely dressed, wearing a clean shirt. His picture, too, was made.

"I will send for your children as soon as I can," Lil promised.

As they drove to the airport, the nurse confided, "I heard why the little boy was late. When we came, he was stark naked. He went off to borrow clothes from a neighbor in order to have his picture taken."

Lil said to Jim when she got home, "I've decided it's time to start that orphanage on the Pescadores."

"Where?" Jim asked.

"That's what I don't know yet."

In October, 1961, Lil planned to fly in one day and out the next—CAT was now scheduling daily service. But she had barely arrived when the winds mounted and the sky grew black. "Typhoon coming," Pastor Lim announced comfortingly. "We're supposed to be right in the center."

"No use doing it halfway," Lil shrugged. Then she remembered uneasily that the highest point on the Pescadores was only fifty feet above sea level, and the average height twenty feet. But after all, the islands had been here a long time.

"No planes or boats are going out," the pastor reported that evening as they sat in the Lims' home in Makung. The wind shrieked outside in one continuing high-pitched wail like a siren that someone had forgotten to shut off.

That night, two visitors came calling, leaning into the wind. "We have heard that you want to start an orphanage here," said one.

Nothing wrong with the island's communications system, Lil thought.

"We have a building—" said the other. "We started to build it and can't finish. We would be glad to sell it to you."

Lil could almost feel the nudge at her shoulder.

"Can you come to see it in the morning?"

Lil looked out the window and listened to the wind. "I'm sure I can't go anywhere else."

By the next day the worst of the typhoon had passed. Planes still were not flying—that had something to do with the direction in which the one runway had been built, fine for windless days, but hazardous when crosswinds passed twenty-five knots—but things seemed no more cyclonic than normal. Signs had blown down, and a few shutters and roof tiles littered the streets. "We're used to typhoons," Pastor Lim said. "We batten down, haul our boats up on the beach, and wait. It's hard to blow away a coral house that has had practice all its life standing up to the *kong hong*."

The building offered for sale was indeed unfinished. The owners had put up only the coral-reinforced concrete walls; there was no roof or floor. The windows and doors were packed away in a friend's house, they said, and were a part of the deal. Building, doors, windows, and the land could be had for thirteen hundred dollars U.S. Just in front of the site, the land sloped down to a pretty bay.

Something told Lil, "Take it." She did.

Getting the orphanage completed proved to be no small matter. Other activities delayed Lil's return until early 1962 to sign a building contract, and even after the formal start had been made, there were delays. Lil wanted a fireplace; she'd had one or more in each of her schools and orphanages. During the cool time of the year, they not only took the chill out of the air, but added a friendly, homey touch. It was the fireplace that gave the local builder trouble, for in all the Pescadores there was none. "Four by six feet," Lil had specified, keeping it down to child-scale. When in July she returned from a trip to America, she found that he had followed her directions, but had reversed the dimensions; the fireplace was four feet wide and six feet high. Glumly, the contractor ripped it out and tried again. Lil had designed the building so that the kitchen would be added to the existing structure off the living-dining room, and the bathroom off the dormitories. Again, he had got his specifications crossed. There was no way of correcting *that* mistake, Lil decided on an inspection tour. But she could do something about the yawning open doorway between dining room and bathroom. "We must have a door there," she said.

The contractor, proud of his work, wanted to keep it all beautiful. "How about a glass door?" he suggested helpfully.

"Just an *ordinary* door, please," said Lil.

When the children moved into the completed building in October, 1962, a year after she had bought the bare walls, Lil was there for the dedication. She brought along curtains decorated with animal cutouts and supervised their hanging. A picture was ready to go over the rebuilt fireplace. Again marooned by the wind, she spent the extra time shopping for clothes and tennis shoes for the first nine boys and one girl who initiated the orphanage. Most of them had never worn shoes before.

Also, there was rattan furniture to be bought for a corner of the living room, to help give the place a lived-in look. In Makung, there were no department stores; each shop specialized, and in many cases its product was made on the spot. At the rattan shop, Lil watched a young apprentice putting a chair together, using his bare feet and toes as a vise to steady lengths of wicker while with pliers he crimped the pieces into graceful loops. Completed chairs hung from ceiling hooks and several were brought down for her inspection. Soon after she placed her order, the chairs and a table were delivered at the orphanage, piled high on a three-wheeled bicycle.

At one point in the shopping tour, Pastor Lim's wife called a halt, directing Lil's attention to a slight woman sitting on a low stool on the sidewalk opposite, busy at shoe repairing. "That's the mother of Tan So-ngo, the girl we took into the orphanage last night. Her husband, a shoe repairman, died of tuberculosis in July. She lost his shop and their home, but took over his trade. She's on that corner every day."

Lil said impulsively, "She's probably hungry. Let's get her some cookies." They walked down the street until they found a bakery, where they bought a dozen cookies and a bag of candy. Then they walked back to the corner where the shoe repairwoman was working. A shoe iron, a box of nails, knives, and a supply of tire rubber for half soles were spread in front of her. Shoes to be repaired were lined up at one side. A sunny smile lighted the woman's face as she motioned Lil to the wicker chair, which she kept for customers.

Lil presented the gift. Then she had a motherly thought. Opening a package, she said, "This is the sweater and material for a skirt and the shoes we have just bought for your daughter. Do you think she will like them?"

The woman beamed with pleasure. She was still nodding and smiling after they had gone on, and Lil turned to look back from the next corner. Then the woman turned to her work, neither her heart nor her hammer quite so heavy.

When the children moved into the orphanage, its fresh paint and new concrete floors looked and smelled so luxurious to them that one little boy sat down and shook with excitement. Lil walked through the dormitory rooms, where she saw new double-decker beds with their fragrant tatami mats. The fresh, clean smell of varnish hung over the rooms. Each child had his own cupboard. Lil opened one of the cupboard doors. Inside, carefully folded, was a shirt, a pair of trousers, and one lone marble.

"We forgot something," Lil said suddenly, and tore back into Makung to buy an armload of toys.

The next morning she said to Pastor Lim, "I'm getting worried about things at the office in Taipei—I expected to get back today. Aren't any planes flying—even any boats sailing?"

He went to check. A short while later he returned, shaking his head. "The wind is still too high. No planes. There *is* a little freighter that *may* go out. But it's very little—maybe one hundred tons. And no one can go on it unless he's accompanying cargo."

Lil pondered a moment. "I could buy a shipment of peanuts. Better try to get me passage."

But the freighter did not sail; the winds and waves were too much for it.

On that night, October 25, American-Cuban-Soviet tension reached its 1962 crisis. Pastor Lim tuned in a Japanese station and pursed his lips thoughtfully. When the newspaper came, he translated freely for Lil, running his finger down the column, right to left, as he spelled it out: "American ships waiting. Russian ships coming. When they meet—*poof!*" On that uncertain note, she went to bed, feeling that the Pescadores, close to the Communist China mainland, were very exposed and that she should at least pull down the window shade.

Morning brought better news from the Voice of America, but no moderation in the howling winds. The agent at the local office of CAT held out no immediate hope. "You know what I think CAT means?" Lil said to him. " 'Can't Always Travel.' " Morning brought the news, also, that the night before, a freighter of one hundred sixteen tons had gone down off the Pescadores, with all hands lost. Pastor Lim looked at Lil strangely. "Just as well our boat *didn't* sail," she said grimly.

A phone call to the Mustard Seed office in Taipei was not reassuring. "We have no problems," her helpers told her, "except that we're running out of money." Only she could sign checks, and they had used up the supply she left with them.

Perhaps a military plane would be taking off, Lil thought. A dash to the American armed forces hostel near the airport brought courteous attention but the nonplusing question, "What is your rank, Mrs. Dickson?"

"I'm a nobody," she admitted.

The captain smiled. "Dickson—I think I have heard of you. *Reader's Digest,* wasn't it? We could do with a few more nobodies like you." Then he said, more soberly, "As of now, nothing is moving. If anything comes up, I'll be in touch with you."

"Well, it was a nice try," Lil said to Pastor Lim when she came back out to his jeep. "But you can't expect a miracle unless you at least put yourself in the way of one that might come along."

At five minutes past noon, a message came from the captain. "Be at the Chinese military operations building by twelve twenty-five—a plane will take you to Taiwan." The plane, bucking the wind, was landing just as the jeep raced Lil into the airport. Signing a statement releasing the Chinese government from liability, she lined up with the military personnel who were leaving and went aboard. Inside the military transport plane, Lil strapped herself into a bucket seat, and, like the Chinese troops aboard, clung to an overhead handhold as the plane scurried into a takeoff and rocked into the air. Below, the only evidence of the unrelenting wind was whitecaps on the water. When the plane landed minutes later in the carefully guarded military zone of the airport at Tainan, the wind was as quiet as if they had flown to another continent.

Walking nonchalantly past an armed sentry, Lil made her way through a gate in a high board fence to the civilian sector of the airport. As she settled into a seat on the Civil Air Transport plane for Taipei, the window curtains were drawn closely. "Military secrets," the stewardess explained sweetly as they took off.

Lil smiled to herself.

When she arrived late that afternoon at the Mustard Seed office, the staff young people were standing around looking worried. Before she scarcely had a chance to sit down, Tan Sian-si thrust a checkbook in front of her. Monthly funds for the operation of the clinics were due. More than twenty-eight thousand patient visits a month were now dependent upon Mustard Seed. "And they wouldn't eat tomorrow at the Boys' Home and Annex, if you hadn't got back," Tan Sian-si said. The boys in that one project ate up two hundred dollars worth of groceries every week. "Two hundred dollars *gold*" is the way Lil often puts it when she wants to emphasize the figure, distinguishing from New Taiwanese dollars, which by comparison become astronomical and seem unreal.

The boys at Rescue Home were smaller and fewer in number, but they too managed to stow away rice in large quantities. Catherine, one of Lil's "young people," who had been in charge, reported that the Rescue Home pastor was anxious to talk about one of his boys, Hun-khai, "the one with the harelip."

"He ought to have another operation," said Lil. "It's bad enough to have only one leg—but a harelip, too. I'll see the pastor tomorrow . . ."

Her "street boys," Lil called the youngsters at Rescue Home. They had a warm place in her affection. The idea for a rescue home had resulted in early 1961 from stories about juvenile delinquency that began appearing with alarming frequency in Taipei newspapers. Lil had an interest because many of the boys at Boys' Home had once been on the streets. She was concerned about the others who had not been rescued, many of them small youngsters.

To Jim, she declared, "I heard a policeman say that there are over a hundred little boys on the streets, stealing for a living, doing just enough work to get along; sleeping at night in the railroad station or under boards and boxes along the streets. Over a hundred!"

"A civic group is appointing a committee to make a survey of juvenile delinquency," Jim observed. "I heard about it the other day."

"It takes a committee forever!" Lil exclaimed. "And the chances are that if they do make a survey, they'll consider their job done. There isn't time to wait. I'm going to do something about it!"

She knew a pastor who was the kind she felt would work nicely with boys. "You need a certain type—somebody with quiet, friendly eyes, who looks *very* kind," she said to Jim. "I have that sort of pastor. We're opening a place in the area of Taipei where our lads from the Boys' Home used to wander around. The pastor will live upstairs and downstairs will be the Rescue Home."

But the boys didn't respond. They thought that after they came in, someone would tell the police and they would be taken to jail. "They have been treated very badly by the police," Lil pointed out, discussing the problem with the pastor. "How do we show that we want to help them?"

The pastor's daughter solved it for them. As she came home late one night from a music lesson, she saw six boys sleeping under boxes. Tapping on one of the boxes, she awakened them. "My father has a much better place. If you want to come, I'll take you."

She heard them talking among themselves. One of them said, "If it's a trick and she's trying to take us to the police, we can still run away. Let's follow her and see."

So they came along—and stayed the night. The next morning, they were given clothes and food, and the pastor explained what it was all about.

One boy said, "How could anyone do all this for us?" And then the pastor had a perfect opening to tell them why Christian people were interested. The six boys stayed, and later became "missionaries" themselves, finding other boys and bringing them in—skeptical in the beginning, then secure and happy.

"It isn't a good enough location," Lil said to her staff one day. "There's no place for the boys to play."

"But there isn't any other place," Tan Sian-si pointed out. He wasn't sure of this project anyway. He had said, "These boys will always be a problem. You don't know what you're getting into—and besides you have no support for it."

But Lil had gone ahead anyway. And now she said, "Let's go hunt for a place." Lil and three of her staff got in the car and went out. On the way up to the campus where the Dicksons lived they found a building that was just right, on the edge of town, where there was room to play and run. Furthermore, it was for rent.

"We moved our boys over there," says Lil, beaming. "More came in—we've had over one hundred twenty since we started. The pastor always interviews them first, and because he's kindly and friendly, they tell him their whole story. If they've run away from home and are afraid to go back, he acts as the middle man. If they come from broken homes, as often they do, and they're not wanted, we keep them. Those who can be trained to qualify are entered in the public school. Those who can't immediately qualify are taught in our own school at the home. Our object is to make them all into normal boys who can take their places with others."

The youngest lad in the Rescue Home—brought to the Dicksons' door by a sympathetic policeman—was only five when he came. He had stolen two bananas on the street because he was hungry. The fruitstand man had beaten him so badly that his body was black and blue. The boys are not afraid of policemen now. If one asks, "Where is your home?" they tell him proudly, "*I'm* from the orphanage!"

The day after Lil's return from the Pescadores, the pastor came in to talk about Hun-khai. "He ought to have another operation for his harelip."

"He has such a sweet smile," Lil said.

Misfortune had dogged the boy's steps. His father died when he was a baby. His mother became mentally ill when the boy was seven; she took her children to relatives in Kaohsiung, in the southern part of the island. There, while Hun-khai was gathering dry sugar-cane press for firewood, the sugar mill train ran over him and he lost his left leg. Using a stick as a crutch, he followed his second older brother to Taipei. There Hun-khai shined shoes, supplementing his meager earnings by begging. For this he was picked up by the police, and at twelve, came to Rescue Home.

"I saw in the paper," Lil said to the pastor, "that Dr. Ralph Blocksma, a great plastic surgeon, is to be in town next week, doing volunteer work at Mackay Hospital. "I'll tell you what you should do," she went on, adopting Jim's expression. "Call the hospital and see if you can make an appointment for him to see the boy."

The next week had almost gone by before the pastor admitted defeat: "He is a waif with no one to fight for him."

"Well, I'll fight for him!" Lil said. "You have him at the hospital at three o'clock and I will meet you there." Meantime, she tried to call Dr. Blocksma at the home of the doctor with whom he was staying, but was unable to reach him. She concluded that he must be at the hospital.

At the scheduled time, Lil, the pastor, and Hun-khai met in the lobby of Mackay Hospital. Lil strode to the desk and asked for Dr. Blocksma.

"He's in surgery," the nurse said, "and can't be reached."

"We'll go up," Lil declared, heading for the stairway. Lil felt at home there; she had been racing around that hospital for many years. The pastor followed her, and Hun-khai, hopping along on his one leg and crutch, followed the pastor. Up the stairs Lil led the way, like a field officer leading a charge. On the second floor, past a surprised nurse they swept, Lil's expression brooking no interference, the mild-mannered pastor in tow, the one-legged boy hopping along behind. Through a ward they went, then through a door leading to the operating-room corridor. Lil was brought up short only by a locked door; through its glass she could see two doctors washing up at the end of the long corridor. Stopped for only a moment, she spied another door at the side and hurried into what proved to be a room for the sorting of masks and gloves for the operating room. A dignified missionary nurse looked up in astonishment.

"I want to see Dr. Blocksma. It's important," Lil announced.

"But, Mrs. Dickson, the doctors are washing up for an operation!"

"I have a little boy who needs surgery. I'm sure that if I could talk to the doctor—"

"I'll see what I can do," the nurse said with a sigh, moving off. Presently, she returned. "Dr. Blocksma says he can see you for a few minutes tomorrow morning, just before his plane leaves."

"That will be too late!" Lil exclaimed. "I have a little boy with only one leg and a harelip—"

The nurse sighed heavily, and went away again. This time the two doctors, dressed in blue gowns, face masks in place, their arms soaped to the elbows and turned upward so the water wouldn't drip, followed behind her. "I'm sorry I can't shake hands," said Dr. Blocksma wryly.

"I'm Mrs. Dickson," Lil began.

"I know. This is Dr. Nordhoff, staff surgeon." He indicated his colleague.

Lil explained about the boy. "I wanted an expert to operate on him. He had an operation once before, and it wasn't successful, and he's afraid."

"We discussed him," Dr. Blocksma said. "His case is not exceptional. Dr. Nordhoff has been throwing me the curves to handle while I'm here."

"I want the best for my boys—" Lil began.

"We are booked up solid today, Mrs. Dickson. But Dr. Nordhoff worked with me in America, and he has worked with me here. He will do the very best job that can be done. He's an expert."

Lil looked at the second doctor who said, "I can do it within a week or two—whenever you say. You just let me know."

The two doctors moved away, to face the lesser terrors of the operating room.

As Lil went down the corridor, through the ward, past the reception desk, the pastor and Hun-khai fell in behind her. She turned to the pastor as they went down the stairs. "I guess Dr. Nordhoff will do. I'm very particular about my boys." She waited until Hun-khai caught up, and patted his shoulder. "It's going to be all right."

At the end of the school term in 1963, he went into the hospital and Dr. Nordhoff operated with skill. "His smile is even sweeter now," Lil told the doctor when she saw the boy's almost perfect lip a few weeks afterward. Later on, when the time was right, she would get Hun-khai fitted with an artificial leg, and perhaps he could put aside his crutch.

That made her think of the artificial legs that had come in one of the "missionary barrels." She had sent them down to Pak-mng on the Salt Coast. If they could be used anywhere, it would be at Pak-mng, Lil thought, where doctors had encountered one of the most baffling diseases to be found anywhere.

Lil's interest in Pak-mng had started with a phone call from a visiting American she never met nor heard of; he was simply a voice.

"I've been visiting in the Tainan Theological Seminary," the voice said. "I went with one of the students to the Salt Coast. Have you been there?"

"No-oo," Lil said. "I've been so busy in the mountains and other places—"

"They have a terrible disease down there called blackfoot. It's the only place in the world where this disease seems to occur, and the only relief—and a temporary one, at that—is amputation. After amputation, these people, who were very poor to begin with, have no work to do. Could you possibly think of a way of providing a ward for them so that when they have their operation they will have a place to stay, and some kind of occupational therapy, so they can earn money after the amputation?"

"I'll look into it," Lil promised.

When she visited the Great Salt Coast, on the western side of Taiwan, she found it just as the visitor had said. The soil was sandy and too poor to raise vegetables. Some of the residents along the shore tried to fish, but the sea was often stormy and most of them did not have boats. Available work was mainly in the government-controlled shallow brine vats, stretching along the coast. Here, ocean water was allowed to evaporate until the salt remained. Working barelegged in the brine, year after year, was enough to aggravate any ulcer that might appear, Lil decided. When she saw beggars sitting on the narrow streets, blackened stumps where their feet or legs had been, she felt a deep sadness. Where did one even start with a problem like that?

Her medical adviser, Dr. Tang, said, "Start with milk and vitamins. Whatever the immediate cause of the disease—and so far no one has been able to discover it—malnutrition is probably an underlying factor." Lil promptly set up twenty-five milk stations along the Salt Coast, where children were provided not only milk, but vitamins three times a week, and the Gospel. Locating a Christian doctor, she opened a free clinic at Pak-mng, in the heart of the blackfoot area, providing wards for men and women. Adjoining, the Christian people of the area built their own church.

What she could learn about the disease was discouraging. It was something like gangrene, affecting feet, legs, and hands. Relentless, it seemed to mark Salt Coast people as its own, even though some moved to other areas to try to escape. No victim of blackfoot was found anywhere on the island who had not grown up on the Salt Coast. A team of American military doctors pointed the finger of suspicion at the drinking water, which in that one part of Taiwan contained as much as 1.0 to 2.0 parts per million of arsenic, when the acceptable maximum was 0.2.

The Christian doctor at Pak-mng explained to her how the disease progressed. "In the early stages, the patient may complain of the toes or fingers—it is sometimes also called blackhand disease—being cold, numb, or itching. There is a bluish discoloration, tenderness, hot sensation, and in the foot intermittent limp. Severe, agonizing pain begins—one of the most hellish pains possible.

In the dry type, the part becomes as hard and as black as coal, and finally drops off—but the pain persists. The moist type has a foul odor. The patient loses his appetite, he can't sleep, some of them lose their minds. Amputation is no guarantee against recurrence."

Lil saw for herself one man who had had his leg cut off in seven different amputations. Another was blind—and with toes gone, leg gone, fingers gone. Nor was the disease limited to the aged. A girl of twenty-one was a patient in the women's ward; part of her foot and several fingers had been amputated.

The doctor taking Lil on rounds on one of her visits stopped in front of a woman with a bandaged leg stump. The toes on the other foot were cold to the touch and growing dark. "We will have to take off her other leg tomorrow," he said in the matter-of-fact tones of a medical man.

When, in the men's ward, the patients sat on their beds to sing as a tribute to Lil, "My Heart Is So Happy My Mouth Must Sing," her own heart was as heavy as lead. Someday, perhaps she could build a new clinic, replacing the makeshift facilities, where the disease could be fully understood and conquered.

"Where are your projects going to stop?" Lil's sober business friends wondered.

"Why should they stop anywhere?" Lil demanded. "Do we think that God can supply two dollars but not three dollars? Or that, when we see a hungry or sick child, He may say, 'You don't need to care about *that* child—you're doing enough already'? Is any need, anywhere, beyond the love of God? And if it is His concern, should it not be ours?"

"You can't take on the whole world!" they argued.

"I can't," Lil agreed. "God can."

22. How Long?

On a recent trip of Lil's to the States, an American woman tourist boarded the jet plane just ahead of her. The street boys had come down to sing Lil off, using the hymn that had become a theme song for all Lil's humble people—"God Will Take Care of You." The woman tourist had heard the singing, had seen the lei around Lil's neck, had watched her wave and wave again to the boys as she went out to the plane and climbed the loading ramp.

"They must like you," she said. "Have you been here long?"

Lil waved once more, and turned and said quietly, "Thirty-five years."

Young Lillian LeVesconte had once written to her fiancé, distance runner Jimmy Dickson, "We have only one life to live. Let's go where there is the greater need." That had been a long time ago, Lil mused on a Sunday morning in late 1963 after the alarm clock rang, giving fair warning that the busiest day of her week was about to begin. One life. It was not very much. One had to make the most of it.

After she had a quick breakfast, Tiu Sian-si picked up her accordion and put it in the back of the station wagon. They drove along the campus road, past the big classroom building, with Jim's Oriental chapel on the crest of the slope behind it. The chapel was vine-covered now; on the front lawn enormous hibiscus blossoms set their bushes aflame. Overhead, acacia trees rattled their leaves and palms swayed gracefully.

Jim has worked hard, Lil said to herself. And always against obstacles. Her heart glowed when she thought of him. A plaque in the Chi-oang Memorial Church in Hwalien honored his work in evangelizing the mountain tribes. Two tribes—the Ami and Taroko—had formed presbyteries, tribute to Jim's efforts to make the churches self-governing.

To her left, the campus hill dropped off into the valley, a vast flatland that Lil had seen in typhoon time become a lake, with only the red-tiled roofs of houses showing and untold misery under those roofs. When "Gloria" struck in September, the result had been the worst flood in the history of Taipei, piling water nine feet deep in some of the low-lying downtown streets and causing damage estimated at ten million dollars U.S. Lil had managed to get off a cable with her tragic news to the Glendale, California, office of Mustard Seed: FOUR ORPHANAGES SUBMERGED. HOUSE MOTHERS HELD 50 CHILDREN ALL NIGHT IN RAFTERS OF HOUSE ONE FOOT ABOVE THE WATER. TWO CHILDREN DROWN. When the water subsided, she went sadly about her work of rescuing, comforting, rebuilding, rehabilitating, setting things to right. This, too, was mothers' work, and a mother's work was never done nor her own sorrows ever wholly comforted. But God had not promised "skies always blue." Christians were marked, not by the way they were delivered from trouble, but by the way they faced it. Would not God, Lil wondered, also weep for two lost children?

Ahead in the distance rose Tai-tung Soa. Someday, Lil supposed, the mountain would be covered with houses, and the wild life would have to go farther back into the mountains to find refuge. This is what always happened to mountain things and mountain people. What would happen when the last mountain was reached? Would all on the island learn to live together then?

On the way to the women's prison, her first visit of the day,

Lil stopped at a flower shop to buy a bouquet for the plain table that would serve as altar, lectern, and pulpit. "Flowers are cheap, and they add color to drab places," she told the chaplain, who was waiting for her at the shop together with the girl who had volunteered to play the pump organ.

Guards at the prison gate passed them through. Some of the women inmates were working at the sewing machines as the visitors entered the cell block at the end of which was the assembly room large enough to accommodate the meeting. "We'll be ready for you in a few minutes," a khaki-skirted attendant said, showing them into a small waiting room adjoining her quarters.

A tawny kitten meowed anxiously, and swayed against Lil's legs. "Look," she said gently, "it's blind! A blind kitten—in prison."

It was time for the meeting. The organist played while Lil accompanied her on the accordion. The women, ranged on benches, sang, "There's a land that is fairer than day . . . in the sweet by and by." Some were young, others wrinkled and old. A boy of four toddled from one woman to another—his mother was probably a newcomer. Somewhere a baby whimpered. The chaplain preached, accenting his remarks with movements of the folding fan he held in his right hand—now closed and used as a pointer for emphasis, now flung open and vigorously fanning his perspiring face.

Women crowded around Lil after the service, asking about the babies they had entrusted to her keeping. A pleasant-faced young inmate packed Lil's accordion into its case, walked with the visitors to the farthest gate where she reluctantly handed it over to Tiu Sian-si, and then turned back to the monotony of another week. The chaplain went on to a service on the men's side of the big prison.

Tiu Sian-si drove the station wagon away from the prison gate. Downtown they picked up the missionary Lil had asked to preach at the leprosarium that Sunday morning, and headed south. The next stop would be the Boys' Home, where the organist would get out and walk up a flight of stone steps to the church prayed into reality by little boys, crowning the hill where once there had been only a pigpen. The boys from Boys' Home Annex, two miles distant, would also be there, having sung their way along the road. It was their church, too.

The leprosarium entrance was just a block beyond. Tiu Sian-si turned the car into the gate. It was raining. The church elder—one of the patients—was waiting with an umbrella. Coming past the clock tower, Lil and the elder stepped onto the concrete paths she had built years before. They went down Lillian Walk past a pond that was once a swamp. A fountain played in the center, its spray shimmering into the rain-dappled water where lily blossoms that looked like great magenta rain-filled cups rested upon glistening lily-pad saucers.

The congregation had already gathered and was singing to while away the time. As Lil climbed toward the Church of the Lepers, their words became clearer: "This is my story, this is my song, praising my Saviour, all the day long—" Lil could distinguish between the high-pitched voices of the children and the more mellow ones of the men and women.

With the arrival of Lil and the preacher, the service officially opened. The bell on the wall outside was rung, the organist played, "The Lord is in His holy temple, let all the earth keep silence before Him."

The Lord's Prayer was prayed simultaneously in Taiwanese and Mandarin. The God who understands all languages heard His people say, "Give us this day—" Some who were praying in the audience, or lying on their tatami mats in the Ward Nearest Heaven's Door, listening to the service over the loudspeakers, literally had to be given their bread. And all required a daily ration of hope. The older ones, who would be here for the rest of their lives, desperately needed it; the younger ones, though they would, by the miracle of modern drugs, almost assuredly be cured, would need hope, too.

The congregation stood for a unison Bible reading, then the Doxology. "Praise God from whom all blessings flow." What blessings? Count them: A bed. A roof. A meal. A friend. A faith. Once, no one had cared for them—the ultimate despair.

The adult chancel choir at the left of the sanctuary sang, "There is sunshine in my soul," blending their voices beautifully. Then the men's choir sang, and finally the children's choir, the collars of their white surplices refusing to lie down. The brass band, organized years before by Lil so that their talent would not be lost, and to give meaning to lives that had become empty, played, "We should never be discouraged—"

During the sermon, Lil's eyes took in the familiar sight. The men sat together on the left, the women on the right. Many of the men wore army uniforms. The pastor was speaking in Taiwanese, the interpreter translating into Mandarin. Lil's eyes sought out a beautiful, untouched face in the congregation—a woman with almost classic features. Lil breathed a silent prayer for that woman, and felt humble in her presence. Her husband, years before, had contracted leprosy, and she too was hospitalized with the lepers for observation, though she showed no sign of the disease. In six months she was pronounced clean, and Lil took her to her home for such women; Lil already had their two boys. When the woman learned that her husband had quit going to church and begun gambling, she resolved to return to be with him, to keep up his morale, to share his destiny. Now they were living in a cottage just outside the leprosarium. He was still a patient. What a sweet, understanding face she has, Lil thought.

After the sermon and another hymn, the offering was taken up in two long, brass-handled velvet bags. Some of the congregation had to use both hands held carefully together to drop in their gifts, mostly bills the equivalent of two and a half cents U.S., precious in the Lord's sight.

At the conclusion of the service, Sister Alma introduced Lil to a boy of about eight who had joined in the service for the first time and had sung in the children's choir. His mother died on the mainland, Lil learned; he teamed up with soldiers with whom he came to Taiwan and from whom he contracted the disease. An orphan, a strange land, now leprosy, Lil pondered sadly. Another "blind kitten."

"There's something else, Mrs. Dickson, that I should mention," said Sister Alma. "The loudspeakers in the wards are getting old. They should be replaced—perhaps the whole system."

"Replaced?" said Lil. "We just installed them."

"It has been at least ten years," said Sister Alma gently.

Lil shook her head in amazement. Ten years! They would have to start over again soon, go through the whole leprosarium, find out what required replacing. That was one thing about need: you meet it once, but it doesn't necessarily stay met. " 'It doesn't say forever,' " Lil mused.

Now, the leprosarium administration was honest and compassionate; a fine new superintendent was in charge. Even a brickyard had been set up to provide work for some of the men patients; customers had no hesitancy about buying their brick, for all could see that a kiln was an effective sterilizer. But no matter how efficient the administration, the leprosarium could provide only the bare necessities, not the small, thoughtful comforts Lil offered to make life happier for these people and to give them a sense of dignity.

The lepers walked companionably through the rain with Lil to her car, and sang their benediction of faith.

After a hurried lunch, she drove past Rescue Home, where some of the boys outside recognized the station wagon and waved, and continued on to the Mustard Seed office. As Tiu Sian-si swung the car from the express lane of North Chungking Road into the parallel service lane next to the sidewalk, Lil looked up at the Mustard Seed building, to the large painting of Christ and His disciples, wired between the center second-floor front windows. The picture showed up well, she decided.

It was one of Frank's—he prominently signed each of his pictures with that one name. Lil had discovered his talent when he was a patient in the leprosarium; he previously worked as a billboard artist for movie houses. Lil took him paints, brushes, canvas, to lift him out of his despondency, and he began doing religious paintings for her. He could not paint an original picture, but he could copy anything, enlarging it square by square to any size. "Billboard evangelism!" Lil said to Jim. "There's a church downtown at the corner of Sin Alley, where we can put up a different religious painting every week or so."

"You had better get a police permit," Jim advised.

"If other people can put up pictures, surely we can do it on a church!" Lil retorted. She talked the police into agreeing with her.

When Frank was released from the leprosarium and was about to return to commercial art in order to make a living, Lil hired him—possibly the only oil painter on a missionary payroll in the world. He has proved invaluable in a country where if you want a large poster of any kind, religious or otherwise, the easiest way to get it is to have it hand painted. Frank's copies add color and visual-teaching impact to each of Lil's orphanages, clinics, and schools. Eventually, she hopes to have one in each mountain church. One of his Christmas scenes identifies each "Room for Mary."

The painting hanging on the Mustard Seed office building was an example of "fighting fire with fire." Lil had come back to the office from lunch one day to discover that the movie theater across the lane from the Mustard Seed building had put up not only a lurid burlesque-type overhead sign, but had mounted a cutout of "a naked woman" on a pillar of Lil's building. Marching into Mustard Seed, Lil recruited her workers and started downstairs to do battle. Iu Sian-si, the moderate mailman, held up his hand in a delaying action while he telephoned the theater manager. "He says he didn't know the sign was on our building," Iu Sian-si reported. "His people will move it."

"Good!" said Lil. "We will help them!"

But even with the offending cutout moved fifteen feet distant, Lil was still not happy. The signs were still there, right next to her building, though not now attached to it. Summoning Iu Sian-si, she pointed to one of the six-foot-high paintings Frank had just finished. "We'll compete with them!" she directed. "See if you can think of a plan to get that picture hung on the front of our building." For Iu Sian-si it was easy. Not only that, when the picture was in place, he rigged a spotlight so that it could be lighted at night—putting Christ and His Disciples one up on the competition, which had no lights.

"I have another trick up my sleeve, too—" Lil said darkly,

thinking of her successful encounter with Sin Alley. A Presbyterian church is located at one corner of that street, and just opposite, the seminary stood until the move to Grass Mountain. Sin Alley was known for its bars and brothels—eighteen bars alone. The street, which brazenly catered to American servicemen, angered Lil every time she went by. She had put up Frank's religious paintings, but they weren't enough. Calling in her electronics expert, Eng-cheong, she told him what she wanted. Soon he had an amplifier playing hymns at the time of heaviest evening patronage. A sailor or soldier would swagger into one of the bars, order a drink, and suddenly hear, "Jesus Is Tenderly Calling Thee Home." Somehow, he lost his thirst. One after another, the saloons began going bankrupt.

"Can't you play your music a little *softer?*" the survivors pleaded with Lil. When the number dropped to three, she turned off her amplifier. Although she hates bars in any quantity, apparently three were a manageable number.

Lil's reserve weapon was not necessary this time. The stage show played out its engagement and moved elsewhere, taking its advertisements with it. The lighted religious paintings stayed.

Waiting at the Mustard Seed office this Sunday afternoon were several of the girls of the staff, and Iu Sian-si. All was in readiness —the big hampers just inside the door, filled with cups, saucers, a teapot, flower vases, coverings for piano, altar table and lectern, lace tablecloths for the tea tables. Iu Sian-si and the driver loaded the heavy hampers in the back of the station wagon, the girls got in the front, Iu Sian-si returned to his job of being office watchman. They were on their way to the Y.M.C.A. for "vespers and fellowship."

Lil looked at her young people proudly as the station wagon headed downtown toward the "Y." Martha and Catherine, valued members of the staff, came along every Sunday afternoon, on their own time. Go Sian-si, he whose diapers Lil had changed in airraids, had married Catherine; he spent part of his Sunday teaching the An-Lok children. Thinking about the young couple, Lil reflected sadly that the boy's mother, a minister's widow, was deeply opposed to the marriage; Catherine was of the new generation, not of the old in which a bride became the underprivileged member of the family, the abject handmaiden of her mother-in-law. Some of the older women, who had given traditional servitude and looked forward to receiving it, did not take kindly to the new ways. Lil had proffered her own home for the wedding of these two fine youngsters, so that it would be happy and memorable.

Deborah was another of Lil's fine girls. A year ago Deborah and her husband had brought Jim, who had married them, a chicken. It was the preacher's fee, which he did not collect until a boy baby was born.

Hoa-te was another of Lil's blessings—he of the Boys' Home. Two evenings a week, on his own time, he went out to a Taipei slum to run a milk station. Preparing the powdered milk and serving it to long lines of dirty, lovable youngsters who brought all kinds of pans, cans, and cups in which to receive their portions, was not a cheering task. The lines of children had to break ranks and flatten against the walls of the shabby houses when coolies came by pulling carts heaped with garbage. In heavy rains, the water rose out of the sewage canals and spilled into the houses, leaving a stench that could never be completely obliterated. Here, Hoa-te, the boy who felt himself privileged because he grew up in a Christian orphanage, passed out hot milk and bright Christmas cards and Christian love.

The station wagon stopped again at the flower shop, this time to pick up an assortment for the meeting at the Y.M.C.A. The florist was a Christian. When Lil once remonstrated at his low prices, he said, "Whatever I give you beyond what you pay for is my contribution." Lil bought roses, gladioli, lilies, to beautify the austere chapel. Another quick stop was made to pick up mimeographed bulletins, especially prepared for the week's service. At a bakery, she bought an assortment of cookies and doughnuts to go with the tea, then the station wagon drove on to the "Y."

There, the arrangements went ahead like clockwork. Tiu Sian-si carried in the heavy baskets. The girls spread the lace cloths on two large tables at the back of the chapel, arranged the flowers in the vases that were hung on the bare walls on either side of the pulpit, covered the upright piano with a rich scarf, spread another on the table just below the pulpit and placed two offering containers on top.

They took out the plates and cups, arranged the cookies and doughnuts, put water to boil for tea.

"Many pastors come to these vesper services for English-speaking Chinese," Lil pointed out to Jim. "They see what a nice service can be like. And it all costs only about twelve dollars U.S. a month."

It was Jim who got Lil into it in the first place. The Sunday vespers had dwindled in attendance to a mere handful of missionaries talking to missionaries. "The service is stuffy," Jim said to her. "If we just had someone who would take it in hand—"

Lil called the man in charge. "I am appointing myself social chairman of the vespers until the end of the year," she said. Delighted, he turned over the whole responsibility to her. Broadly interpreting her assignment, she painted the chapel, put in a new floor, decided to have a "nice" service with a fellowship time afterward. The formal hymnbooks she locked away in the balcony, and bought hymnbooks with simpler, more singable hymns.

Attendance mounted, and for three years the chapel had been filled every Sunday afternoon. One old gentleman who admired the dignified failures of the previous era mentioned one Sunday afternoon to Lil, a teacup in his hand, "The other hymnbooks were *very* superior."

Lil, reporting this to Jim, added, "He's terribly theological!"

When the cups and saucers and all the other equipment had been gathered up after the service, repacked, and returned to the Mustard Seed office—to be washed and prepared for the next week—there was just about time enough to get back to the leprosarium for the evening service. Not until late Sunday night, when Lil was home again, was there opportunity for a sandwich and a few relaxing moments while she and Jim sat deep in the chairs of their living room retelling the adventures of the day.

Looking up, Lil said, "They've been good years, Jim." She had much to be thankful for. People, for one. Marilyn and Vernon were back, living in the cottage next door; Vernon was taking charge of the training schools. Ronny and his wife were doing well in San Francisco. Don and Betty Williams had at their own request moved deep into the hills, to live among the mountain people so they could serve them better. Glen and June Graber were doing a fine work for the Christian Children's Fund at Taichung.

There were things as well as people to be thankful for, but things always involved people. The fine new clinic at Pak-mng, paid for by a Sunday-school class of the Hollywood Presbyterian Church, was completed, but what a time she had had with that! When the contractor submitted the building plans, he had left off all dimensions. "How," she asked him, "is one to make sense of plans that do not show how big anything is?" Her own loyal staff helped her through that project, as they helped her through every other. "They are the smart ones," Lil repeatedly says with deep affection. "They know how to get things done."

At Pak-mng, too, Lil had found a use for the hundreds of aluminum pie pans sent to her from America. She took them down with an assortment of the prettiest Christmas cards and ribbons she could find and sample Christmas tree ornaments as models. The ingenious patients turned the pie pans into beautiful silver bells and angels that brought in more money than most of them had seen in a year, proving that they were still resourceful.

The tuberculosis clinic at Hwalien had two new buildings—tripling its capacity to one hundred twenty-five. At Koan-san, the bamboo-and-mud wards for tuberculosis patients had been replaced. The old buildings had begun to lean precariously; the nurses' aids had a dark, unlovely room in one of them. Now there were bright, clean buildings for sixty patients, with a little apartment for the nurses' aids who already had shown a large measure of devotion by volunteering to work among active tuberculosis cases. It's as dangerous as walking into a den of lions, Lil often thought, marveling at their dedication. If only she could afford now to bring up electric power lines from the village, so that the patients could have the comfort of adequate lighting in the dark, mountain nights. At Sin-Khang there were now seventy patients.

The Pescadores Children's Home already had twenty youngsters. The building had been planned so another floor could be added if necessary. Tan Sian-si would shake his head if he knew she was even thinking about that!

More than a hundred mountain churches—Jim's pride and joy—had been rebuilt by the people themselves after Lil had rounded up gifts to pay for cement. Donations from America, stones from mountain streams, strength from mountain muscles, motivation from mountain devotion—the churches were built of these. Two of the stone churches and three kindergartens were on Orchid Isle, five hours by small boat off the southeast coast—inhabited by the Yamis, most primitive tribespeople of all.

When drums of chick peas were brought to Mustard Seed by the U.S. Navy for distribution, Lil told her staff, "American Aid will not be here forever. Rather than just divide them for our clinics and homes, I have a plan—" She sent some to every village in the mountains, to the Salt Coast, and to the Pescadores with the message, "Plant—don't eat!" They produced manyfold, and in the Pescadores—as in the Biblical parable—a hundredfold.

Training young people was also a way of sowing seed. At the Hwalien Girls' School, a needed new dormitory was built, so that more mountain girls who applied for nurse's aid or kindergarten teacher training could be accommodated. These girls come from primitive homes—opening day is devoted to removing lice from their hair—and they go out competent young women, many returning to their villages to lift the level of living and vision.

The Boys' School had an attractive classroom and library building, and two new dormitories. Built of concrete block, the buildings were utilitarian, but Lil did not forget the happy touches—attractive lighting fixtures in the dining hall, graceful wrought-iron railing spindles that she insisted replace ones made of reinforcing rods welded together. The chapel at the Boys' School at Hwalien, built of Taroko marble—simply because marble was near at hand for the taking—was one of the prettiest on the island. Now if the boys just learned to take care of their church— The rule that they must remove their shoes before they entered might help; in the mountains, they were used to chickens and pigs walking right through the church.

God had been good.

Yet, there was so much more that could be done. For one thing, beautifying the mountain churches. The churches were in breathtaking, natural settings, but the churchyards were not beautiful. Some of them were wallows for water buffalo. "We could have competitions by districts to beautify the church grounds," Lil told Jim. "I would like to bring a landscape architect out here to steer the project. As awards we could give books, and these would be the start of church libraries. The churches ought to be plastered and whitewashed once a year. Let the young people do that—it will give them something to do. And the landscaping wouldn't cost anything—plants and trees and bushes are already in the mountains. All they would have to do is transplant them."

"What's all that?" Jim asked.

"I'm just dreaming," Lil replied.

She had dreams, too, of a great school that would accommodate five hundred boys, and another for a similar number of girls.

Lil had finally acquired land for a Christian cemetery in Taipei; a road had been bulldozed to the top. Someday a beautiful chapel would crown that "Gate to Glory" hill. That was a dream, too.

She had a dream of several schools that would need to be little more than private homes, mothered by women who could teach girls to be good homemakers, showing them how to brighten their homes at small expense. "The people out here," Lil often said, "like to have gold or silver crowns put on their teeth—the more prominent the better. One of those costs twenty dollars or so, U.S. If a young wife could take even the cost of two or three of those decorative teeth, she could do a lot in her home."

Sitting there near Jim, her thoughts ranging far, Lil remembered a time when Dr. Poling was once visiting Taiwan and he and she were returning to Taipei in a small government plane from the south. Taipei was closed in by fog, and their plane began circling.

For thirty-five minutes it circled, the pilot growing more ashen by the minute. Lil said to Dr. Poling, "When our time comes"—and privately she thought this might be it—"our jobs won't be done." Then a mere elevator shaft of visibility opened in the fog, and the pilot headed down sharply to a safe landing.

Tasks undone! Lil had ended one of her newsletters with the plea, "Stay with us during the harvest! We do not know how long we have."

Looking down over the lights in the valley below, Lil wondered about the future. What did it hold for Taiwan and its twelve million inhabitants whose destiny was not in their own hands.

Who could be sure of the destiny of any island or continent anywhere, East or West? Formosa's—Taiwan's—history from the beginning of history had been one of turbulence, of servitude, of conqueror replacing conqueror. Some of Lil's friends back home wondered if this pattern would not repeat itself, and the Communists someday engulf the island. They questioned whether it made economic or perhaps even humanitarian sense to spend too much effort, love, and money.

Lil's mother instincts rose up against such a philosophy. A statement she once made summed it all up:

"Sometimes in a home a mother puts all her children to bed, and then in the darkness she hears one crying or perhaps two of them. She goes softly to their bedside and comforts them. I know that many people think that night is reaching out its long arms toward this island. But if we hear people crying in distress in the darkness before night, let us comfort them as a mother might, for Christ's sake, until they fall asleep."

Jim, sitting there in the living room, nodded when Lil, going through some of her old letters, found that paragraph and read it aloud.

"But," said Jim, "it may not be the darkness before night. It may be the darkness before dawn."

"Besides," said Lil, putting aside her papers and taking off her glasses, "tomorrow there will be work to do."

Institutions Under Mustard Seed Care, in whole or part (figures as of November 1, 1962)

IRO–IRO "Miscellaneous" COMPOUND, 195 children
- Iro-Iro Children's Home
- Phok-Ai "Great Love" (for babies of prisoners)
- Phok-Ai Annex
- Children's Shelter (for small girls rescued from prostitution)
- Babies' Home
- Babies' Home Annex

AN–LOK "Peace and Happiness" COMPOUND, 55 children (for children of leper parents)
- An-Lok Annex
- An-Lok Babies' Home
- Children's Haven (for the handicapped)
- Christian Herald Home

PU–LI, 35 children
- Grace Home
- Mountain Babies' Home

also

- Room for Mary (Maternity Ward for Mountain Mothers)

KAK–PAN
- Mountain Mobile Clinic base

PESCADORES
- Children's Home, 20 children
- Au-Liau Kindergarten
- Liong-Bun-Kang Kindergarten
- Makung Mobile Clinic

PAK–MNG
- Mercy's Door Clinic (for Blackfoot Disease)
- 24 Milk Stations in this Great Salt Coast area (free milk and vitamins)

TAINAN
- Prison Work—evangelization

PING–TUNG
- Mountain Clinic, 75 in-patients
- Mountain Mobile Clinic goes out from here into mountains
- Room for Mary

KIM–LUN
- Mountain Clinic

TAITUNG
- Mountain Clinic
- Room for Mary

KOAN–SAN
- Mountain Clinic
- Tuberculosis Sanatorium
- Room for Mary

SIN–KHANG
- Mountain Clinic
- Tuberculosis Sanatorium

KONG–HOK
- Mountain Clinic

HWALIEN

- Mountain Babies' Home
- Boys' School for Aborigines, 150 students
- Girls' School for Aborigines, 172 students
- Tuberculosis Sanatorium for Aborigines
- Room for Mary

IN THE MOUNTAINS

- 183 Kindergartens
- 140 stone churches built since 1952. (Mustard Seed supplies cement; churches supply labor and rest of materials.)

TAIPEI

- Mercy's Door Clinic (in Mustard Seed headquarters building)
- Bang-Kah Mobile Clinic
- Prison Work (Mustard Seed supports chaplain and conducts weekly services)
- Rescue Home, on north edge of city, 55 boys
- Milk Stations in slum areas

YANG MING SHAN

- Taiwan Theological College, which Dr. James Dickson heads, but which is not a part of Mustard Seed

SOUTHWEST OF TAIPEI

- Leprosarium (under Nationalist Government, but Mustard Seed has been active in religious and humanitarian program)
- Boys' Home (supported principally by World Vision), 40 boys
- Boys' Home Annex (supported principally by World Vision), 65 boys